MICHAEL RAMSEY

A PORTRAIT

Elgar: The Man
Denton Welch: The Making of a Writer
The Honours System
Acting as Friends: The Story of the Samaritans
Eddy: The Life of Edward Sackville-West

MICHAEL DE-LA-NOY

MICHAEL
RAMSEY

A PORTRAIT

COLLINS
8 GRAFTON STREET, LONDON W1
1990

William Collins Sons & Co Ltd
London · Glasgow · Sydney · Auckland
Toronto · Johannesburg

First published 1990

ISBN 0 00 215332-7

Set in 11pt Linotron Garamond

Made and Printed in Great Britain by
Billing & Sons Ltd, Worcester

For Michael and Jindra Burton

(Paris, 1970)

CONTENTS

LIST OF PLATES

Francis Dodd's preliminary study for his 1927 portrait of Michael's father, Arthur Stanley Ramsey (which hangs in the Combination room at Magdalene College, Cambridge). Reproduced by courtesy of Dr Bridget Barcroft.

Michael's mother, Mary Agnes Ramsey

A family holiday at Little Holland Norfolk, Michael is fourth from the left. His brother Frank and his mother are on the right.

The Mitre House photograph, taken at Repton when Michael Ramsey, seated third from the left, was 18. On his right is a boy who arrived the same day, Hampton Gervis. The boy at the extreme left of the back row is now Sir Desmond Lee. Alan Thornhill, who sang duets from Gilbert and Sullivan with Michael, is fourth from the left in the second row.

Frank Ramsey by the Cam, with his wife Lettice on the left and his mistress, Elizabeth Denby, on the right. Photograph by courtesy Frances Partridge.

Michael's aunt, Lucy Ramsey, in the garden of her house in Mount Pleasant, Cambridge.

Michael's elder sister, Bridget photographed by her sister-in-law, Lettice Ramsey

Michael's younger sister, Margaret

Michael and Joan on their wedding day in 1942

Michael Ramsey, Archbishop of Canterbury, in episcopal

evening dress with the Queen. The orders he is wearing were presented by the Orthodox Church. Photograph *The Sun*.

On 18 November 1967 the Archbishop was the guest at the Greek Orthodox Cathedral in London of His All Holiness the Ecumenical Patriarch, Athenagorus 1, Archbishop of Constantinople, seated. On the left is Mrs Ramsey. Behind the Archbishop is the general secretary of the Council for Foreign Relations, John Satterthwaite, now Bishop of Gibrolta in Europe. Photograph *Guardian*.

On 6 February 1969 the Archbishop spoke at a press conference at Lambeth Palace conducted by his press officer, Michael De-la-Noy, seated beside him, on the results of voting in Diocesan Conferences on the Scheme for Anglican-Methodist Reunion. Photograph Sport & General.

In the garden at Lambeth Palace, in full flight from Jane Bown, preparatory to walking back towards her up the garden path.

In the study at Lambeth. Photograph *Daily Express*.

A portrait study of Michael Ramsey by Jane Bown.

ACKNOWLEDGEMENTS

My first and most profound words of gratitude must be reserved for Lady Ramsey, who gave her blessing to the concept of my book from the start but never once attempted to influence its contents. She has written and spoken to me on a variety of matters, and her affectionate support and practical help have only increased a debt I already owe, for the confidence, encouragement and fun she always provided during the years when I had the privilege of serving as her husband's press officer. Although this is in no sense an official biography, Lady Ramsey has expressed her approval of its contents.

I am also extremely grateful for the kindness and help I have received from Lord Ramsey's two sisters, Dr Bridget Barcroft and Mrs Margaret Paul. Dr Barcroft has permitted reproduction of the drawing of her father by Francis Dodd, and Mrs Paul most generously lent me a typescript copy of her father's unpublished memoirs. This has proved a valuable source of information regarding the family history, and both Dr Barcroft and Mrs Paul have supplied from their own memories much interesting detail about Michael Ramsey's childhood. I am also indebted to one of Lord Ramsey's nephews, Mr Michael Barcroft, for his time, hospitality and the loan of photographs.

His Grace the Archbishop of Canterbury has been kind enough to give me an interview. Other people who have gone to considerable trouble to help me, none of whom bear responsibility for any errors of fact or for any opinions expressed other than their own, and to all of whom I have reason to be extremely grateful, include Sir Norman Anderson, the Rt Rev. Cuthbert Bardsley (formerly Bishop of Coventry), the Rev. Lord Beaumont of Whitley, the Very Rev. Trevor Beeson (Dean of Winchester), Mr William Brough, Mr Robin Catford (the Prime Minister's Secretary for Appointments), Dr and Mrs Wilfred Chapman, Canon Frank Chase, Mrs E. M. Coleman (Assistant Librarian at the Pepys Library, Magdalene College, Cambridge), Mr E. W. Crosskill, the Rev. Philip Crowe, the Rev. Don Cupitt, the Rev. Gordon Defty, Mr S. K. Ellison (Assistant Clerk of the Records at the House of Lords), Canon Peter Fluck, Mr Douglas Fryer of the Central Board of Finance, Canon John Garton, Mr Hampton Gervis, Mr Nils Halker, the Rev. Donald Harris, Canon Tony Hart, Mr R. J. Henderson, Canon Christopher Hill, Dr Brenda Hough (Archivist to the General Synod of the Church of England), the Rev. Professor Leslie Houlden, the Rt Rev. John Hughes (formerly Suffragan Bishop of Croydon), Mrs Rebecca Hurry, Mr Jonathan Inkpin, Mr Micheàl Jacob, Canon Eric James, the Rev. Graham James, the Rt Rev. David Jenkins (Bishop of Durham), Miss Rebecca Jenkins, the Very Rev. Noel Kennaby, the Rt Rev. John Kirkham (Suffragan Bishop of Sherborne), Mrs John Kirkham, Canon Ray Knell, Sir Desmond Lee, Mr Andrew Lewis, the Rev. Professor John Macquarrie, Canon Tony Meakin, Mr John Miles, Mr Richard Murray, Canon James Owen, Dr Bernard Palmer, Mr Andrew Parker, Mrs Frances Partridge, Mr Gerald Peacocke, Mrs Mary Phipps, the Rt Rev. Simon Phipps (formerly Bishop of Lincoln), the Rev. Wayne Plimmer, the Rev. Robert Pollock, OP, the Rev. Brother Reginald, SSF, Mrs Phyllis Richardson, His Grace the Duke of

ACKNOWLEDGEMENTS

Richmond and Gordon, Dame Betty Ridley, Miss Elizabeth Simons, the Rev. Victor Stock, the Rt Rev. Mervyn Stockwood (formerly Bishop of Southwark), Mr William Surtees, Canon John Turnbull, Mr John Walker, Mr Robin Waterfield, Mr Cyril Watson, the Rev. David Webster, the Rev. Harry Williams, CR, Mr and Mrs Patrick Woodward, the Rev. Francis Woolley and Dr P. N. R. Zutshi (Keeper of the Archives at Cambridge University Library).

Photographs are reproduced by courtesy of Dr Bridget Barcroft, Mr Michael Barcroft, Miss Jane Bown, Mr L. W. Brough, the *Guardian*, the *Daily Express*, Mr Hampton Gervis, Mrs Rebecca Hurry, the *Daily Mirror*, Mrs Frances Partridge and Sport & General.

Michael De-la-Noy
Windsor, 1989

CHAPTER ONE

CHILDHOOD

The saints show us the spirit of Calvary caught in human lives
which show suffering transformed in love, sympathy, creativity. This is itself a part of the Mystery of Life, for the mystery
includes not only the problem of evil but the astonishing
problem of good. *Canterbury Pilgrim.*

Arthur Michael Richard Ramsey was baptized Arthur after
his father, but was invariably known as a boy as Mick, and
in adult life as Michael. He wrote half his considerable
output of books under the name Arthur Michael Ramsey,
but until he made his Will at the age of 82, no mention
was ever made of the name Richard. He was born on 14th
November 1904, the younger son of Arthur Stanley
Ramsey, a mathematics lecturer at Magdalene College,
Cambridge, and of Mary Agnes Wilson, a former teacher
of history at East Putney High School. Among his fore-
bears, on both sides of the family, was a veritable phalanx
of clergymen.

They belonged, however, to two very different traditions. Michael's father was a Congregationalist, and his
paternal grandfather, Adam Averell Ramsey, who was a
Congregationalist minister, had been named in honour of
the Reverend Adam Averell, a famous preacher who
became the leader of John Wesley's followers in Ireland.
Adam had been the second of four sons (there were two

15

girls as well, and the family lived on £70 a year) of the Reverend John Ramsey, who early in life, and following the example of Adam Averell, had quit the Church of England to work for the Irish Home Missionary Society. Thus in 1837 Michael's grandfather, Adam Ramsey, was born in Ireland, at Downpatrick. He spent an itinerant childhood, but eventually the family settled in Dublin where, after visiting the sick, Michael's great grandfather died during an epidemic of scarlet fever.

Missionary fervour seems to have gripped all the men in John Ramsey's family. Adam Averell's eldest brother, John Charles Ramsey, and the third boy, William Henry, both worked for the Home Missionary Society, and John, who remained a Nonconformist all his life, became minister of the French Church in Cork, a building once used by Huguenot refugees. He was later minister of the Independent Chapel at Stonehouse in Gloucestershire, where in 1874 he died of consumption. For a short time, Henry was minister of the Countess of Huntingdon's Chapel in Cheltenham, but was eventually ordained in the Church of Ireland, and after emigrating to California he became archdeacon of Santa Barbara. The youngest of Michael's four great uncles, Andrew, not content with such a resounding second Christian name as Borrowdale, called himself Chrysostom* as well, graduated from Trinity College, Dublin, was ordained in the Church of England, embraced the Anglo-Catholic cause, and became vicar of St Botolph's Church in Lincoln.

Michael's father has recorded that his own father, Adam Averell Ramsey, grew up to be a most earnest evangelical preacher.[1] In his early twenties, from the steps of the

---

* John Chrysostom, born in 347, first became bishop of Constantinople in 398. He was deposed in 403, recalled, and again deposed in 404, dying in exile in 407.

Custom House in Belfast on Sunday afternoons he would preach to large crowds, and according to the *Belfast News Letter*, at Lisburn in June 1859 Sunday services conducted by Adam, when he was only twenty-two, went on "all day and all night". By 1863 he had moved to England, where for a year he served as minister at the Countess of Huntingdon's church in Gloucester, and from 1864 to 1872 he took charge of the Adelphi Congregational Chapel in the Hackney Road, in London's East End. Here he met and married Michael's grandmother, the sixth of nine children of Samuel Sargeant, a successful coal merchant. She was a beautiful young woman, though unfortunately burdened by her own devout, puritanical and "Godfearing" Congregationalist parents with the name of Hephzibah.

Adam and Hephzibah were married, in 1865, at the Adelphi Chapel. Aided by Hephzibah's private income, derived from her father's coal wharf, they made their home, according to Arthur, their second child and Michael's father, in St Thomas's Road, "which", he has written, "abuts on Victoria Park".[2] Although no such road is nowadays adjacent to Victoria Park, at all events it does seem to have been within easy reach of the park, with its lake and green open spaces, and it was here that the oldest children of a typically large Victorian family were born.* The first child was a girl called Phebe, who had an aunt whose name was similarly spelt. Michael's father, who was

---

* Arthur Ramsey's memory may have been unreliable when recording his childhood at the age of 81, for he refers also to his nursery "at the top of our house in Alfred Terrace", but there is no Alfred Terrace anywhere in London. He says, however, that in about 1933 "I made a special visit to Hackney to see once more the scenes of my childhood. St Thomas's Road was still there, but the houses had been renumbered and it was not possible to identify the house in which we lived. It looked a pleasant road as such roads go, and Victoria Park was close at hand."

born in 1867, Arthur Stanley, was named, for some obscure reason, after Queen Victoria's favourite dean of Westminster, and by 1878 the family, numbering eight in all, was complete. The last child to be born, Lucy, was to play a sad domestic role in the adult life of Arthur.

In 1872 Adam and Hephzibah moved to Dewsbury in Yorkshire, where Adam took up his duties as minister of Trinity Congregational Church. Twice a day, after breakfast and tea, Adam conducted family prayers, and with his two brothers and five sisters Arthur took it in turns to read a verse from the Bible. Like all middle-class families at that time, they were ministered to by maids and a nursery governess, and apparently the children "lived a happy carefree life mostly in the open air", with frequent seaside holidays at favourite Yorkshire resorts like Filey. Alas, this carefree life in the open air failed to stand Arthur's brothers in good stead. Frank died from meningitis in 1894 at the age of twenty-three, and in 1903 his younger brother, Harold, who had become a Congregationalist minister at a church in Lewes Road, Brighton, developed tuberculosis of the hip, from which he too died, after many months of acute suffering.

Early in 1877, when Arthur was still only nine and at a formative age, an event occurred which may have accounted for his life-long adherence to religion of a rather puritanical kind. At his father's church a week-long series of evangelistic mission services were held. It seems that "people flocked to the services and night after night the church, which seated twelve hundred, was crowded in the pews, the aisles and the gallery steps, and towards the end of the week there were overflow meetings going on at the same time in a large schoolroom".[3] Phebe and Arthur caught the mood of the moment and began to harangue their pagan friends, conducting prayer meetings in the street and encouraging much ardent hymn singing on the way home from school. In 1882, when he was fifteen, Arthur was admitted as a full communicant member of the Congregational Church. He attended his father's church at 10.30 a.m. every Sunday and again at six o'clock in the evening, and after the evening service he used to take part in an extempore prayer meeting.

From the age of twelve Arthur was educated at Batley Grammar School. His headmaster, the Reverend L. S. Calvert, a graduate of Trinity College, Dublin, was, according to Arthur's adult recollections, "a man whom we all respected and in time came to love".[4] Although ready to teach any subject, his specialities were chemistry and mathematics, and presumably it was under Calvert's influence that Arthur developed his own enthusiasm for mathematics, by which he was to earn a considerable reputation as a lecturer at Cambridge. With five other boys, including one called Henry Spencer, who was later to become his brother-in-law and a Congregationalist minister in Liverpool, Arthur formed a small sixth form, and apart from reading some Greek and Latin texts, his time, he tells us, was now wholly given to mathematics.[5] When he was seventeen he tried for a scholarship to Jesus College, Cambridge, where he had a cousin, Charles Heath, in residence. He came out fourth. A year later he tried for Pembroke, again without success, coming third. At the same time, at King's, he was placed fourth, and a few months later he just failed to secure a scholarship to Christ's College. After such a frustrating series of failures – or near-misses as they actually were – Arthur was fortunate to find four scholarships in mathematics vacant at Magdalene, and he scraped in fourth on the list. His award was worth £45 a year. As it turned out, the early failures proved providential, for there was to be no vacancy as a college lecturer in mathematics at Jesus College until after the Great War, at Christ's College for about thirty years, or at King's for almost forty years, when by chance, in 1924, it was filled by Arthur's elder son Frank. And at Pembroke there was to be no lectureship in mathematics vacant until after Arthur's own election to Magdalene.

So in October 1886 Arthur Stanley Ramsey began his long and distinguished connection with Magdalene College, Cambridge, of which he was to be President from 1915 to 1937. He took up residence as an undergraduate in attics on C staircase, one of several sets of rooms assigned by tradition to Charles Kingsley. Here he remained for four years. His arrival coincided with the retirement of a "very old man", William Walton, who had been eighth wrangler* in 1836 "and had long passed his best days"; he was to be replaced by the Senior Wrangler of 1882, William Welsh, who in the opinion of Arthur Ramsey was "one of the best teachers of mathematics there has ever been".[6] Life in a small Cambridge college in the dying years of the nineteenth century was taken at a leisurely pace. It was not until Arthur had been in residence five terms that he and the other scholars were summoned to the Master's Lodge by its clerical occupant, the Hon. Latimer Neville, for formal admission as scholars and to write their names in the College Order Book.

In 1888 Arthur's father received an invitation to build up a fledgling congregation in Dulwich, so he and his wife, the beautiful Hephzibah, and their younger children now moved back to London. Within three years the Reverend Adam Ramsey had raised the money to build a new church in Barry Road, Dulwich, later bombed in the Second World War. In the year following the family's removal south, Arthur sat the mathematical tripos. He tells us he did not find either part of the examination to his liking,

---

* A wrangler is a holder of a first class honours degree in mathematics at Cambridge.

and "consequently it was a great surprise, when the list was read in the Senate House some ten days later, that I found myself bracketed sixth wrangler. I could not but conclude that the standard must be very low."[7]

Arthur returned to Magdalene for a fourth year to read for the second part of the tripos, choosing to study applied mathematics, and was placed in the second division of the first class. Faced with the immediate need for employment, in September 1890 he obtained a teaching post at a public school, Fettes College in Edinburgh. One of the house-masters there was Kenneth Wilson, who had a sister, a Church of England communicant called Agnes, but it was to be eleven years before an introduction was made between Agnes and Arthur. By that time Arthur had gone back to Magdalene as a Fellow, but within a week of meeting Wilson's sister during a return trip to Fettes in 1901, Arthur had impetuously proposed. Agnes asked for time to consider the matter; but within a few months they were engaged, and in the spring of 1902 they were married by Agnes's father in his own parish church at Horbling in Lincolnshire. Arthur was thirty-four, Agnes was twenty-eight.

Mary Agnes Wilson was the eighth of the nine children – there were six sons and three daughters, and Agnes was the youngest daughter – of the Reverend Plumpton Wilson, whose wife, much loved by her grandchildren, particularly Michael, was known as Mimi. "I think we loved our grandmother Mimi almost as much as we loved Mother herself", Michael warmly recalled in old age. It was a mixed marriage in several ways. Arthur Ramsey, descended from ardent Nonconformist stock and a practising Congregationalist, had chosen as his bride not just the daughter of an Anglican priest but a young woman with a pronounced preference for the Anglo-Catholic wing of the Church of England; she enjoyed attending celebrations of the Eucharist where vestments were worn and incense was burnt. But they did have much in common. Both enjoyed sport (Arthur played cricket and Agnes hockey), and although academically neither of them would ever have claimed to hold a candle to either of their sons, both were extremely able; Agnes, who had been educated at Redland High School in Bristol, had taken a Second in Modern History at St Hugh's College, Oxford. But as with religion, their allegiances diverged again when it came to politics, in which both were keenly interested, Agnes being the more politically active of the two; Arthur was a Liberal, Agnes a suffragist and ultimately a socialist.

Arthur and Agnes made their first home at 71 Chesterton Road in Cambridge, and here they lived from 1902 until 1909. The house had been built in 1883 opposite a footbridge crossing the River Cam, and it was only a three- or four-minute walk from Magdalene College. There was a small rear garden, and unimpeded views from the front windows across to the cricket grounds of Jesus College. Arthur rented the property from two of his unmarried sisters. It stood on four floors with a breakfast room in the basement and a nursery at the top, and it may have had as many as six bedrooms, all still lit by gas. During the Second World War the house was converted into flats and became somewhat dilapidated, but since 1979 it has been carefully restored and is today a comfortable guest house. The present owner, on her own initiative, has had a plaque placed beside the front door, commemorating the fact that it was in this house, in 1904, that Michael Ramsey, Archbishop of Canterbury, was born.

But the first of Arthur and Agnes's four children to arrive, in February 1903, after a labour lasting almost forty-eight hours, was Frank. He became something of a giant, both intellectually and physically; his frame was large and ungainly, he grew six feet three inches tall, and weighed 16 stone. There was also little dispute that he was a genius. But he was born with jaundice, and in his boyhood he also suffered from poor digestion. The child was baptized at Horbling by his grandfather, whose own Christian name of Plumpton he was given in addition to Frank, Frank no doubt being chosen in memory of Arthur's ill-fated brother. His father records that the boy's intellectual development was remarkable, and that he learnt to read almost as soon as he could talk.[8] Apparently he also "always had a great regard for truth". Agnes took him to a children's service at her parish church, St Giles's,* on the corner of Chesterton Lane and Castle Street, and on leaving Frank is supposed to have protested, "It's no good that man saying that we are the children of Abraham because I know we're not. Abraham came from Shem and we came from Japhet." Although he was confirmed as a boy, further pursuit of truth led Frank in early manhood to abandon Christianity entirely.

A nagging concern over his health now prompted Arthur to take on pupils from Newnham and Girton as well as male undergraduates from colleges other than his own, in order to earn extra money he could put aside in case he found himself unable to work at all.† He was in fact suffering from appendicitis, which went undetected for six years and was only finally cured by an operation in 1908, performed at 71 Chesterton Road. In the meantime, in order to try to keep fit, Arthur played strenuous rounds of golf, and was lucky not to end up with peritonitis. Exhausted after examining in the Mathematical Tripos, Arthur went on holiday to Scotland in the summer of

* Now the Parish of the Ascension, part of the team ministry of St Augustine's, St Giles's and St Luke's.
† There was also a falling off of work available at Magdalene. During the academic year 1903–04 there were only twenty-eight undergraduates in residence.

1904, and it was then that he first met A. C. Benson, with whom he was to work at Magdalene for twenty years. Benson's father had been Archbishop of Canterbury from 1883 until 1896. In his diary, Benson described Arthur Ramsey at this time as "A quiet, sad, pleasant, donnish man, who finds the world rather hard." Arthur's donnish life was nevertheless falling into a pleasant enough pattern. He and his wife attended dinner parties in Cambridge at which ten courses were regularly served, and they entertained Magdalene undergraduates to tea on Sundays. Towards the end of 1904, on 14th November, Michael, their second child, was born.

Like Frank, he was baptized by his grandfather, Plumpton Wilson, at the parish church in Horbling. And again like Frank, Michael was to grow into a large and ungainly shape, but not so tall. His square jaw and hooded eyes, which became such distinctive features, were later shared to some extent with his younger sister, Margaret, born in 1917, although there seems to have been little physical resemblance between Michael and his elder sister, Bridget, born in 1907. But the fact that Frank and Michael were strikingly gauche and ungainly, and to some degree shared with Margaret recognizable facial characteristics, would indicate a strong genetic link with some forebear or other, most probably on their father's side, for a maternal cousin and exact contemporary, Roger Wilson, who became bishop of Chichester, bears no resemblance to Michael at all. It cannot be said that either boy looked remotely like either parent, even though in old age Arthur Ramsey, like Michael, lost his hair and sprouted bushy eyebrows. Arthur was essentially a spruce, rather gaunt figure, not in the least like the popular concept of an absentminded professor. Agnes was by far the more attractive of the two, with fair wispy hair and bright, alert eyes. Her daughter Margaret (who was only ten when her mother died) has described Agnes Ramsey as "very outgoing, full of interest in public affairs, extremely amusing and lively",[9] characteristics she thinks were particularly inherited by Bridget's family, but it could undoubtedly be said of Michael, too, that he was amusing – if not outgoing – and very interested in public affairs.

It was certainly from his mother that Michael inherited or acquired his youthful fascination for history, and possibly too his desire to write; at Oxford she had known Charles Dodgson, then a don at Christ Church, and she edited textbook editions of Charles Lamb and Browning. (His father wrote prolifically, but titles like *Electricity and Magnetism* or *Hydrostatics* would hardly have been likely to stir his imagination.) He was to root his theological quest for the nature of Jesus and the Church in a comprehension of history, and he used to tell ordinands that "However contemporary we may try to be, our authority rests upon an 'old, old story'. And all this amidst a generation for whom the sense of the past is very faint. I would say that one of the biggest differences between the up-and-coming generation in England and its predecessors is that it has a thick curtain between itself and past history or tradition. My own generation felt itself to belong to a stream which flowed through past time: this generation has its consciousness filled and absorbed by the present."[10]

It was from Agnes too that Michael inherited his concern for social justice (he never exhibited even a subconscious trace of racial prejudice, which was rare for a middle-class Englishman born at the turn of the century). Agnes could see no reason why women and children condemned to the workhouse should have their lives controlled by exclusively male Boards of Guardians, and got herself elected a Guardian of the Poor. She became secretary of a committee that boarded out workhouse children in homes in the villages of Cambridgeshire, and as secretary of a committee of women school managers she set about distributing milk to schoolchildren. She also served on the committee of management of a nursing hostel in Thompson's Lane, just off Magdalene Street. In 1918 she joined the Labour Party, and five years later she had Hugh Dalton to stay.* She was considered an excellent public speaker, another gift for which Michael became heavily indebted to her.

Bridget, whose memory of her mother may be taken to be clearer even than Margaret's (she was nineteen when Agnes died), confirms her sister's impressions. "Everybody was very fond of my mother. She was a very lovable person. Everybody in Cambridge loved her, and if I went to a party with her it was she who collected a crowd of people around her. She had a tremendous sense of fun and humour."[11]

In some quarters, Arthur Ramsey, on the other hand, acquired a reputation for rather austere behaviour, yet young visitors to the house, his daughters' friends in particular, liked him. But there seems no doubt that the early death of his wife caused him to withdraw emotionally. Even when Agnes was alive, Margaret thinks he was "rather withdrawn and cross, raging at my mother over the dinner table, mostly over trivia, getting absurdly cross if the maid had not placed the butter knife in the right position. After my mother's death he became extremely gloomy." Fussing over the precise position of objects on the table may well have been indicative of the neat, formal mind of a mathematician.

Again according to Margaret, Arthur Ramsey would never have described himself as brilliant, although he was "a very good expositor of mathematics at undergraduate level". But he knew from early on that he had not one but two sons to contend with both far cleverer than he, one of

---

* At Howfield in Buckingham Road.

them, the elder, almost certainly a genius, the other, Michael, both clever and wildly eccentric. With the elder, however, he shared his life-long passion for mathematics, and had he not died, Frank, who won a scholarship to Winchester and entered Trinity College, Cambridge at the age of seventeen, would almost certainly have developed into the most brilliant mathematical philosopher of his generation. And whereas Frank might have disappointed his father by his loss of faith, Michael, although he chose allegiance to his mother's Church, showed an early attachment to Christianity and was to prove the only one of the four children to retain, as did Arthur and Agnes, a lifetime's commitment to religion. In Bridget's opinion, "Father was rather aloof. I think he admired Michael, but they were not very close. Nobody got very close to my father."[12] It seems that Arthur, like many married men from large families, was essentially friendless, and probably more interested in his wife as a companion than in his children. When he lost both her and the son with whom he shared his academic interests he must have been fairly isolated.

Michael was only four when he left Chesterton Road, but he remembered as a child crossing the footbridge to play on the common. One day, in retirement, he and his wife were spotted by the present owner, standing outside. She hesitated whether to ask them in, and by the time she had plucked up the courage, they had gone. Almost all Michael's memories of childhood, and indeed of his life until leaving home at the age of eighteen, would have been centred on a rather grim and unimaginative house his father built in 1909 at the end of a short *cul-de-sac*, Buckingham Road, just off the Huntingdon Road and still only a matter of five or six minutes' walk from Magdalene. The plot that Arthur purchased was part of a two-and-a-half acre site owned by the College on which already stood the new vicarage of St Giles's Church and a house called The Orchard, owned by Sir Horace Darwin. An architect was employed, but little in the way of design transpired. The rooms were small and square, the kitchen quite hideous, the hall and staircase mean. The overall effect was one of dedicated joylessness. Margaret remembers a big house, but childhood houses and gardens are often recalled as having been far larger than they really were. With three children to be accommodated (four after the birth of Margaret), together with a cook and a housemaid, called Doris, and at times Alice, a nurserymaid as well, Howfield, as the new house was called, may well have been rather cramped. Downstairs were a sitting room, dining room and study. A small veranda led to the garden, where the children used to knock their tennis balls against a sloping roof, and in the garden, which had to be created from scratch, there was space for a grass tennis court and some forty fruit trees. Michael is said by his father to have given a hand with a spade and barrow, working "for hours side by side with the gardener, filling his barrow as the gardener did, wheeling it to the right spot and emptying it there".[13]

As for life indoors, Margaret remembers that "Father was rather mean, particularly about heat. There was never more than one fire on, which was in his study, and he would sit in the study in front of this one fire with the family around him. Two bells were rung for meals, one five minutes after the other. As she rang the first bell, the housemaid went into the dining room and lit a rather small gas fire. By the time we left the room it was just beginning to warm up!"[14]

When Arthur Ramsey died, on the last day of 1954, Howfield was sold to the English Dominicans, who extended their frontage to link Howfield with The Orchard. The whole property is now called Blackfriars, and while it may seem appropriate that Michael Ramsey's childhood home should end up as a monastery, his Congregationalist father, broadminded though he was in ecclesiastical affairs, might have been a little surprised at the prospect of the Roman Catholic Mass being celebrated on premises where he had lived for forty-five years. The house, at any rate, is dedicated to St Michael.

In 1910 Arthur and Agnes took their children for the first of several summer holidays to Perranporth on the north coast of Cornwall. One year they were joined by two of Arthur's sisters, Mabel and Lucy, by Agnes's parents, and by several of Agnes's brothers and sisters, including her third brother, the Reverend Clifford Wilson, a Bristol parish priest, so that Michael was enveloped by relatives, including Clifford Wilson's son, his cousin Roger Wilson, eight months his junior.

In 1949 Roger was consecrated bishop of Wakefield.* Michael, like many boys of his age, was addicted to playing with lead soldiers, and one day he and Roger placed some of the soldiers in a boat, which capsized. The soldiers were naturally presumed drowned, and the two nascent clergymen conducted a funeral service. Under more normal conditions, on dry land at home, Michael used to appoint one of his lead soldiers commander-in-chief and insist that the soldier make a speech before commencing battle. His father asserts that once an interest in politics had taken hold, Michael "arranged his soldiers as a House of Commons and made them harangue one another". There is a story that on a "mound" at Magdalene, Michael preached a youthful sermon, but the mound has been difficult to identify, as has the text.

Michael's mother enjoyed giving garden parties at Howfield in aid of Labour Party funds, and in disgust her Liberal husband would stalk off to dine in college. The

* From 1958–1974 bishop of Chichester.

impression is certainly given in Arthur's memoirs that on
these occasions he drank claret and port with the best of
them, but there seems to have been little alcoholic refreshment served at home. Undergraduates were frequently
entertained at Howfield to lunch and tea, but almost
certainly nothing stronger than cider was provided, and it
was more likely soft drinks. Clearly there was never much
money, for Agnes took to bicycling round Cambridge in
search of minute economies on food. The atmosphere
seems to have been rather stark, and Margaret's remark
that "a good standard of behaviour was expected" puts the
general ambiance neatly. She adds that her father was
broadminded, "a very good, generous man".[15]

Of enormous influence on Michael was his mother's
observance of Anglo-Catholic worship. After the birth of
Frank she was churched at St Peter's,* the little church
that stands back from the Huntingdon Road, just round
the corner from Howfield, but she more generally
remained faithful to her old parish church of St Giles's.
On festivals, however, she took Michael with her to Little
St Mary's, on the corner of Trumpington Street and Little
St Mary's Lane. It was at Little St Mary's that Michael
frequently preached when appointed Regius Professor of
Divinity at Cambridge, and this was the Cambridge church
for which, partly because of his childhood connections
with it and partly through a friendship formed late in life
with the vicar who was inducted in 1974, Canon James
Owen, he reserved a special affection. The church dates
from the twelfth century. In Michael's boyhood the vicar
was the Reverend Andrew Allen. He was succeeded in
1917 by Geoffrey Clayton, who became archbishop of
Cape Town, and on Clayton's death Michael Ramsey was
to refer to him as one of the Church's heroic figures.[16] An

---

* Now in the care of the Redundant Churches Fund.

interesting literary link was forged when in 1924 the Reverend Cyril Hankey, later dean of Ely, became the incumbent: he was married to the daughter of Oscar Wilde's notorious biographer, Frank Harris. Michael may well have been present in 1913 when the new High Altar, designed by Sir Ninian Comper, was installed, and in retirement it was he who, in 1978, dedicated the present organ. Three years later he was invited to dedicate the engraved glass doors at the west end.

Father Clayton, who was also dean of Peterhouse, had been responsible for the introduction into Little St Mary's of two ugly statues of dubious artistic merit, a truly horrible one of the Good Shepherd and one of Our Lady. Michael Ramsey used to recall a story dating from his first year at Magdalene, which nicely combined academic with ecclesiastical scratchiness. "During Clayton's time, when I was an undergraduate, there was a very, very low church archdeacon. Very low indeed. And the low church archdeacon came into the church and he said to Clayton, 'These statues, I suppose the poorer and more ignorant people in the parish say their prayers to them.' And Clayton said, 'Oh, no, no, no, no, mainly Fellows of Corpus.'"

The extraordinary contrast was that when he was not being introduced by his mother to the mystique of high church liturgy, or was not attending Canon L. G. Mannering's children's services at Holy Trinity Church, between Market Street and Sidney Street, Michael would be taken by his father to Emmanuel Congregational Church, practically next door to Little St Mary's, a towering and rather forbidding edifice on the opposite corner of Little St Mary's Lane, to which, in about 1914, Arthur was elected a deacon.* To say there was a tug of war between his

---

* A deacon in the Congregational Church is a layman. Arthur Ramsey

parents over Michael's denominational allegiance would be to exaggerate the situation, but he must have felt a sense of divided loyalties. It may well have been a situation he shared with his paternal relatives, for over the years a steady drift to the Church of England of Arthur's brothers and sisters took place, until eventually, when Michael was parish priest of St Benedict's in Cambridge (often referred to locally as St Benet), he actually received his own father.

On Palm Sunday 1977 the congregations of Little St Mary's and Emmanuel joined forces, which was a moving ecumenical experience for Michael Ramsey, who had been invited to preside. "This could never have happened twenty years ago", he remarked. An old lady from Emmanuel remembered him as a naughty little boy in the front pew, a recollection that sparked off in Michael his inimitable habit of repeating a phrase, his own or someone else's, in his unique and attractive sing-song way of speaking. "Well, well, well, fancy that. A naughty little boy. Fancy that!" He loved Little St Mary's, and in retirement he was often invited to celebrate at the 8 a.m. Mass. One morning Enoch Powell, who was staying next door at Peterhouse, and whose views on racial integration had been anathema to Michael (he had described Powell's infamous "rivers of blood" speech, made in Birmingham in 1967, as a counsel of despair), appeared at the altar rail. Afterwards, in the vestry, Canon Owen said to Michael, "Did you see Enoch?" "Enoch?" replied Michael in tones of mock incredulity, having just given him communion, "Was Enoch there?"

---

also served as church secretary during the First World War, and remained a deacon of Emmanuel Congregational Church for about thirty years, until, he says, he found himself "too deaf to take an intelligent part in meetings".

In 1976 Michael noticed a poster in the church advertising a list of open lectures. With carefully nurtured exaggeration he went through the list of distinguished names. "He doesn't believe in the Incarnation. He doesn't believe in the Resurrection. He doesn't believe in God. Oh, and *he* doesn't believe in anything. He doesn't believe in anything except himself. He does believe in that quite considerably!" This was typical of the "nonsense humour" that always convulsed those attuned to it, partly by the way the lines were delivered, and partly by the sheer enormity of the libels they contained.

Eight months before Michael died, the Michael Ramsey Society was established at Little St Mary's, with the purpose of holding two open lectures a year relating to the basic understanding of Christianity.* The aim is simply to perpetuate the teaching of Christianity conducted by Michael Ramsey in Cambridge over a period of thirty years. "These lectures", Canon Owen has explained, "are intended to fill a basic need. In cultural terms, most undergraduates these days don't even know what Christianity is."[17] The Bishop of Edinburgh, Richard Holloway, lecturing on 30th November 1988, remarked, "When I am at my lowest point of tolerance for institutional religion, and especially the form of it to which I belong, there are one or two places that bring me back to a sort of good-humoured resignation, and there are one or two people, some of them dead, who also have that effect, people to whom I can turn. Michael Ramsey and Austin Farrer† are two of them."

---

* A similar lecture society has been established in Durham, and at the time of writing an appeal has been launched to establish a Chair in Anglican and Ecumenical Theology in Michael Ramsey's name at the University of Kent in Canterbury.
† A Fellow and Chaplain of Trinity College, Oxford from 1935 to 1960, and Warden of Keble College, Oxford from 1960 until his death in 1968.

While he was becoming accustomed to the smell of incense, Michael was also learning to smell books. He owned a set of history books, including *Our Island Story*, into which, both metaphorically and literally, he used to bury his nose, and when he was an adolescent he would play a game with his young sister Margaret. He would shut his eyes, tell Margaret to place any one of the history books against his face, and then he would tell her which one it was by its smell. One of these history books, *The Story of Rome*, was rescued from the loft at Howfield by Michael's nephew, Michael Barcroft, who became head-master of Peterborough Cathedral Choir School. In 1976 Michael Barcroft invited his uncle to open a new building at the school. At a tea party afterwards, in front of the civic dignitories of Peterborough, Michael Ramsey allowed a scarf to be tied over his eyes, smelled the book, and after sixty-one years correctly identified its title. The book had been an eleventh birthday present from his parents, and it carried the rather odd inscription, not in Michael's hand-writing, "The Rev. Arthur Michael Ramsey from Father and Mother, November 14 1915".

In 1982, while talking to an American guest in Durham, Mrs Laurie Kahn-Leavitt, who was researching the life of his brother Frank, Michael recalled he had gone through a phase of reading "rather pious books about being kind to the poor. Then I dropped that and for several years was very fond of G. A. Henty."* He recalled, too, both he and Frank attending a couple of schools for very young children, one of them at 197 Chesterton Road, where they were taught the rudiments of arithmetic and, rather sur-prisingly, French. In 1911, when he was eight, Frank was

---

* A biography of Frank Ramsey has now been abandoned by Mrs Kahn-Leavitt and is being undertaken for Duckworth by Frank's sister, Margaret Paul.

sent as a day boy to King's College Choir School,* whose
new buildings had been opened in West Road in 1878,
within easy walking distance across the Backs for the
sixteen choristers who regularly sang in King's College
Chapel. This was also the year in which the school,
established in 1441 by Henry VI, had been reconstituted
as a boarding preparatory school. By the time the preco-
cious Frank was ten he was at the top of the school in
mathematics, so he was transferred to a preparatory school
called Sandroyd, at Oxshott in Surrey, where one of the
joint headmasters was his uncle, the Reverend Charles
Wilson.† But Sandroyd too failed to keep up with Frank's
fertile brain, and he entered Winchester with a scholarship
at the age of twelve. This was the academically brilliant
brother with whom Michael had to compete. In 1914,
when he was nine, Michael followed Frank to King's
College Choir School, also as a day boy, a rather despised
species within the school hierarchy. The choristers were
regarded – mainly by themselves – as the crème de la
crème, and looked down their noses at the five non-
scholarship boarders, whose fees helped to pay for the
choristers' places. Everyone affected to despise the seventeen day boys.

In the Lent Term of 1914 Michael was placed in the
Upper Fourth Division, and among his seven classmates
was a boy called Oswin Harvard Gibbs-Smith, later to
become dean of Winchester. In the Third Division was
William Baker, consecrated bishop of Zanzibar in 1943,
when he was forty-one. Another exact contemporary,
placed in the Lower Fourth Division, was Henry Barcroft,
who became a most distinguished doctor and Michael's

* Now known as King's College School.
† The other headmaster was W. H. Hornby. The school later moved to
Salisbury.

brother-in-law, for he married his elder sister Bridget.* "At King's Michael was terribly teased by my husband and others", Dr Bridget Barcroft now confesses.[18] But one boy who arrived in October 1915 and refrained from calling Michael Ramsey a mouldy day-bug, for which Michael remained grateful ever after, was Donald Harris, later archdeacon of Bedford. He recalls Michael standing in the playground "not looking like a boy at all. He seemed to have a very short neck, and he just stood there sort of heaving his shoulders up and down."[19] It was often the custom for day boys to invite boarders home for tea on Sundays, and Donald Harris, a choral scholar and therefore a boarder, was often invited by Henry Barcroft to meet his parents (his father was Sir Joseph Barcroft, Professor of Physiology at Cambridge). "But," Father Harris recalls, "I don't believe Michael ever invited anybody home. There was a great detachment about him. Even in those days he seemed to live in his own mental world. I don't remember him talking to any other boy. He was very solitary."

Bridget confirms that "Michael never brought a friend to the house. I'd have loved to have met his friends, but he didn't seem to have any. I think he had a lonely childhood. Frank had flown the nest [by the time Michael was eight, Frank was already at boarding school] and was too clever by half, and Michael would have said I was a silly girl. He suffered very much from being in the middle, and from not being as clever as Frank. Everybody admired my beauty but nobody admired him for anything very much."[20] A flavour of Michael's relations with his younger sister, Margaret, can be glimpsed from the diaries of Frances Partridge. In March 1928 she lunched at Howfield,

---

* From 1948 to 1971 Henry Barcroft was Professor of Physiology at St Thomas's Hospital Medical School, London.

recording afterwards, "There was a brother of Frank's called Mick, a most curious-looking young man with a mobile white face and small red-rimmed eyes; he is said to be very clever as well as deeply religious. He seemed devoted to his little sister Margie, and I noticed him give way to an irresistible impulse and quickly and furtively stroke her cheek."[21] "I think he liked me as a sort of pet", is Margaret Paul's adult assessment of their relationship at the time.[22]

Michael Ramsey's headmaster at King's, Charles Jelf, a classical scholar with undoubted teaching ability but all the hallmarks of an unimaginative authoritarian, had been appointed in 1912. One of his first innovations was to introduce a regular morning assembly at which he would expound the scriptures and commend to the boys the virtues of hard work, honesty and thrift. He had the unpleasant habit of dissecting in public the shortcomings of individual boys, "their catalogue of offences being recited at length with the aim, often achieved, of making them feel a great sense of shame".[23] He was the vicar's warden at St Giles's, but apparently his Anglo-Catholicism marched hand in hand with a streak of evangelicalism that "produced an attitude of derision towards the chapel services".[24] His contempt extended to the University of Cambridge itself, and he even provocatively wore an Oxford hood when attending services at King's College. He abominated motor cars, but he did condescend to install a telephone.

Jelf sounds like a thoroughly unsuitable headmaster to be in charge of a child as sensitive and odd as Michael Ramsey. R. J. Henderson, the compiler of the history of King's College Choir School, has written: "He was unapproachable and would not have had much time for the boy who was unhappy, the boy with a problem or simply the boy who wanted to talk. He would have been horrified by the suggestion that a boy liked him and showed little or no interest in them as individuals." Discipline under this martinet was as severe as the high choker collar he wore, his Victorian button boots and his starched cuffs. Henderson says, "His panacea for any form of irregular behaviour was the liberal use of the cane, and there were several instances of eight strokes being used. These beatings were supplemented by the continued use of ostracism, drills and lines." No wonder Donald Harris recalls that "most of the boys were frightened of him."[25] Mrs Jelf seems to have been made of similar material; she was in charge of the catering, and Father Harris says she looked like a squeezed lemon. Although efficient, according to Mr Henderson she "performed her task with little humour or kindheartedness. Indeed, it was quite impossible for the boys to view her as a mother figure, and she had little patience with demands for her attention."

Michael's mother dressed him in woollen combinations, no doubt to ward off the cold from the classrooms, rooms which seem to have been heated as sparseley as Howfield itself. "The heating was as unsatisfactory as the food", R. J. Henderson has written. "Most rooms were heated by a radiator, warmed by a row of gas jets. The amount of heat was controlled by the flow of gas, which, owing to Jelf's frugality, was normally kept as low as possible. Only the schoolroom, with a fireplace, was properly heated in winter. The iron room was particularly icy, being heated by an inefficient tortoise stove, which frequently broke down." Long trousers, compulsory at eleven, may have helped the boys to keep warm; less welcome would have been Jelf's insistence on stiff Eton collars. Academically, it is fair to say that in some respects Michael Ramsey must have benefited from attending King's, where much of the teaching was carried out by undergraduates, for half the school periods were devoted to Latin or Greek, and Jelf himself excelled as a teacher of Latin. But mathematics and French, in neither of which Michael became at all proficient, were allocated about five periods each every week, and geography and history – in which he was extremely interested – only one. Science was ignored altogether, and it was also assumed that if the boys mastered classical grammar they would need no tuition in English. The oddest feature of Charles Jelf's grim regime was the high academic standards later attained by so many pupils who had been subjected to an outmoded and intolerant system of teaching by rote. One boy, Francis Parsons, was awarded the Victoria Cross, but by and large Michael Ramsey must be the most famous boy the school has ever produced, and although he could not have carried away from it many happy memories, he agreed to become president of the King's College School Association, launching a centenary appeal at a dinner at King's College in 1978.

At the age of nine, Michael won the hundred yards race, a feat that does not in the least surprise Donald Harris, for when he and Michael Ramsey were undergraduates at Cambridge they both returned to King's on two successive occasions to attend the school sports days, competing in the old boys' race, and on both occasions Michael beat Donald – who had played outside three-quarter for Haileybury – into second place. By the autumn term of his first year he had been moved up to the Third Division, and when he left, at the end of the summer term of 1916, by which time numbers at the school had risen to forty-eight, he was one of only four boys in the First Division. What possessed his parents to disrupt his prep school education at this point was probably their desire for him to gain a scholarship to a good public school, and even though Frank had already moved on to Winchester, Michael was whisked away from the relative security of

King's, not more than a ten-minute walk up Queen's Road from his home, to Sandroyd and the dubious care of his uncle Charles. The need for a scholarship was quite simply shortage of money with which to pay school fees. Arthur reckoned that but for the war Magdalene would have had a hundred undergraduates in residence in October 1914. As it was, by the Easter Term of 1915 only twenty-nine remained, and to compensate Arthur for the loss of tutorial fees, one of the first things A. C. Benson did that summer, on receiving a gift of £40,000 from an enormously wealthy American lady, was to make Arthur a present of £100.* When later that year Benson was offered the Mastership of Magdalene, he declined most of the salary and arranged, on the strength of the consequent savings, for Arthur's pay to be increased.

The journey to Sandroyd, in purple school cap and plus-fours, would have been undertaken by train to Liverpool Street and by a journey across London to Waterloo to catch a second train to Oxshott, where on Sundays strictly supervised walks were permitted in the pinewoods. Public beatings occasionally took place, when as many as ten strokes might be administered, but a spanking in the dormitory by matron with a hairbrush was more usual. Sandroyd was Michael's first experience, at the age of twelve, of being away from home, and he was desperately home-sick. "He was frightfully unhappy there," according to Margaret, "and wrote a letter home in his first term to say he was crying and that if his mother did not come and fetch him there was no saying what might happen. Mother went post haste to the school but she didn't bring him back. Uncle Charlie said if he ever wrote a letter like that again he would thrash him to within an inch of his life."[26]

---

* As a result of Arthur Benson's windfall, Magdalene College received much generous financial consideration, culminating in a legacy of £35,000.

Uncle Charlie's partner, W. H. Hornby, taught history, and Charles Wilson classics. His wife, Aunt Lily, seems to have exercised a reasonably human influence ("the fact that she was there and sometimes spoke to one in a friendly and kindly way made a bit of difference", Michael remembered in old age),[27] and it has to be said that with the passing of the years, he modified considerably his first impressions, impressions which may have given rise to an unfair image of Uncle Charlie held by other members of the family. He told Mrs Kahn-Levitt, "Uncle Charlie was basically a very just, fair and kindly person. He wasn't cruel or tyrannical at all, but he had rather a sort of deep, gruff voice, and his voice was rather frightening. I used to think he was sort of bellowing at us, but he wasn't really bellowing at all, it was just that he had rather a deep voice." What seems particularly to have upset Michael was that for some reason his uncle called his cousin Roger Wilson, who also went to Sandroyd, "Roger", but insisted on calling Michael "Ramsey".

When, on 4th December 1962, as archbishop of Canterbury, Michael gave the Waley Cohen Lecture on "The Crisis of Humane Freedom" he recalled that amongst the memories of his very young school days was "the occasion when the familiar essay was set: 'Would you have been a Cavalier or a Roundhead and why?' I wrote: 'I would have been a Roundhead because the Roundheads were more tolerant than the Cavaliers', and the master wrote in red ink in the margin, 'I doubt this'." The master was probably right but the cause young Ramsey chose to support suited his personality. It may well have been at Sandroyd that the essay was written, and it is interesting to note that in his entry in *Who's Who* he omitted any reference to being educated at his uncle's school.

"He wasn't well adjusted to life" is how Bridget Barcroft succinctly describes Michael as a boy. "I think sending him to Sandroyd was probably a mistake, because Uncle Charlie was a really tough gamesey chap, and the boys there all came from very expensive homes and Michael never got asked to stay with any of them. Uncle Charlie didn't really appreciate Michael very much."* At about this time, Michael's own father, far from possessing an expensive home himself, was so short of tutorial fees that he and Agnes decided to take in Indian and Siamese students as lodgers. Arthur of course coached them for university entrance in mathematics, Agnes in French. Many years later, when he was archbishop of Canterbury, Michael Ramsey gave refuge to a Siamese at Lambeth Palace. It may in fact have been his parent's partiality for Indian and Siamese students that made racial integration seem so natural to Michael from a very young age. When in September 1916 the family went on holiday to Old Hunstanton, on the Norfolk coast, they took an Indian pupil with them. It was here that they had their first experience of an air raid. A German Zeppelin, apparently intent on destroying Sandringham House, where Queen Alexandra continued to live as a widow, dropped a bomb about half a mile from their rented bungalow. Despite the bungalow rocking and the thud of gunfire, Michael, rather typically, remained oblivious to danger and slept through the raid.

Sometimes during the school holidays Michael escaped from the family to stay with a rather more agreeable uncle than Charles Wilson, Dr A. W. Wilson. He was organist at Ely Cathedral, and Michael regarded Uncle Archie as "my greatest friend in the family".[28] On the visits to Archie Wilson he spent many hours alone cycling through the Cambridgeshire villages to visit parish churches so that he

---

* Charles Wilson, a graduate of Trinity College, Cambridge, was a cricket blue, captain of the Cambridge Rugby XV, and a Rugby International.

could make brass rubbings. This absorbing pastime gave him an enormous sense of satisfaction, and in later years, at the Old Palace in Canterbury, he would proudly show off rubbings of medieval knights produced on hands and knees when he was a boy.

CHAPTER TWO

REPTON

We are all of us infinitessimally small and ludicrous creatures within God's universe.   *The Christian Priest Today.*

Just as Arthur Ramsey's initial failures to gain a scholarship to Cambridge had proved providential in the long run, so too, while at Sandroyd, Michael had a youthful experience of good coming out of evil. He attempted to gain a scholarship to Winchester, where Frank was covering himself in academic glory, but he came thirteenth, and that year only a dozen boys were accepted. It would, however, almost certainly have been a mistake for Michael to follow so closely in his brother's footsteps. In 1915 Frank had been placed first on the roll at Winchester, and after a term, still aged only twelve, he had mastered algebra up to quadratic equations and progressions. When he was fourteen, merely, it seems, for practice, he sat the scholarship examination for New College, Oxford, and when he did the same thing a year later, this time taking the mathematical papers in the scholarship group to which Magdalene, Cambridge belonged, he was a long way ahead of all the other candidates. At sixteen he headed the list for the college he was eventually to enter, Trinity, and in his last year at Winchester he won the German prize. Had Michael gone to Winchester he would, being only eighteen months younger than Frank, have been continually exposed to comparison with him.

Arthur Ramsey has described Michael as "much more normal in his attainments",[1] but he was hardly "normal" in the social sense. "He was far more eccentric as a boy than as an adult", his sister Bridget recalls.[2] "I remember him in his teens when I had a patch of really quite disliking him. He was appallingly messy. He spilled food all down himself. He would jump up in the middle of a meal and when you talked to him you couldn't feel he was attending. He was peculiarly cut off from people. I don't think Mick and I were very good friends. I was very popular and sociable, and I used to ask a lot of girls to the house, and I can remember them saying, 'What shall we do this afternoon, shall we tease Michael?' And we would chase Michael round the garden. But he didn't want to play hide and seek or any normal game. He was very aloof. He had this extraordinary habit of running. He would suddenly get up while we were having a meal and run round the garden. I used to get very annoyed with him on the tennis court because I was much better and could beat him, and he would drop his racket and tear off round the vegetable garden. He had one friend later on at Magdalene called Gilbert Ponsonby, whom he brought home, but I don't remember him having any friends as a schoolboy at all."

Speaking perhaps with the benefit of family folklore, for she was not born until 1917, Michael's younger sister Margaret nevertheless confirms the eminent teaseability of her brother. "As a child," she says, "he was very timid physically. He was teased for being timid. He was fearfully teaseable. He was a natural butt as a child."[3]

This then was the introspective, rather fearful boy, insecurely squashed between a brilliant elder brother and a boisterous, attractive sister, no doubt in awe of his withdrawn and donnish father, and no doubt also drawn to the humanity of his mother without being able to claim much physical maternal affection, who at thirteen did succeed in gaining a scholarship to a public school, one which was to have a most extraordinary bearing on his life. In September 1918 he entered Repton. A former headmaster (from 1910 to 1914), William Temple, was to become bishop of Manchester in 1921, archbishop of York in 1929 and thirteen years later archbishop of Canterbury. The headmaster when Michael arrived at the sixteenth-century Derbyshire establishment was a thirty-one-year-old Triple First, Geoffrey Fisher, who had succeeded Temple three years previously.* In 1932, Fisher was consecrated bishop of Chester. He was translated in 1939 to London, and in 1945, following the sudden death of Temple the previous year, he became the ninety-ninth archbishop of Canterbury. From 1956 to 1961, the year that Fisher retired as archbishop of Canterbury, Michael Ramsey was to serve under his former headmaster as archbishop of York.

Arthur Ramsey has written of Michael at the time that he entered Repton as "always dreamy and inattentive, with a keen sense of the ludicrous and prone to laugh out loud whether it be in church or in form." He thought he might have been as good at games as Frank had he been able to attend to the game, "but he always seemed to be thinking about something else . . . There was always a good deal of independence about his character and disposition." Arthur Ramsey blandly recalled that "When the time came for him to go to Repton as a new boy he did not seem to mind the fact that neither his mother nor I were able to escort him and that he was the only new boy at his house to arrive without a parent in charge."⁴ But children often do mind about these things far more than they let on.

* Repton went in for youthful appointments. William Temple was only twenty-nine when he became headmaster.

46

As Michael was later to wear one, it was an odd coincidence that from a choice of eight boarding houses he should have entered the Mitre. The housemaster for the past two years had been Harold Hayward, a fine tennis player in his youth, who taught modern languages and was a great expert on butterflies and moths.* But although regarded "as the finest type of Christian schoolmaster", with "unfailing courtesy and good manners", some of the boys thought him not entirely fit to be a housemaster, partly because he was diabetic, and ironically because they considered him "too much of a gentleman".[5] It was his wife, irreverently known to the boys as Ma Hayward, who apparently ran the house. A boy who arrived at the Mitre the same day as Michael, who was just one day older and knew him well at school for four years, Mr Hampton Gervis, says, "We adored Harold Hayward, but he had a very strong-minded wife. We were terrified of her. She was down on any boy who looked untidy, and Michael was awfully untidy."[6] Bullying was strictly taboo in the Mitre, and although it seems that Michael was sometimes laughed at when he first arrived, as he made his way through the school he acquired the cautious respect of other boys. And as his intellectual abilities began to blossom under a variety of sympathetic teachers, especially on the classical side, his most rewarding relationships were almost certainly forged with masters.

"He was a very honest and rather shy person who seemed to live rather in a world of his own", Mr Gervis recalls. "I would say his friends were really his books. We always thought he was a bit curious. He did such odd

---

* When Harold Hayward retired from the Mitre in 1934 he was succeeded as housemaster by A. P. Wilson, a cousin of Michael and a graduate of Pembroke College, Cambridge, who was already teaching at Repton when Michael arrived. Also on the staff in Michael's day was the future left-wing publisher, Victor Gollancz.

things. His mannerisms were curious, especially his springy walk and the way he threw back his head. He gave the impression of acting slightly beyond his years." One of the odd things he did occurred within a very few weeks of his arrival. When in November 1918 the armistice was announced, Michael came firmly to believe that permission had been given for boys to fool around in fancy dress, and he was discovered most convincingly attired, and parading the streets of the village, as an old woman with a bag over his arm. Hampton Gervis hustled him back to the Mitre.[7]

The school uniform consisted of a starched Eton collar, tails and a straw hat. Equally uncongenial to any boy of a fastidious temperament would have been the degrading condition of many of the boarding houses, including Michael's, a former coaching inn, which was by 1918 already in a pretty dilapidated and depressing condition. A new Mitre House has since been built, and Michael's old boarding house, close to the main school buildings, today provides accommodation for bachelor masters; the former boys' portion of the house is completely derelict. A boy who shared a study with Michael Ramsey, Ted Crosskill, has recalled how his own heart sank when he first saw the Mitre. "The dark passages, cramped quarters and, worst of all, the primitive 'loos' across the yard, which were just earth closets, shocked me to the core. The front door opened from the street into the housemaster's comfortable quarters, while a shabby one, which should have carried a notice saying 'Abandon hope all ye who enter here', or perhaps, 'Put your penny in the slot', led to ours."[8] Mr Gervis adds, "How the school got away with such insanitary conditions, I don't know."[9]

The boys had a dining room, a small, sparsely furnished common room which also served as a library, and eight studies. The one shared by Ted Crosskill and Michael Ramsey also housed two fags, who were responsible for dusting the room, and who occasionally cooked the older boys scrambled eggs. The school food was generally regarded as "reasonable", except that on Fridays a substance known to the boys as Peasant's Revolt was served – some sort of yellow-looking pudding they did not care for. Crosskill remembers Michael Ramsey as "strangely reclusive. Each of the four of us worked at his own particular 'Prep', but our conversation never rose to a level beyond day to day matters, so our relationship never developed further than to one of friendly dissimilarity."[10]

It was, however, through the matter of prep that Michael Ramsey did get on to terms of some useful familiarity with other boys. "We always thought he was a little short of money", Mr Gervis recalls.[11] "He often went without jam and things like that. But because he was so bright with his classics we paid him 6d [2½p] from time to time in exchange for his help. He probably spent it in the tuck shop. I suppose I would call him a buffoon in some ways, but he was respected, because he was so useful to us. He was much laughed at, but never teased."

Sir Desmond Lee, later a distinguished headmaster, who arrived at the Mitre in 1922 when Michael Ramsey was seventeen, says, "We all thought that he was pretty clever, but he wasn't regarded as quite normal. But in the Mitre in those days being clever was not something for which you were persecuted. There's no doubt the housemaster was on the side of people who wanted to be intelligent about things."[12] So far as Michael Ramsey's schoolboy oddities of behaviour were concerned, Sir Desmond Lee formed the impression that he was always hitching up his trousers. He thought Michael displayed a streak of originality, whereas he considered the headmaster, Geoffrey Fisher, "very conventional and ordinary in his tastes". But he thought Fisher an excellent teacher, "a very good headmaster indeed". In view of the rather unpastoral impression of Fisher that has tended to come down in history, it is worth recording that many boys who knew him at Repton have retained pleasant and often admiring recollections. Hampton Gervis, who later became a prep school headmaster, thought Fisher, at Repton, was "first rate",[13] and recalls that Fisher was one of three men around whom Michael's life revolved at school. Another was Laurence Burd, for thirty-seven years form master of the Classical Sixth. Burd had arrived at Repton in 1886 from Balliol and Clifton College, and was considered by everyone not really to be a schoolmaster by inclination but a scholar whose talents were largely wasted at Repton, and whose presence there for so long seemed something of a mystery. His time was devoted solely to classical teaching, and although it was generally agreed he was kind and gentle, in the daily life of Repton he was said to be "friendly but aloof". His features were dark and aquiline, and he was known to the boys as the Auk. For twenty years he acted as librarian, and today there is a small library at Repton in a building dating from 1172 (the site of Repton School was originally a monastery) named after him.

Another classics teacher, and the third man around whom Michael's life centred at school, was the Reverend Henry Balmforth, a High Anglican who later became headmaster of St Edmund's School, Canterbury and Principal of Ely Theological College. From 1920 to 1932 Balmforth ran the Civics Class. His influence and encouragement persisted long after school. It may well have been of his abilities as a teacher that Michael was thinking when, while lecturing at the University of Athens on 7th May 1962, he said, "It was from the Greek tongue that I learned to love the beauty of words and the meaning of clear thinking." Previously, on 28th July 1957, when Michael, by then archbishop of York, preached in the school chapel, he had specifically recalled "the flawless scholarship" of Laurence Burd and "the gentle courtesy" of Harold Hayward.

Although it is probably true that Fisher was by instinct a disciplinarian, both Mr Gervis and Sir Desmond Lee dismiss as a travesty of the truth[14] a grotesque portrait painted of Fisher in a generally jaundiced memoir of childhood written by Roald Dahl, who entered Repton in 1929.[15] Dahl, primarily a writer of highly fantasized fiction, describes Fisher as "a rather shoddy bandy-legged little fellow with a big bald head and lots of energy but not much charm", and depicts him as a sadist.

Mr Gervis, on the other hand, remembers Fisher as "firm when necessary but never brutal", and recalls, when being told to attend in the chapel to practise reading the lesson, that he arrived early, only to find Fisher already there. The headmaster explained, "You are not late. I am early because I did not want you to arrive to an empty chapel and become more nervous than you are now, by having to wait for me."[16] An equally sympathetic picture of Fisher's character has been drawn by another Old Reptonian, Denton Welch, whose asperity when observing human foibles could, if the occasion demanded, leave little to the imagination. Denton Welch was an exact contemporary of Roald Dahl, and in 1933 he went to tea with the Fishers while they were on holiday at Minehead. Alas, he disgraced himself by spilling his cup. To cover Denton's embarrassment, Fisher, by then bishop of Chester, sliced a piece of bread and threw it down the table to his wife, who deftly caught it, still pouring out with the other hand. "Now", Denton wrote, "the whole table was laughing and gay and boisterous; my awful accident had been merged and incorporated into the Bishop's wild bread-throwing. It really was the most charming and brilliant thing to do."[17]

No one recalls Michael Ramsey as particularly religious

at school, but possibly because he came under the influence of Henry Balmforth he did ask permission to be confirmed when he was sixteen, and that was the point at which he made a firm decision to remain in the Church of England, in which he had been baptized, rather than join his father's congregation. It is unlikely that Fisher contributed greatly to this decision, for although Fisher might be said, as a bishop, to have passed for Central Church, he was at heart an evangelical, and his temperamental attitude to religion did not commend itself to Michael.* But confirmation at school for public schoolboys already baptized was in those days virtually routine. What was far from routine was the day in 1919 (22nd June) when the former headmaster, William Temple, was invited to preach. He did so on a text taken from John 17:22: "The glory which thou hast given me I have given unto them." This must almost certainly have been the first occasion on which Michael Ramsey set eyes on his future hero and heard him preach. The subject of Glory was to become an abiding theological topic. And surely this must also have been a unique occasion in the annals of the Church of England, for three future archbishops of Canterbury (Temple, Fisher and Ramsey), none of them yet even consecrated, to be together at one service. All three were to contribute a prayer for the School Prayer Book. Ramsey's was the shortest: "Jesus Lord and Master, who served your disciples in washing their feet; serve us daily, in washing our motives, our ambition, our actions; that we may share with you in your mission to the world to serve others gladly for your sake; to whom be glory for ever."

---

* As Edward Carpenter has written in *Cantuar: The Archbishops in their Office* (Cassell, 1971), Fisher was "no speculative theologian . . . His faith was essentially simple, sincere and uncomplicated." Asked by Bishop Mervyn Stockwood what his father's faith had been, one of Fisher's sons replied, "Gentle Jesus, meek and mild . . . !"[18]

Michael seems to have opted out of the School Officer Training Corps, for not only was he notoriously unsmart, he was considered too gawky to drill, with no proper control over his limbs. He went, however, for long walks, a habit formed early and enjoyed on holiday for the rest of his life. The only recreation he ever listed in *Who's Who* was walking. Hampton Gervis sums up his schoolboy recollections of Michael Ramsey by saying, "I thought he would be a don. I thought he was too dotty to be a bishop. I also assumed he was a confirmed bachelor. He never showed any interest in young ladies. On the whole, I had the impression at Repton that he was quietly happy."[19] In an annual series of house photographs Michael continually gives the impression of being rather wistful, shy and sensitive, a good deal better looking than one might expect, indeed a good deal better looking at school, and far more intelligent, than many of his contemporaries.

There were two school activities, apart from the classroom, where Michael made a mark. One, which will come as no surprise, was in the debating society. The other was as an exponent of Gilbert and Sullivan. At house suppers he would take the soprano role in duets with Alan Thornhill (small and dark, a very intelligent scholar with a rather slow, deep voice, who was later ordained), and the two of them reduced the company to hysterical laughter. Michael's falsetto was said by all who heard it to have been a theatrical hit, and his enthusiasm for the lyrics and music of Gilbert and Sullivan persisted into retirement, when gramophone records of the *Mikado* and other favourites could be heard echoing through 16 South Bailey in Durham. But it has to be said that the Savoy Operas, which had been great favourites with his parents too, were the only music to which Michael Ramsey was ever remotely attuned.

Michael was fifteen when, on 10th February 1920, he

took part in his first school debate, speaking against a motion proposing that Great Britain's only chance of future prosperity lay in a strong oligarchy. He said that if we were oligarchs the League of Nations would be ineffectual. Three weeks later he was again on his feet to display his budding interest in politics; he explained that the Labour Party had both a sober and an unconstitutional element, and it was the latter that held sway. His knowledge of English literature proved no less impressive on 13th October when, during a debate on the motion "The cult of Shakespeare is an outworn and over-rated fetish", he said he thought "Shakespeare could not depict character as compared with Shaw and Galsworthy".

As in later life Michael Ramsey was not well known for his interest in fiction (apart from theology he seldom read any books other than biographies) it is interesting to note that on 18th October 1921 he read a paper to the Repton School Literary Society on the subject of the historical novel, but his main allegiance seems to have been to the debating society, where he developed the enviable gift of being able to think on his feet. He came rather to dread making speeches in the House of Lords, but as an after-dinner speaker he often excelled.

Michael's childhood saw cinema-going become a way of life. By 1917 there were over three thousand cinemas in the country, and it was estimated that about half the population went to the cinema once a week. At a Repton debate he was to second the opposition to a motion which declared the influence of the cinema to be pernicious, saying that in spite of the paucity of his experience, he thought the public house was much more pernicious than the cinema, which actually kept men from the pubs. Aware, perhaps, that during the war cinemas had been supplied with propaganda material by the Cinema Division of the Department of Information, material which glossed over the reality of the fighting, he added that (by 1920) the cinema "did much to show people the horrors of the war".

In another debate he denounced capitalism as selfish in its essence, "for pursuit of gain was its only stimulus", and he got into "an altercation ... which was, however, quashed by the President" when, on 6th October 1921, he opposed a motion which said that the abolition of welfare would not benefit society. When the House deplored the appearance of women in public positions he no doubt had his mother's altruistic actions in mind when he retorted that women had not yet had a proper chance, and that some public positions, such as the management of work-houses, were better filled by woman's experience. Denying that democracy was played out, he later told the House that democracy allowed mankind to understand citizen-ship in the widest sense, and when it came to the idea that England's greatest hope of future prosperity lay in social-ism, the future speaker for the Liberal cause in Cambridge said that private enterprise and competition alone could bring efficiency.

Michael's academic achievements at Repton were impressive. In 1920 he was awarded a Foundation Schol-arship. In 1922 and again in 1923 he won the Harford and Wightwick Political Essay Prize, and also in 1923 the Latin Verse Prize, the Douglas Marriott Exhibition and a Leav-ing Exhibition. The fact that in 1923 the Mitre was awarded the coveted Cattley Shield, presented each year to the house with the best academic record, was largely due to Michael's contribution to the tally of points, and although Hampton Gervis was head of the house, he invited Michael to collect the shield on Speech Day. He thought that Michael's modesty would prevail, and as he had really been looking forward to going up to the platform to receive the shield himself, he was rather mortified when Michael cheerfully accepted the honour. "My only worry", he recalls, "was whether he would make a hash of it, by dropping the shield or something like that, but fortunately he didn't."[20]

As top boy of the Classical Sixth, Michael was due to be appointed head of the school, an honorary position since abolished. This meant he would automatically become a school prefect, but as he had not even been appointed a house prefect Gervis had to go to Hayward and ask that this be done. No one ever regarded Michael as a disciplinarian exactly, but there were no riots when he was in charge of the other boys, only a few laughs when he took the roll call, for invariably he got someone's name wrong. As a school prefect, another of his duties would have been to read the lesson at Matins.

Whatever the truth of Michael Ramsey's relationship with Geoffrey Fisher, as bishops they certainly had a good deal less in common than had been the case in younger days, when teaching and absorbing the classics was all that mattered, and Michael did not hesitate to make fun of his old headmaster's alleged lack of judgement of his true potential when he was made archbishop of York and was elected to a private dining club, milking his carefully prepared quip for all it was worth. Fisher was present, and introduced him. Replying, Michael told the assembled company, "When the Archbishop of Canterbury was my headmaster at Repton, he wrote my final report. And he said in this report, 'This boy has an uncouth and ungainly appearance, but if he can get over that he might do quite well.'"

CHAPTER THREE

MAGDALENE

Through the years of my priesthood the paradox has more
and more come home to me: the paradox that divine power
and love, the resources of heaven itself, can use, and use not
in vain, wayward, sinful human nature like our own.
Westminster Abbey, on the fortieth anniversary of his ordi-
nation to the priesthood.

In December 1922 Michael sat an examination for Magdalene College, Cambridge, founded in 1542 by Lord Audley
with an endowment of £20 a year for the maintenance of a
Master and four Fellows. He won a Major Scholarship in
Classics and History, and the following October, shortly
before his nineteenth birthday, he went into residence. For
the first two years he lived at the top of the eighteenth-
century Pepys Building, in rooms next door to Selwyn
Lloyd, later to become Foreign Secretary, and with a
reproduction of Perugino's *Crucifixion of Jesus* on the
wall.* When the willow trees on the bank of the Cam,
which flows at the end of the college gardens, were not in
leaf he may just have been able to glimpse the house in
Chesterton Road where he had been born. Other famous

---

* The Pepys Librarian when Michael Ramsey was an undergraduate at
Magdalene was Owen Morshead, who in 1926 was appointed Librarian at
Windsor Castle. By an odd coincidence his nephew, Mr Andrew Lewis, is
currently housemaster of the Mitre at Repton.

contemporaries were Francis Wormald, later a professor of English, William Empson, the philanthropist Guy Clutton-Brock, and Lord Burghley (later Marquis of Exeter), the athlete. His father, whom Michael described as "a kind of caring tutor [who] could look fierce in argument",[1] had by now been a resident Fellow for a quarter of a century. A few days after Michael's arrival he and the other freshmen were fortified with sherry in the college hall by V. S. Vernon-Jones the Praelector, and given a little lecture on undergraduate behaviour. Vernon-Jones said that when they went out to lunch with one of the Fellows they should always leave at 2.15 p.m. "unless the general conversation was particularly good, in which case we could stay till 2.30 p.m." Then they trooped off to the Senate House to matriculate.

Michael now came into close contact with Arthur Benson, Master of the College since 1915, whose acutely depressive father, Queen Victoria's archbishop of Canterbury Edward Benson, had produced a brood of very extraordinary children, including E. F. Benson, author of the Mapp and Lucia novels (he wrote a hundred books altogether), and Hugh, a Roman Catholic monsignor.* Arthur Benson, who wrote the words *Land of Hope and Glory* to which Elgar set his 1902 *Coronation Ode*, had inherited his father's depressive tendencies, and two years after becoming Master of Magdalene he had been compelled to take extensive leave of absence to recover from a particularly severe nervous breakdown, very probably caused by tension resulting from the suppression of his emotional and sexual instincts; he was, like his brother Edward, homosexual. Michael Ramsey thought that by 1922 Benson had "recovered full happiness, a radiant

---

* For a portrait of the Benson family the reader is referred to *Genesis and Exodus* by David Williams (Hamish Hamilton, 1979).

happiness it was, full of joyful energy."[2] Writing in retirement in 1986, Michael Ramsey said he believed that Benson
had been largely responsible for a growth in the prestige
of Magdalene among the smaller colleges, by giving "his
own style of cultural leadership by the reading of essays,
by discussion with students, by lectures on literary subjects
from time to time in the college hall, and by his links with
the wider world of letters through his own writings and
his many friendships."

Many of Benson's friendships with the undergraduates
at Magdalene were delicately referred to as "romantic".
Michael Ramsey recalled that Benson "had his 'romantic
friendships' and he enjoyed writing about them. But he
impressed not a few of us by the range of his friendships
to many [sic] who were not romantic in the least, and this
is the Benson whom we remember." Benson found
Michael Ramsey "a friendly boy but slightly priggish",
and Michael was certainly not one of those undergraduates
by whom Benson was smitten. After a visit to Howfield
for lunch in 1923, when the entire family was present, he
left a distinctly chilling account of the occasion in his
diary, a diary that ran to four million words and was kept
under lock and key until 1975.

> Curious how the amenities are neglected. The drive is like a sea-
> beach, the shrubs sprawl, dead leaves pile up, flowers straggle.
> The house is bare and unbeautiful. It was something of an ordeal.
> R genial but a little frozen. Mrs R very voluble and emphatic,
> Frank solid and *very* clever, Michael a distressing object, so
> sharp-faced, dull-eyed, spotted. Bridget charming and long-
> limbed, and Margary really pretty. But this silent circle was
> alarming and I grew nervous in drawing-room after.*

* The family's nickname for Margaret was in fact Margie. After her
marriage, Bridget was known as Biddy.

Benson died from pleurisy in 1925, the year that Michael, having won the Latin Verse Prize in his first term, took a second class degree in the Classical Tripos, and he recalled that his death had been "shattering". His successor as Master was, like Benson, a former Eton housemaster, A. B. Ramsay, whom Michael Ramsey described as a "pedagogue who pressed for compulsory attendance in chapel". He also required classical scholars (including Michael, presumably) to recite lines to him from time to time, "giving them marks for 'accuracy', 'eloquence' and 'deportment'!"

As for Benson's unflattering description of Michael Ramsey aged nineteen, a college photograph taken two years later shows him as a decidedly serious young man, still with plenty of hair, parted to the left and brushed across his forehead, but exhibiting the beginnings of a double chin. He wore a tiepin clipped across his collar.

Frank, who seemed to be living his life as though he knew time was in short supply, married (at a registry office) in 1925, when he was only twenty-two. His bride was a fellow militant atheist, Lettice Baker. She had taken Honours in the Moral Science Tripos at Newnham College, and in glaring contrast to her father-in-law and brother-in-law she – and Frank – felt thoroughly at home on the fringes of Bloomsbury. Lettice had been educated at Bedale's School with Frances Marshall, who in 1933 was to marry Ralph Partridge, the intimate friend of Lytton Strachey and former husband of Dora Carrington, and after Frank's death Lettice became a well-known professional photographer. A daughter, Jane, was born to Frank and Lettice at Howfield thirteen months after their marriage, but within a very short time of getting married they had both taken lovers, and they lived a thoroughly Bohemian life. (Only a year after Frank's death, Raymond Mortimer, later literary editor of the *New Statesman*, was reporting to the novelist and critic Edward Sackville-West on what he called "a sort of sub-Bloomsbury party" where he had found "Lettice Ramsay [sic] with her skirt round her neck and Julian Bell* round her waist". Frank, Lettice and Frank's mistress, Elizabeth Denby, both young women dressed in almost identical skirts and cardigans, and obviously the best of friends, would all gaily trip along the bank of the Cam together, and Frank and Lettice thought nothing of wandering around the freezing corridors of Howfield stark naked. It was a world of intellectual freedom and permissive conduct alien to anything that had begun to cross the mind or experience of Frank's chaste and "slightly priggish" younger brother. By the same token, Frank had left Michael standing academically. While an undergraduate he had translated what was to many people Ludwig Wittgenstein's virtually incomprehensible *Tractatus Logico-Philosophicus* from German into English by dictating to a typist, and by twenty-one he was a Fellow of King's College, his lectures on the Foundations of Mathematics becoming a new feature in the University lecture list.

On 27th February 1978 Radio 3 broadcast a portrait of Frank Ramsey, in which Michael said, "I was aware that he was far cleverer than I was and knew much more . . . he never made me feel inferior though I was vastly below par intellectually." He added that Frank rejected religion "as an unsound and irrelevant occupation. He was certainly sorry that I went on being religious. He was very sorry that I decided to become a priest in the Church of England, but quite tolerant." Michael's own tolerance towards Frank's teasing was noticed by the historian Sir Lewis Namier, who, while on holiday with Frank in the Tyrol in 1924, met Frank's parents and Michael, "whom he found

* Elder son of Clive and Vanessa Bell and a nephew of Virginia Woolf.

an impressively religious youth able to bear with a dignity rare in one so young the raillery of his brilliant, irreligious big brother."[3]

Almost immediately following Frank's wedding in September 1925, Michael set sail for America, to take part in debates in no fewer than thirty universities. It was his first visit to the United States, and if he developed an especial love for any country (he became, as archbishop of Canterbury, far and away the most widely travelled Church leader at a time when it was unheard of for the pope even to leave Italy) it was for America. While in New York in 1925 Michael paid a visit to the Anglo-Catholic Church of St Mary the Virgin on 46th Street, an experience which is said to have had a profound – but surely not decisive – influence on his decision to be ordained. His taste for debating at Repton had naturally drawn him to the Union debates in Cambridge, where his sister Bridget remembers that "he had such a reputation as a wit that everybody started to laugh before he even opened his mouth".[4] She thought this was not quite fair, but members of the Union must have become used to anticipating some amazing absurdity. Apparently on one occasion he recited as follows:

> Oh oh oh my sweet Hortense,
> She ain't good-looking but she's got some sense,
> She has got two teeth in her mouth,
> One points north and the other points south.

Bridget says, "He did it in such a way that the undergraduates became quite hysterical." In the Lent Term of 1926 Michael became President of the Union, the first Magdalene president for almost sixty years. The historian Charles Smyth, who became a Fellow of Corpus Christi and wrote the life of Cyril Garbett, had left Repton in 1921, and Michael used to say that he had pushed out Charles Smyth, whose last opportunity it had been to become President. "Poor old Charles," Michael Ramsey used to say, "I don't think he's ever forgiven me." Indeed, Canon Smyth used to get his own back by declaring that Geoffrey Fisher had been the greatest archbishop of Canterbury of all time, but no great rift in friendship really seems to have occurred, and as young men they went on retreat to Cowley together.

While at Cambridge, Michael assisted a Fellow of Magdalene, Frank Salter, in his Liberal campaign for the Cambridge constituency, and it has frequently been stated that Michael himself seriously considered a political career. He was in fact asked if he would accept nomination as a candidate, but wisely declined. By temperament he was quite unsuited to the cut and thrust of the House of Commons – or in many crucial ways to the general rough and tumble of any sort of public life; for one thing, he reacted very badly indeed to adverse criticism, and it is absurd to believe, as one obituary claimed, that he "would have risen to public eminence whatever career he would have followed". What he did do in 1926 was to toy with the idea of a career at the bar, and he began to attend lectures for the Law Tripos. He told Sir Norman Anderson, at one time chairman of the House of Laity of the General Synod, that had he not been ordained he would have become a lawyer.[5] But legal affairs exerted their attractions for a very short time. His final decision was to read Theology, and that switch was probably brought about by coming to know and admire several influential men while at Cambridge. One was an Anglo-Catholic baronet, Sir Edwyn Hoskyns, dean of Corpus Christi. Another was Eric Milner-White, for twenty-three years dean of King's.

Michael had first met Milner-White (later, when Michael himself was Primate of England, dean of York) early in 1914, when, at the age of nine, he had enrolled as a pupil   *d. 1963* at King's College Choir School. Two years previously Milner-White had been appointed chaplain to King's College, and he taught the boys scripture. "If you can't stop laughing you'll have to stand on the desk", Milner-White used to say to Michael.[6] Within a few months, however, Milner-White was serving in the trenches as an army chaplain, and when he returned to King's College in 1918 (by this time Michael was at Repton) he did so as a hero, for he had been awarded the DSO.* He was twenty years older than Michael, was said to have inspired more affection from King's College Choir School boys than any other teacher in the school's history,[7] and certainly Michael seems, even during the few months he knew Milner-White as a boy, to have turned him into something of a father-figure. "Michael really loved him," Lady Ramsey has recalled, "and he adored Michael. They were tremendous friends."[8] But contrary to popular belief, it was only after Michael had gone up to Magdalene in 1923 that he got to know Milner-White well, and to share with him his interest in history (from 1912 to 1914 he had been a lecturer in history at Corpus Christi), as well as his theological outlook, for Milner-White had trained for the ministry at Cuddesdon, where Michael was to follow. Michael kept Milner-White's photograph on his mantelpiece all his life.

Another man who was to influence Michael Ramsey at Cambridge, and perhaps decisively, was William Temple,† for it was in 1926, the year that Michael decided to read Theology, that Temple, by then bishop of Manchester, arrived to conduct one of his famous and inspiring missions. Although only archbishop of Canterbury for two

---

* It was Eric Milner-White who in 1918 introduced to the chapel at King's the Christmas Eve service of nine lessons and carols, although the first such service had actually been instigated by Arthur Benson's father in 1880 when he was bishop of Truro.
† Son of Frederick Temple, archbishop of Canterbury from 1896 to 1903.

and a half years, Temple became something of a legend in his own life-time, and if any one event can be said to have brought together the strands leading to a sense of vocation in the case of Michael Ramsey it was most likely Temple's mission to Cambridge. Partly Temple was admired as a result of his leadership of the Life and Liberty Movement, dedicated to freeing the Church of England from the "intolerable hindrance" under which it worked while tied as closely as it was to the restraining powers of parliament, but also he was an avowed socialist whose personal goodness and sincerity moved and impressed all who met him. "Prodigal in his gifts, lavish in his generosity, wide in his interests, abundant in his energy, holy in his dedication" is how a former archdeacon of Westminster, Edward Carpenter, has described William Temple.[9] Asked what it was about Temple that had so struck and impressed Michael's generation, Michael Ramsey's cousin Roger Wilson replied, "You simply knew you were in the presence of a man of God."[10]

The mission was centred upon the University Church of Great St Mary. Here, says Donald Harris, Michael Ramsey was to be seen in the third row of the congregation every night.[11] As President of the Union he had been asked to chair the opening meeting of the mission in the Guildhall, and according to his father's recollections, the place was packed, Michael read the opening prayers, "and then spoke impressively to his fellow undergraduates about their attitude to the mission, warning them if they felt critical to beware lest they be found to be fighting against God."[*]

---

[*] University missions were generally well attended and good preachers appreciated. In 1887 Arthur Ramsey, although a Congregationalist, recorded in his diary hearing sixteen University sermons at Great St Mary's. Unfortunately Temple's addresses for his 1926 mission to Cambridge were not published, as they were after his even more famous mission to Oxford in 1931, in *Christian Faith and Life*.

In addition to Temple there had been two other mission-
ers, one a fiery preacher from Northern Ireland, who
announced at the opening meeting that he had been born
in 1891 and again in 1919. According to Michael Ramsey's
doubtless embellished recollections, this born-again Christian was booked to preach at Holy Trinity, where Michael
had sometimes attended as a child. "Well, I thought I'd
better hear the man at Holy Trinity. So I went in, and he
was getting very worked up. Very worked up indeed. He
was using very foul language. And there were a couple of
rather rough chaps from Magdalene, whom I knew, in
front of me, who were crying. Which surprised me. Which
surprised me a good deal. After singing a hymn, this
evangelical preacher said, 'Now hypocrites, go back to
your women and cigarettes.' I thought to myself, well, I
haven't got a girlfriend and I don't smoke, I can stay. After
another verse of the hymn the preacher said, 'All those
who wish to declare, stand up.' And all around me, it was
very alarming, all around me people were jumping up, and
I thought I might be impelled to do so by mistake!"

Ramsey's inherent distrust of instant conversion
remained with him always, and although he was fond of
Billy Graham, whom he once invited to address the
General Assembly of the Church of England, he never
missed an opportunity to poke fun at him, or at the Bible
Belt of America.* In 1981 he shared a mission to Great St
Mary's in Cambridge with Dr Graham. "Billy thinks that
everything in the Bible is true", Ramsey remarked. "Well,
Solomon had a hundred and twenty wives, so I suppose
we must all have a hundred and twenty wives!"

In the summer of 1927 Michael redeemed his second

---

* "An area characterized by ardent literal interpretation of the Bible; *esp*
such an area in the southern USA." *Longman Dictionary of the English
Language* (1984).

class degree in Classics by taking a first class degree in the Theological Tripos, and he was accepted by James Seaton, Principal of Cuddesdon Theological College since 1914, to be trained – rather swiftly, as ordinands were in those days – for the priesthood. Seaton left Cuddesdon in 1928, the same year as Michael, to be consecrated bishop of Wakefield at what today would be regarded as the advanced age of sixty. He kept a register in which he normally wrote down nothing but the name and college of his students. But in the case of "Michael Ramsey, Magdalene College, Cambridge" he broke his own rule, and added, "a very good candidate".

An event occurred just before he entered Cuddesdon, on 30th July 1927, that explains one of the most unusual interviews Michael Ramsey ever gave as archbishop of Canterbury. (The interview took place in 1968, at Uppsala in Sweden, during the Fourth Assembly of the World Council of Churches.) In order to learn German (and the reason he wished to learn German could have been in order that he might read books of German theology in their original language) in 1927 Michael went to Sobernheim, in the Rhineland, to stay with a schoolmaster called Dr Dörner. There, it would seem, he mastered sufficient German to understand the language but not enough confidence to speak it. While in Uppsala forty-one years later he was invited to broadcast for a German radio station. The interviewer put the questions in German, Ramsey sat sagely nodding, clearly understood exactly what he was being asked, and replied in English. A dubbed translation of the Archbishop's remarks was later supplied for the benefit of his German audience.

According to the recollections of Bridget Barcroft, who would have been nineteen at the time, "One day, sitting in front of the gas fire in the dining room, mother said, 'I think

Michael's going into the Church.'* She was very disappointed. She didn't want him to go into the Church. I don't know why. Perhaps she'd had enough of the Church with her father and brothers. And father used to bully her into going to Emmanuel Congregational. She didn't like that."[12] Arthur Ramsey's version of events is a little different. He says that he and Agnes "rejoiced" that Michael had felt a call to Holy Orders.

The nature of a call to any vocation is always hard to articulate, but there are certain features of the priesthood which serve to make ordination seem an attractive prospect for the wrong reasons to a great many of the men who are ordained. (Some, but not so many, may today also apply to women.) This is not to belittle the genuine desire most ordinands feel to serve the Church in a particular way, but any candidate for ordination may be tempted by some of the easy options and emotional outlets, and these would have been weighed by Michael Ramsey. For one thing, until recently the Church was an almost entirely male-dominated organization, the perfect haven for men who do not care for the company of women, or who are in some cases attempting to avoid the issue of their own homosexuality. It is equally obviously a perfect haven for those who have acknowledged their homosexuality, for those who wish to preach to other people from six feet above contradiction, and for anyone unlikely to rise very far in the hard-headed world of trade or commerce but for whom prospects of "promotion" in the enclosed, relatively easily manipulated world of ecclesiastical politics seem not too difficult. A desire to dress up, common to the clergy, judges, actors, anyone who wears uniform, can legitimately

* "Going into the Church" is a commonly but inaccurately applied expression to denote "seeking ordination". Michael, like any other Christian had been a member of the Church since baptism.

be indulged in church. The social position of an Anglican parish priest also confers upon him in his town or village a status he might not enjoy under other circumstances. It is also almost impossible as an Anglican cleric to get the sack, for the parson's freehold confers tenancy of a parish for life, and it is a very modern idea for bishops to retire at sixty-five, or even seventy. Randall Davidson (1903 to 1928) was the first archbishop of Canterbury ever to resign, and then he was eighty when he did so.* In 1955 Cyril Garbett, then also eighty years of age, had to be asked by a deputation of his clergy to vacate the archbishopric of York. Shute Barrington died in harness as bishop of Durham in 1826 at the age of ninety-two.

In Ramsey's day there was no question of a candidate for ordination spending two or three days in residence at a selection conference, or of those candidates selected for training, by a board consisting of a bishop and assorted clergy and laity, spending two or three years at a theological college. Providing he could find a bishop prepared to lay hands on him, Michael's academic attainments, particularly taking into account his first class degree in Theology, would have been considered such that after rather less than a year at Cuddesdon he would be fit for ordination as a deacon. The amount of pastoral training relating to the needs of the secular world that he was likely to receive, scant even now, would then have been almost non-existent. As it happened, those ten months, from 30th July 1927 to his ordination at Trinity 1928, were marred by a tragedy that occurred just a fortnight after his training had begun, and he later told several people that it had "completely messed up" what should have been a crucial period of peaceful preparation for a life devoted to the ministry.

---

* Two archbishops of Canterbury have been murdered, one burnt and one beheaded. So far, ninety-two others out of a total of a hundred and two have died in office.

In 1925 Arthur Ramsey had built a garage on to Howfield and had purchased a motor car, an open Morris Oxford. There were by this time perhaps about one million cars on the roads, but despite a speed limit of only twenty-two miles an hour, fatal accidents were alarmingly common. There were over seven thousand road deaths in 1934, 1,950 more than there were in 1988 and scarcely fewer than the 7,779 deaths recorded in 1972, when by that date there were eight times as many vehicles on the roads. The reason for so many accidents was almost certainly because, unbelievable though it may seem, it was not until 1935 that drivers had to take a test. And accidents were not confined to bad driving. One day while cranking the car, Arthur Ramsey managed to break his wrist. On 15th August 1927, the year of their silver wedding anniversary, the Ramseys, together with the minister of Emmanuel Congregational Church, the Reverend Henry Carter, his wife, and a Danish friend of theirs, set out to have a picnic at Stamford. Arthur and Agnes had both learnt to drive, but apparently Agnes said, "It's Arthur's picnic so he must drive", and the three ladies got into the back of the car. As the weather looked doubtful, Arthur draped a raincoat over the back of the passenger seat. About ten miles from Cambridge on the A604, somewhere near Hemingford Grey, according to Arthur Ramsey's account of the tragedy a sudden gust of wind flung the raincoat over his hands, and when he recorded the event twenty-one years later he wrote, "Instead of instantly stopping the car I tried to free my hands and the wheel while driving; this took my eyes off the road for a few seconds and when they returned to the road the car was just about to hit a telegraph post head on." The car turned over. Mr Carter escaped injury, but his wife's arm was damaged. Arthur found himself trapped beneath the engine with broken ribs. Agnes was killed outright, and the Danish lady later died from head injuries. But according to Frances Partridge, the family were in no doubt at the time that "a sudden gust of wind" had little to do with the accident, and that Arthur Ramsey had been needlessly looking over his shoulder. Apparently Frank told Frances his father was filled with remorse to begin with "but forgave himself very quickly".[13]

Probate on Agnes's estate of £7,192 9s 6d was granted to Arthur and Frank. When Arthur was released from Huntingdon Hospital he recuperated at Seaford, and then he had to consider who was to keep house. Frank and Lettice were living in Bridge Street, two or three minutes' walk away from King's, and Michael had two weeks previously taken up residence at Cuddesdon. But Bridget was only in her first term at Newnham, and Margaret was still a little schoolgirl. For a year, Frank and Lettice gave up their rooms in Bridge Street and moved into Howfield to look after Arthur and Margaret. The arrangement, according to Margaret, was "a total disaster. Father and Frank got on very well and Frank didn't want to move out, but Lettice hated it." The final solution was one hit upon by many a Victorian family. Lucy, Arthur's youngest, and still unmarried, sister, music mistress at Penrose College, Colwyn Bay, was prevailed upon to give up her career and independence and become her widowed brother's housekeeper, a post she retained until the end of his life.

Aunt Lucy had already embraced the Anglican Church, and like her recently deceased sister-in-law Agnes, she had become an Anglo-Catholic. Hence she was more close to Michael than any other member of the immediate family. Margaret admits she behaved very badly towards Aunt Lucy as a child, which was a perfectly natural reaction for a girl of ten who had virtually had a stepmother thrust upon her, and says, "She had a sort of crush on Michael.

71

There's no other word for it. But she tended to have crushes on young curates anyway." By then aged fifty, she had presumably given up all hope of marriage, but not, it seems, of romance. After several years of solitary servitude at Howfield, Aunt Lucy made a dash for it to the Isle of Wight, becoming housekeeper to a former curate from St Giles's called Ross Wilson. "There was", Margaret recalls, "a colossal family scandal. After a year she came back with her tail between her legs. Father was awful to her. She hadn't a very good brain and he made her do the accounts. It was all very sad." By 1930 Michael was writing to his aunt to commiserate about the difficulties of her life at Howfield, and he remained more fond of Aunt Lucy, who lived to be ninety-three, than of his sisters or their children, frequently going to see her in her house in Mount Pleasant, Cambridge, where she moved in 1955 after Arthur's death. Lucy used to say whenever Michael had been to stay, "He's left a sock under the bed and a handkerchief under his pillow." In 1971 Michael took her funeral service at St Giles's. When he came to the passage commending the soul of "our dear sister departed" he somewhat startled the congregation by departing from the words of the funeral service. In a moment of inspired abstraction he commended to God the soul of "our dear Aunt Lucy".

Michael was twenty-three when his mother died, or to put it in crude psychological terms, his father killed her – killed, that is, the only woman who in twenty-three years he had loved. Agnes may not have found it easy to show Michael maternal affection, for he was a shy and awkward boy, desperate for love but unable physically to respond. Nevertheless much of his personality was moulded on hers, and what warmth and genuine humanity had flowed through the chilly rooms of Howfield had been provided by Agnes. "It was a reasonably happy marriage," says Bridget, "but there was no demonstrable warmth between my parents." The removal of Agnes had been violent and without a moment's warning. Considering the guilt his father must have felt and the degree of blame the children must inevitably have imparted to Arthur, the death of Agnes, still a comparatively young woman, could only have caused an emotional trauma for all concerned. Bridget says, "I can remember Frank and me sitting and howling in the sitting room, and her brothers arriving and being very upset." What Michael seems to have done, instead of having a good howl, was to bottle up his grief, and certainly from then on he found it almost impossible to identify with the suffering of other people at a deep and personal level. In fact, he came to avoid the subject of pain and bereavement as much as he possibly could. His immediate reaction in 1927 was to take himself off to be psychoanalysed.

In 1924, Frank had spent six months in Austria, ostensibly to sit at the feet of the wealthy, unstable, thirty-five-year-old genius Ludwig Wittgenstein, who had turned up at Cambridge as long ago as 1912 to make the acquaintance of Bertrand Russell, and who in 1930 became a Fellow of Trinity.* But during this period Frank also underwent psychoanalysis, which was highly fashionable; it was in the same year, 1924, that Lady Ottoline Morrell, soon followed by cohorts of sub-Bloomsbury satellites, including Edward Sackville-West, was traipsing off to Freiburg to place her susceptible psyche in the dubious hands of a charlatan called Dr Marten. In Michael Ramsey's case it seems almost certain it was not solely the death of his mother that occasioned a need for help, although this may have been the event that brought other problems to the surface. Much of his youthful conduct had frankly bordered on the mentally unbalanced. "At night," Margaret

---

* Ludwig Wittgenstein was a Fellow of Trinity College from 1930 to 1936, and Professor of Philosophy at Cambridge from 1939 to 1947.

recalls, "he would keep father awake. He had an attic bedroom above father's room, and he would rush up and down for hours in the night banging on the walls."[14] Identical conduct was reported when he was sub-warden of Lincoln Theological College, and at times of great agitation he never lost the habit of pacing rapidly up and down his study, twisting and twirling the sash of his cassock. He returned one evening from a City dinner, and still resplendent in purple gaiters was observed prancing round the study, shadow boxing with an imaginary punch-bag. Frank wrote to Lettice, shortly after his mother's death and at a time when Lettice was staying in Dublin, to say that "Michael was getting very odd, and he was afraid he was not going to a good analyst."[15] Perhaps what he needed more than anything was simply a sympathetic person to talk to; he had spent a week on holiday in the French Alps in 1926 with his Magdalene College friend, Gilbert Ponsonby, and maybe during his sessions in London with the psychoanalyst he at least underwent some process of self-discovery. Apparently he once said to a member of the family, "I want to tell you the big secret of my life", and then never did.[16]

Preaching at Cuddesdon in 1958, when he was arch-bishop of York, Michael Ramsey recalled his ten months as an ordinand, and perhaps it is not too difficult, in assessing the words he used, to imagine the memory of unhappiness he had at the back of his mind. "It was here", he said, "that we faced the truth about ourselves before the Cross of Christ, and with the painful shattering of our pride discovered that we have no sufficiency of ourselves to think anything of ourselves." He also starkly drew attention to the fact that he had been ordained into one world to minister to another. "I doubt", he said, "if any of us would have guessed that there would be a Second World War within just over a decade, or that Communist

Russia was destined to become so dark a menace to the world, or that vast movements of population in this country were going to alter the shape of our pastoral work. Nor could we have guessed the extent to which industrial development was going to bring about the technological kind of outlook as the mental ethos of so many of the people, nor that the Welfare State would really come to be, and when it came, could produce the mentality of comfort in the way it has. And who would have guessed that the epoch of social security within the State would also be the epoch of 'near-catastrophe' in the world as a whole through the creation of weapons able to annihilate the world itself?"

In 1928 Michael Ramsey's Congregationalist grandfather, the Reverend Adam Ramsey, died at the age of ninety-one, and at Trinity Michael was ordained as an Anglican deacon in the parish church of St Nicholas, Liverpool. When he was bishop of Durham and preaching at the Institution of a vicar to the Church of St Nicholas, Bishopwearmouth, he told the congregation he had always had a special devotion to St Nicholas because of this early association.* In the light of his subsequent lukewarm attitude towards the question of establishment, it is significant that on 14th June, only a fortnight after his ordination, the House of Commons had, for a second time, rejected the Revised Prayer Book Measure, although, following rejection by the Commons on 15th December 1927, the Convocations had passed a slightly modified version of a

---

* St Nicholas was bishop of Myra in Asia Minor, and although he never came to England there were, by the middle of this century, nearly four hundred churches in England dedicated to him. In his memoirs, Arthur Ramsey says that Michael was ordained deacon at Michaelmas, but in old age he was presumably confusing his ordination as deacon at Trinity in 1928 with his ordination as priest at Michaelmas in 1929, and even his consecration as bishop, again at Michaelmas, in 1952.

new Prayer Book in order to try to accommodate Parliament. The issues, and any attempt at apportioning blame for the major rift that occurred between State and Church at this time, are too complex and would be too contentious to go into here, but for many men of Michael's generation the entire matter became a turning point in their attitude towards the Church of England's relations with Parliament. The bishop of Durham, Herbert Hensley Henson, until 1928 staunchly in favour of the Church of England remaining established, now went out on a limb to advocate disestablishment, and Michael was present in Cambridge on 29th January 1929 to hear Henson preach what Owen Chadwick has described as "an electrifying sermon"; according to Dr Chadwick, Michael himself later described it as one of the most powerful and persuasive utterances he ever heard.*

Having been ordained, Michael now exchanged the cloistered atmosphere of middle-class Cambridge for the slums of Liverpool, and the reason he was ordained in the parish church was because the diocese of Liverpool had only been created in 1880, and St Nicholas was still serving as the pro-cathedral. He would have found no difficulty identifying with the parishioners, for he was quite without class-consciousness, and he would have been happily at home too with the churchmanship practised at St Nicholas. This had come about through a comical tussle of wills between Gladstone and Disraeli. Disraeli, who was low church (this was one reason he got on so well with Queen Victoria, who actively disliked the idea of bishops of any complexion), managed to get appointed as the first bishop

* For a detailed analysis of the debates in 1927 and 1928 in the House of Commons on the Revised Prayer Book Measure, their consequences and the handling of the matter by the bishops, the reader is referred to *Hensley Henson: A Study in the Friction Between Church and State* by Owen Chadwick (OUP, 1983).

of Liverpool an aggressive evangelical, John Ryle, famous for conducting running battles with his tractarian clergy.* When Disraeli's ministry fell and Gladstone became prime minister, Gladstone, who was a High Church Liberal, managed to rile Bishop Ryle by securing for himself the patronage of St Nicholas, thus ensuring that a catholic would always be instituted to the living. When Michael Ramsey arrived on the scene, the vicar was John How, and under Father How Michael served as assistant curate for two years.† When he knelt at Michaelmas in 1929 to be ordained priest by Albert David, bishop of Liverpool from 1923 to 1944, he did so in the company of a young philosopher, Alan Richardson, who later became a fellow member with Michael of the Cathedral Chapter at Durham and dean of York. Together with Richardson, Michael Ramsey attended post-ordination classes run by Charles Raven, a canon of Liverpool and a biologist as well as a theologian, whose influence on the still young and inexperienced Ramsey bore fruit when he came to formulate his own theological approach to religion, and survived in fact into Ramsey's episcopate. When, in 1953, the Cambridge University Press published Charles Raven's Gifford Lectures on the theme of Natural Religion and Christian Theology, Michael Ramsey said it had been a long time since he had read anything so fascinating, instructive and challenging.[17] He thought Charles Raven, along with William Temple, one of the best Christians he ever knew personally,[18] and looking back to the post-ordination

---

* Although Benjamin Disraeli was born a Jew he was baptized into the Church of England when he was twelve.

† The custom of appointing evangelical bishops to Liverpool, a diocese heavily populated with Roman Catholics, seems for some reason to have persisted to the present day. When Stuart Blanch, appointed bishop of Liverpool in 1966, became archbishop of York in 1975 he was succeeded by another evangelical, David Sheppard.

classes attended with Alan Richardson, he often used to say, "I think Charles thought we were both promising young men, but a dreadful nuisance."[19] Michael Ramsey and Alan Richardson saw eye to eye on the catholic nature of the Church of England, although when reviewing *An Introduction to the Theology of the New Testament** by Richardson in 1959, by which time Michael was archbishop of York, he did not flinch from bringing to bear a sharp scholarly eye on a book he believed to contain faults.[20] They shared, too, some early ecumenical adventures. At a conference in Denmark attended by them both, an irate Lutheran bishop complained that his slippers had vanished. It was Richardson who noticed that Michael Ramsey was wearing them.

During those two years Michael's reputation must have spread beyond the parish boundaries in Liverpool, for in 1930, when he had only been a priest a year, he was offered not a second curacy, nor even his own parish, which would have been remarkable enough, but the post of sub-warden of Lincoln Theological College. He was only twenty-six, and he was to take a major share in the training of ordinands. But just as he was about to embark on a six-year experience which would culminate in the writing of his first book, *The Gospel and the Catholic Church*, a work which established his reputation as a leading biblical theologian, he suffered a second devastating bereavement.

When Aunt Lucy moved into Howfield, Frank and Lettice had taken a lease on 4 Mortimer Road, just southeast of Parker's Piece, and here, on 28th March 1929, their second child, Sarah, was born. A paper Frank had published in December 1928 in the *Economic Journal* on "A Mathematical Theory of Saving" was described by the editor, Maynard Keynes, as "one of the most remarkable

* SCM Press.

contributions to mathematical economics ever made", and at King's he was acknowledged as an authority on Mathematical Logic and the Foundations of Mathematics. In December 1929 he was taken ill with an attack of the disease with which he had been born, jaundice. In the second week of January 1930 he was moved to Guy's Hospital in London, where he came under the care of a doctor who was an uncle of Lettice. An exploratory operation on his gall bladder was performed, and soon Lettice, at any rate, seems to have believed that Frank would die. She remained constantly at the hospital, and was visited and comforted a good deal by Ludwig Wittgenstein and Frances Partridge.* By 17th January Frank's condition was critical, and Frances recorded in her diary that she could hear his laboured breathing, which she found "very harrowing".[21] The next day he was given a blood transfusion, and Frances says that Lettice's stoical attempts to control herself filled her with admiration. A second minor operation was performed. While waiting for Frank to come round, Lettice, Frances and Wittgenstein went off in search of supper and found sausage rolls and sherry in a station buffet. By the time that Lettice and Frances returned to the hospital, Frank was delirious, and Frances found herself moved "by the extremely gentle, cultivated sounds of his voice coming from behind the screen". She was, she wrote, painfully conscious of the struggle for life going on, and the sounds of laboured breathing and hiccups were worse than before. Frank died at three o'clock on the morning of 19th January. He was twenty-six.

Arthur Ramsey records that he and Bridget went to the hospital, but there is no mention in his memoirs or in Frances Partridge's diary of any visit being paid by

* Still in 1930 Frances Marshall.

Michael, which comes as no surprise. Most people dislike hospitals and sickbeds, and Michael was no exception. In fact, he would do almost anything to avoid them, but to be fair, he may have been in Liverpool and unaware of how serious his brother's condition was. Two days after Frank's death, on 21st January, Michael did conduct his funeral service at Golders Green Crematorium. It took place in thick fog and was attended by representatives of Bloomsbury, among them Maynard Keynes and Alec Penrose. Richard Braithwaite, a friend and contemporary who later edited a volume of Frank's papers, and wrote in the *Cambridge Review* that Frank's death at the height of his powers had deprived Cambridge of "one of its intellectual glories", was seen to be "shedding tears into a pocket handkerchief". Frances Partridge thought that Michael "read some of the Psalms very well", but she also noticed that as the coffin disappeared "Michael's face was contorted by grief and he practically ran out of the chapel".

The death of Frank, like that of his mother, was entered on the list of those topics which for Michael Ramsey became virtually taboo. Was it a sense of guilt from which he suffered most? By his own acknowledgement Frank had been his intellectual superior, yet it was Frank who had died; Frank had been far closer to his father than Michael was, and Arthur, already a rather lonely widower, had been deprived of the son, a fellow mathematician, with whom he had most in common. The girls, too, had found Frank "a very kind person", and following Frank's death Bridget, who used to preach in the open air outside a public house in Battersea, actually lost her faith. Frank's grasp of philosophy and mathematics had gone hand in hand with a passionate love of Wagner and Beethoven, and indeed his was a far more rounded personality than Michael's. He had left a very young widow and two orphans, towards whom Michael may have felt a certain sense of responsibility but little affection. At twenty-five, he must have been under considerable pressure to try in some way to compensate for the loss of such a paragon of virtue. "He loved Frank and admired him very much," according to Lady Ramsey, "but they hardly noticed, perhaps, that Michael was clever too. That's why Michael was shy."[22]

CHAPTER FOUR

THE MAKING OF A THEOLOGIAN

While theology includes a variety of academic disciplines and demands rigorous intellectual integrity it is, I believe, properly inseparable from the knowledge of God through prayer and contemplation and the Christian life.

Preface to *Jesus and the Living Past*.

On 22nd January 1930 a memorial service had been held at King's College Chapel for Frank, although he was an avowed atheist, and it was almost certainly of Frank that Michael was thinking when in 1961 he caused a rumpus by side-stepping orthodoxy to declare that he hoped to meet atheists in heaven. Michael offered the sum of £100 to found a prize in his brother's memory. His father provided an additional £100, King's College added the Ramsey's gift to a bequest from another lecturer in mathematics, Arthur Berry, and a new endowment, the Berry-Ramsey Fellowship, was established.

Before taking up his appointment as sub-warden of Lincoln Theological College, Michael paid a visit to the religious festival at Oberammergau. He then entered upon that part of his career as a teacher which was to last in all for eighteen years, twelve of them spent as a professional theologian. It was primarily due to his gifts as a theologian that he was consecrated bishop of Durham and eventually translated to the see of Canterbury, but no one is exclusively a theologian, and in reality every lay man and woman, as well as every clergyman of whatever denomination or theistic religion, is a theologian, for the dictionary defines theology as "the study of God and his relation to the world". Leslie Houlden, Professor of Theology at King's College, London, has said, "So far as people are reflecting on God and doing it intelligently they are theologians."[1] But the dictionary also defines a theologian as "a specialist in theology", and in that sense Michael Ramsey set out to master more theology than others whose gifts lie mainly in pastoral or administrative fields. To some extent he would have been attracted in this direction because he was an intellectual, and faith alone would have failed to satisfy his kind of enquiring mind.

It may seem strange to some people that not every archbishop of Canterbury rates as a "theologian"; of course, to some extent they all have been, in the sense that all Christians are theologians if they study, as they must, "God and his relation to the world", but some archbishops, like some priests and some laymen, have done it more profoundly than others. In fact, it has been extremely rare for an outstanding theologian to find himself a successor to St Augustine. Anselm, appointed in 1093 and in the view of Henry Chadwick, a former Regius Professor of Divinity at Cambridge, "the greatest philosophical mind to whom England can lay any reasonable claim",[2] immediately springs to mind. Thomas Cranmer, who bequeathed to the Church of England an incomparable liturgy it has been busy in recent years destroying, and who, like so many of Mary Tudor's loyal subjects, died the death of a martyr rather than compromise his principles, was a competent theologian. But Ramsey's only theological peer at Canterbury in recent times has been William Temple, who, like

Anselm, was a theologian trained as a philosopher. In periods of history when the Church was a partner in government, archbishops of Canterbury were more often chosen for their political acumen or, like Thomas à Becket, who rose to greatness by having greatness thrust upon him, for their conviviality. In modern days, factors almost always taken into account have included the "right" public school, university and theological college.* Randall Davidson became archbishop of Canterbury in 1903 as a reward for taking so much care of Queen Victoria when he was dean of Windsor. His successor, Cosmo Gordon Lang, another ardent monarchist who was also a snob and a social climber, a man with severely limited vision who one day gave a luncheon party at Lambeth Palace exclusively for dowager duchesses, had earlier in his career earned Queen Victoria's approbation when preaching before her while he was vicar of Portsea and she was staying at Osborne. He became so popular with the royal family that he was invited by Edward VII to stay at Sandringham, an honour never accorded to Michael Ramsey, whose immediate predecessor, Geoffrey Fisher, far from being a theologian was first and foremost an administrator.

* Schools most favoured in modern times for the episcopate generally have been Eton, Winchester, Marlborough, Shrewsbury, Rugby, Harrow, Westminster, Charterhouse, Haileybury and King Edward's, Birmingham, but not Repton. Trinity College, Cambridge, Christ Church, Oxford and New College, Oxford between them had contributed 25 per cent of those who were bishops in 1952, and more than 25 per cent had been trained at just four theological colleges, Cuddesdon, Ridley, Westcott and Wells. Only by training at Cuddesdon, therefore, had Michael Ramsey been groomed in the mainstream. According to the sociologist Leslie Paul (A Church by Daylight, Geoffrey Chapman, 1973), Ramsey also lacked the two other major advantages in the episcopal stakes, a father in the Anglican ministry and connection by birth or marriage to the peerage or landed gentry.

Michael Ramsey would have grappled with the intellectual content of religious belief from a very early age, long before deciding to be ordained. It would then have been natural for a man of his disposition to attend in great depth to the theological basis on which Christian faith and doctrine had been constructed. The first theological work in which he invested was *Belief in God* (1921) by Charles Gore, bishop, in succession, of Worcester, Birmingham and Oxford, and the founder of the Community of the Resurrection. Ramsey was engrossed in this book in October 1923, when he was still nineteen, only just arrived at Magdalene and reading Classics. "The impression of the book upon me went deep," he recalled in a sermon at Westminster Abbey on 16th November 1971, "and remained throughout the years." In the Preface that he wrote when his 1959 Hale Memorial Lectures were published, Michael Ramsey said he thought that Gore was one of the "greatest of all Anglican thinkers and teachers",[3] a verdict he reiterated in the *York Quarterly* in August 1960: "Charles Gore was one of the greatest figures in the modern Church of England."

But we can trace his early influences further back than that. At Repton, Henry Balmforth demonstrated a sympathetic understanding of the interconnection of apparently distinct faiths, a line of enquiry Michael pursued in earnest while at Lincoln. A theologian with whom he made personal contact while an undergraduate was the Reverend Lionel Thornton, whose essay "The Christian Conception of God"* was published in 1926, about the time that Michael met him. Writing about Father Thornton for the magazine of the Community of the Resurrection in 1961, he said they met while Thornton was staying at the

---

* In *Essays Catholic and Critical*, edited by E. G. Selwyn. Other contributors included Edwyn Hoskyns and Eric Milner-White.

Oratory House in Cambridge on sabbatical leave from Mirfield, and that he found him a lively talker who "always linked theology with a lucidity which his writings sometimes lacked. His talk made me conscious that he stood in a great tradition of Anglican divinity . . . It was a tradition at once ascetical and incarnational, catholic and liberal." This was the very tradition in which Michael was to become absorbed and identified. Edwyn Hoskyns was a biblical theologian whose lectures at Corpus Christi were attended by many undergraduates from colleges other than his own, and in 1981 Michael Ramsey wrote, "I learned from him more than from anyone else that the study of the New Testament is an exciting adventure, and while it calls for a rigorous critical discipline, it is not made less scientific if the student brings to it his own experience of faith."[4] When, midway through his years as van Mildert Professor of Divinity in the University of Durham, Michael Ramsey came to write his second book, *The Resurrection of Christ*, he actually began it with these words: "The writer of this book remembers receiving something of a shock when it was first his privilege to attend the lectures of the late Sir Edwyn Hoskyns. The lecturer began with the declaration that as our subject was the Theology and Ethics of the New Testament we must begin with the passages about the Resurrection. It seemed to contradict all the obvious preconceptions. Was it not right to trace first the beginnings of the ministry of Jesus, the events of His life and the words of His teaching? Here, surely, the essence of the Gospel might be found, and as a finale the Resurrection comes so as to seal and confirm the message. No. The Resurrection is a true starting place for the study of the making and the meaning of the New Testament."

When giving a second series of Hale Lectures at Seabury-Western Theological Seminary at Evanston in the

USA in 1978, Ramsey remembered that Hoskyns used to say "it would be a good thing if a bull could be sacrificed once a year in the college courtyard so as to bring home to all our senses what sacrifice really meant in the world in which Christianity began". Another don whose lectures Michael Ramsey attended with enjoyment was Percy Gardner-Smith, dean and president of Jesus. "There was a very amusing one", he used to recount, "about the Eucharist at Corinth. Old Gardner-Smith used to say, 'The Eucharist at Corinth, according to St Paul's account, must have been a cross between a bump supper and a CICCU* prayer meeting.' That was the line we all went to hear!"

Bearing in mind the Anglo-Catholic influence of both Michael Ramsey's mother and his aunt Lucy, of Sung Eucharists at St Giles's and Little St Mary's, and the High Churchmanship of teachers like Henry Balmforth and Edwyn Hoskyns, it would not have been surprising if Michael Ramsey had been tempted, while at Cambridge, to adopt an extreme Anglo-Catholic stance. He has often been regarded as a High Church archbishop – an expression, however, which means different things to different people – or even as an Anglo-Catholic archbishop, which he certainly was not; that would be to confuse the genuine catholicity of his liturgical bearing with the "great tradition of Anglican divinity" he found so attractive in the theological discourses of Father Thornton. Thornton's Mirfield, and Cuddesdon, where Michael trained, are not Anglo-Catholic institutions but the inheritors of a liberal catholic tradition, and they used to specialize in training for the priesthood a species of Anglican now almost extinct in the Church of England, for in recent years ultra-extreme positions have been taken up by a majority of clergy in

* An evangelical society called the Cambridge Intercollegiate Christian Union.

order to defend or attack such central issues as the ordination of women. Mirfield and Cuddesdon were the expositors of a tradition in which Michael Ramsey found his spiritual home, and from which he sought to preach a "catholic" faith based upon the sacraments of Holy Communion and Auricular Confession.[5] While he certainly shied away from evangelical concepts of instant conversion, and believed the sacraments to be the essential foundations to a spiritual life, he also experienced total incomprehension over entrenched doctrinal positions adopted by extreme high and low wings of the Church of England, an incomprehension never more sorely tried than when both wings combined to defeat the Scheme for Anglican-Methodist Reunion.

But as far as evangelicals were concerned, it sometimes seemed like an incomprehension bordering on the naïve. Michael Ramsey was once invited to address ordinands at an evangelical theological college, Oakhill, and seemed quite surprised by the sort of questions the students had prepared for him.[6] They were impressed by his commitment to worship, but he introduced two sentences from the Collect for that week and then apologized for not taking a text from the Bible. But according to Philip Crowe, the Principal at the time, he did this entirely without guile. Mr Crowe says, "His responses to the students were not in the least typecast but he seemed a bit uncomfortable."[7] While Michael Ramsey's catholic instincts always remained apparent, most evangelicals seem to have accepted that his broad understanding of the nature of the Church was such that it did not confine him within narrow limits, and he himself seems to have assumed that the same would be true of others. At Salisbury and Wells Theological College, to which Mr Crowe later transferred as Principal, two of Ramsey's books, *The Gospel and the*

Catholic Church and *The Glory of God and the Transfiguration of Christ*, remain on the students' reading list.

Michael Ramsey became what is known as a biblical theologian, someone who "tries to look at Christian belief very much in biblical categories rather than philosophical categories".[8] Biblical theology flourished between approximately 1940 and 1960, and Michael Ramsey spent much of his time at Lincoln thinking about belief concerning the Church in biblical ideas. The result was his first, and in the opinion of many people his most important, book, *The Gospel and the Catholic Church*, published in 1936 when he was still only thirty-one. He was to subtitle his second book, *The Resurrection of Christ*, "An Essay in Biblical Theology", and in a Preface to the second edition, which came out in 1946, he wrote:

> It has often been urged that the functions of the historian and the theologian must not be confused, and that it is first the business of the former to establish the facts and only then the business of the latter to come on the scene to interpret them. This seems to me a misleading simplification. For if the most important evidence for the Resurrection is the existence and religious experience of the Apostolic Church, then the study of that religious experience and of the faith connected with it is a part of the study of the evidence. It seems increasingly to be recognized by students of the New Testament that a rigid separation between the facts and their interpretation does not really make the search for the facts as scientific a procedure as was commonly thought.

In later life Michael Ramsey dropped a good many comments on his own faith and on his views about theology itself. When he was archbishop of York he told an audience of students during a mission in the Sheldonian Theatre at Oxford that he was a Christian humanist, for he believed that the Christian faith could "create and liberate the truest and deepest humanism". In 1968 he wrote that "Theology needs openness. So often a lack of openness has vitiated theology in its tasks. Through lack of openness to the contemporary world theology has sometimes worked in a kind of vacuum with neither meaningfulness for itself nor power of self-communication."[9] He was to tell ordinands that while they were pledged to be dedicated students of theology, their study need not be vast in extent "but it will be deep in its integrity, not in order that [the priest] may be erudite but in order that he may be simple. It is", he used to say, "those whose studies are shallow who are confused and confusing."[10] And lecturing at the Trinity Institute in New York in 1970 on the Future of the Christian Church he had this to say about the "false security" of theology:

> Theology is indispensable for the Church and for every member of the Church. But the object of faith is not theology but the God whose theology it is. We can be sound in the theology of the Bible, grasping correctly the biblical words and the biblical thought-forms, Biblical Theology with a capital B and a capital T. Yet our Biblical Theology can be held in a kind of vacuum, without sensitivity to the human context in which theology comes alive. So too it can be used as a thing for the mind, without the knowledge that comes through prayer and contemplation. In those ways theology, divorced both from the social context and from the inner life, can become a thing-in-itself, and be substituted for the God who gave it. The substitution can be made equally by Barthians and by Liberals, by Catholics and by Protestants, each after his own kind.

But one of the best statements on theology that Ramsey ever produced was reserved for a lecture in Cambridge on 21st October 1972, on the occasion of the merging of two Anglican theological colleges, Westcott House and Ridley Hall, with a Methodist college, Wesley House. He remarked, "We are being challenged on all sides both to practical Christian obedience and to theological seriousness. Here in Cambridge the tasks before the new federation of colleges are tasks theological through and through. And the names of Ridley and Westcott and Wesley will stand to remind us that theology is nothing apart from the true liberation of mankind and the call to holiness with the vision of God as its goal."

Writing in the magazine *Theology* when Michael Ramsey died, a Methodist, Gordon Wakefield, described *The Gospel and the Catholic Church* as a minor miracle, and its author as "a theologian in the depths of his being from first to last". Wakefield believed the chief importance of *The Gospel and the Catholic Church* in its time was that it set the agenda for the unity negotiations in England, and he thought he clearly detected Ramsey's hand in a report called *Catholicity* published in 1947, a year after Archbishop Fisher's sermon in Cambridge urging certain Free Church denominations to take episcopacy into their system as a first essential step towards reunion with the Church of England. The Reverend John Macquarrie, who at one time was Lady Margaret Professor of Divinity at Oxford, was invited to give three lectures on Michael Ramsey at All Saints Church, New York in 1988*, and he told his audience, "I am inclined to say that this first book was possibly also his best. Certainly it is the best exposition and defence of Anglicanism that I know, and is quite likely to remain so." He explained: "*The Gospel and the Catholic Church*, though it is unashamedly catholic in its outlook, is not a polemical book. Rather the reverse. It is trying to bring together those whom we would call evangelicals and whose primary concern is with the Bible and the proclamation of the word, and those catholics who

---

* With characteristic generosity Professor Macquarrie made the typescripts of all three lectures available to the author.

certainly prize the Bible but believe that it has its home within the Church and the worship of the Church. The central message of the book is, in fact, that Church and Bible need each other."

In 1903 the Society of the Sacred Mission had moved from Mildenhall in Suffolk to Kelham near Newark, seventeen miles from Lincoln, and while he was on the staff of Lincoln Theological College and writing *The Gospel and the Catholic Church* Michael Ramsey was often to be seen deep in conversation at Kelham with a revered member of the Society, Father Gabriel Hebert. When he came to write the Preface he offered thanks to Father Hebert for "criticism and encouragement at every stage of the writing of the book". Also thanked were Canon Leslie Owen, warden of Lincoln Theological College, his old schoolmaster Henry Balmforth, and Noel Davey, who he was to succeed in 1938 as vicar of St Benedict's, Cambridge. Charles Smyth must have got over his disappointment at not becoming President of the Cambridge Union, for he read the proofs of the book, as did, perhaps even more surprisingly, Michael's father, who modestly fails to mention the fact in his memoirs. Someone else Michael Ramsey met during his visits to Kelham was Father Herbert Kelly, who by 1930 was seventy and deaf, and whom Michael regarded as a prophet. Father Kelly had been one of the founders of the Society of the Sacred Mission, and Michael was deeply attracted to his theological concepts of vocation: "to work without pay, to remain unmarried and to be obedient."[11] Was Michael Ramsey himself tempted to the monastic life? There is no evidence of any desire to marry before he did so at the age of thirty-seven, relatively late for a man of his generation. All the Anglican religious houses were capable of providing the right environment for academic theological study, and those like Mirfield and Kelham provided opportunity for

the training and teaching of ordinands. The worst depri-
vations resulting from a vow of poverty have been known
to be circumvented, and alcoholic refreshment in modera-
tion was one of Michael Ramsey's few genuine concessions
to the flesh. Otherwise, his tastes in food were simple and
his awareness of physical comfort almost non-existent. A
young priest who knew him well in retirement gained the
impression that he would have been perfectly happy to
live in a cardboard box,[12] and Mervyn Stockwood, when
bishop of Southwark, rather dreaded the bishops' annual
residential meetings, held at Cuddesdon for Michael's
benefit, because, he claimed, "we lived in infinite squalor
and slept on pre-Reformation beds!" Bishop Stockwood,
who trained for the priesthood at Lincoln and was
ordained in 1936, thought Michael Ramsey at this time
"very eccentric. In chapel he was always groaning and
moaning." But he later came to recognize him as "a man
of such obvious holiness."[13]

When *The Gospel and the Catholic Church* was reissued
in 1956 the *Spectator* found it hard to believe it had been
written twenty years before, because "It fits so well into
contemporary writing that it seems to have been born out
of due time." And a bishop a generation younger than
Ramsey, Simon Phipps, certainly thought of the book,
when he came to read it, as a seminal work.[14] When Simon
Phipps was bishop of Lincoln and Michael Ramsey was
retired, Michael used to stay at the theological college for
a fortnight on a regular basis, for continuing contact with
students was one of the pleasures of his old age. One day
the Bishop of Lincoln and his wife took the Ramseys for a
picnic, and experienced a common occurrence when
Ramsey was faced with a humorous situation he felt unable
to sustain. "I told him", the bishop recalls, "what we all
thought was a funny story. Ramsey said, 'Very funny,
very funny, very funny, very funny' four times, as a way

of killing the joke."[15] At the bishop of Chichester's dinner table, Mrs Phipps had earlier experienced an unnerving introduction to Ramsey. Simon Phipps was at that time suffragan bishop of Horsham, and as he had a previous engagement he was unable to go to dinner one evening with Ramsey's cousin Roger Wilson and his wife, Joyce, so Mary Phipps, a psychoanalyst by profession and only recently married to Simon, went alone. The Ramseys were staying, and Joyce Wilson warned Mary Phipps the conversation might be stilted. Mary was placed on Ramsey's right. After the soup had been served, Ramsey asked her if she thought depression was the same thing as the dark night of the soul. She said, "No". After some fifteen minutes of further silence, and the serving of the next course, the Archbishop again turned to her, and said, "Good. Neither do I."[16]

Theology, being studied in such depth by Michael Ramsey while he was sub-warden at Lincoln, was to become a kind of yardstick for measuring major issues as well as a prop with which he coped with life. In 1958 Simon Phipps had been appointed Industrial Chaplain in the diocese of Coventry, and discovered that Ramsey "understood what industrial mission was about. Although he had no direct contact with industry he had the shape of mind that could pick it up from someone who was talking to him about it. He was not just a good listener but a very good taker-in, and he was good at this because he had a sort of theological stand-point. I guess he had a Kingdom Theology, a theology that saw the priority as attending to the Kingdom of God. That's to say, attending to the fact that in ordinary secular affairs and circumstances there is a potential that comes to the surface and becomes actual if we live in a certain way, as opposed to attending as a priority to things to do with the Church. You start by trying to perceive what God is saying about ordinary secular affairs and this gives you an immediate link with ordinary people, so long as you can translate that into common or garden terms. I think he was rather good at that, because he assiduously avoided jargon."[17]

Professor Houlden, who was Principal of Cuddesdon when Michael Ramsey moved into the Old Vicarage there in 1974, and so saw a good deal of him in the early days of his retirement, confirms that as a theologian Ramsey "had the gift of avoiding technical shorthand. He had a certain fastidiousness of mind. He was not a person to drop into slogans or unpleasant jargon. He had taste. He was, however, always talking about Glory, which is a very technical term."[18] Indeed, the second book Michael Ramsey wrote while a professor of divinity at Durham was called *The Glory of God and the Transfiguration of Christ*, and Professor Macquarrie told his New York audience in 1988 that this title summed up the central interests in Ramsey's thoughts. "I do not think", he said, "I ever heard him give a sermon or deliver a lecture without that word 'glory' coming into it, probably several times." Ramsey explained in his Preface to this book, first published in 1949, that its purpose was to examine the concept of glory in the New Testament, that behind this conception there lay a fascinating piece of linguistic history, "and within it are contained the greatest themes of Christian Theology". He said the word expressed in a remarkable way "the unity of the doctrines of Creation, the Incarnation, the Cross, the Spirit, the Church and the world-to-come". It has to be said, however, that while this book reveals the quite extraordinary scope of Ramsey's reading and the accumulation, by this time, of a vast erudition, it is not, unlike his other books, readily accessible to someone not already versed in Old and New Testament studies. For Michael Ramsey, the Feast of the Transfiguration was one of the most significant festivals in

95

the Church's Calendar, and it always remained for him a matter of particular grief that the day on which the Transfiguration is celebrated, 6th August, was the day on which, in 1945, the Americans elected to drop their first atomic bomb.

Like Bishop Phipps, Professor Houlden also describes *The Gospel and the Catholic Church* as seminal. "It joined biblical, doctrinal and spiritual strands together, and brought to the fore the question of how you reflect about the nature of the Church. It did it in a way that, because it was scripturally based, appealed widely. And to draw attention to the Church theologically was highly relevant for ecumenical negotiations, because this was an issue we had got to come to terms with. He had the gift, when he was archbishop of Canterbury, of writing very high-class popular theology. He was not a major theologian in terms of his achievements in that particular discipline, but if you put him in the context of an archbishop being a theologian, then he was a major figure. When talking to Pope Paul VI he stood head and shoulders over him in terms of his profundity."[19]

After Michael Ramsey's historic visit to the Pope in 1966 he used to recount how he and the Pope "locked the door of the Vatican church and talked to each other leaning on the vestment chest like two old gentlemen". There is another amusing anecdote connected with that visit. Before he left England, a Baptist peer asked Michael Ramsey, in the House of Lords, if while in Rome he would maintain the fact that he was a protestant according to the meaning of that word in the Book of Common Prayer. Michael Ramsey had read the Book of Common Prayer with rather closer attention than had the Baptist peer, so he was able to rise from his bench and solemnly give the undertaking asked for, knowing full well that nowhere in the Book of Common Prayer does the word "protestant" appear.

While in the broadest sense Michael Ramsey was a very Anglican theologian, there were strands of interest that pointed to a far stronger sympathy for the Orthodox tradition than the public may have realized, for ecumenically the areas where he was most visibly seen to be at work were in striving for reunion with the Methodists and in forging closer relations with Rome. But one only had to see him with the Orthodox, at home in Lambeth or Canterbury or sharing their liturgy, to imagine him, at heart, an Eastern Patriarch. "He was acutely aware of the unspeakable splendour of God," Professor Macquarrie has said, "and aware too of how the humanity of our Lord Jesus Christ was transfigured by that splendour. These ideas are perhaps given more prominence in the Eastern Orthodox Church than in the Christianity of the west."[20] And Professor Houlden has said, "Michael Ramsey very much exemplified the Orthodox tradition of the holy man, one who devotes himself to speech about God. As a result, there's no doubt he was more popular in the Church than any other archbishop of Canterbury has ever been, and revered by a great many clergy, but outside the Church he was regarded as rather mysterious."[21]

Michael Ramsey relaxed by reading theology, but some people believe he might have been better prepared to cope with the theological ferment of the 1960s if he had kept even more abreast of German theology than he did. His favourite modern theologians (although he did become influenced by Frederick von Hügel) were Englishmen, people who shared his own catholic and biblical view of the Church. Ramsey was so impressed when in 1966 he read John Macquarrie's *Principles of Christian Theology* that two years later he invited him to attend the Lambeth Conference as an observer. Another teacher whose present day attempts to demythologize the Gospel have brought him a certain notoriety, David Jenkins, the Bishop of

Durham, was quoted extensively by Ramsey with approval, and undoubtedly became one of his favourite modern theologians. He remained fascinated by the Bishop of Durham, partly because Dr Jenkins came to occupy his old see, partly, one suspects, because he saw that upon David Jenkins had fallen the mantle of John Robinson, the purpose of whose *Honest to God* Ramsey had been far too slow to grasp in 1963. The bishop in turn has said, "Michael Ramsey was a good example of the best sort of typical Anglican theologian, namely that he was very firmly committed to what he would regard as the heart of the catholic tradition, and that that catholic tradition was especially to be found in the Fathers. And if you are in that tradition you are quite as sympathetic to the Orthodox as you are to more recent Roman Catholic developments. And he saw that it is the duty of the Anglican tradition to maintain this particular blend of biblical revelation, traditional Christianity, and the use of reason, particularly related to the way these blend in the practice of worship. He was always writing about Glory and could be accused of being over romantic or unrealistic at times, but none the less it was clearly the heart of him, really.

"As far as my own later pronouncements have been concerned, he would have felt I pushed the critical questioning almost too far and that possibly I was too ready to do that too publicly." Michael Ramsey attended the enthronement of David Jenkins, and commented afterwards on his sermon, "That sounded like William Temple." "I was", the bishop recalls, "very, very touched, as you may imagine. Temple was a hero. But Michael also used to say to me, 'If you are going to speak to miners you will have to speak more slowly.'"[22]

When delivering a lecture in memory of another former bishop of Durham, Ian Ramsey,* whose premature death

---

* Michael Ramsey and Ian Ramsey were in no way related. By chance,

in 1972 almost certainly robbed the Church of England of a leader to follow Michael Ramsey in the form of another William Temple, David Jenkins's rather swift Welsh mode of speech tripped him up, with results that Michael Ramsey was swift to pounce upon. His own inimitable version of the occasion went as follows: "After Jenkins had been in Durham a bit and wasn't behaving very tactfully I saw he was giving the Ian Ramsey Memorial Lecture, so I went along to hear what he was going to say, and there I was, sitting in the front row, and in comes Jenkins, and he sees me, and I think he was rather put off, and he starts his lecture, 'I'm very glad to be here on this prestigious occasion to give the Michael Ramsey Memorial Lecture.' Well, I stood up, and I turned round to the considerable audience, waiting to hear something startling from the Bishop of Durham, yes, I turned round, and I said, 'Well, I'm glad to discover that the Bishop of Durham believes in the Resurrection!' "

The Bishop of Durham thinks Michael Ramsey "did not move theologically fully with the times, and will increasingly be read as a pretty conservative theologian. But because of the immensely deep and warm faith that he had, which was not just piety, there was, with him, an unusual stillness at the heart. You could feel that."[23]

But for someone as radical as the Dean of Emmanual College, Cambridge, the Reverend Don Cupitt, Michael Ramsey simply wasn't a theologian at all. "For me, he's not a theologian because under modern conditions I think a theologian has got to be a heretic. The relation between religious belief and modern culture is so extreme you have to be innovative and exploratory. You have to be all the things that Michael Ramsey abhorred. A heretic, in origin,

---

there was even a third bishop called Ramsey, Kenneth Ramsey, suffragan bishop of Hulme.

is a person who chooses and thinks for himself. The great heretics of Church history have been the great philosophical theologians. Ramsey as a theologian was always first a churchman. He saw it as the task of the theologian to articulate the faith of the Church. I believe a theologian must have a more prophetic and critical role. It is necessary to re-invent and re-imagine the faith of the Church in the face of historical change. There is no such thing as truths that continue unchanged through history. Unless you continuously recreate or re-invent, truth dies. So that, for me, the simple repetition of slogans from the past is not religious utterance at all. You have to remake things all the time.

"At the moment, only a person with a literary education has access to Christian belief because you have to root yourself through the past in order to understand it. The Christian language is entirely phased in terms of a world view that died in the seventeenth century. So when Michael Ramsey spoke of Christ being seated at the right hand of God in heaven he was using forms of words that could only be understood by people who knew how the world used to be seen many centuries ago. And there you've got an acute problem of how you can actually relate such language to your life today. He wouldn't admit the difficulty of that. The problem is that the sort of biblical theology he stood for really disappeared from the intellectual scene in 1960. His books are not intellectually stimulating now mainly because he never really deals with objections. Any deviation from what he reckons to be orthodox is always treated as rather unbalanced or unsafe or extreme, as if, for him, religious thought is a matter of playing safe and going down the middle of the road. He always used those sorts of metaphors of risk and imbalance to describe any adventuresomeness in matters of intellect."

But, Mr Cupitt concedes, "It's not necessarily a good

100

thing for thinkers to be in positions of leadership in the Church, any more than it is in the State. So maybe one doesn't need a theologian as archbishop of Canterbury. The job of an archbishop is to respond to questions of a political and ethical kind, to know what forces in the Church to encourage and which to discourage."[24]

Another view of an archbishop's role was expressed by Bishop Phipps. "It's frightfully important that the archbishop of Canterbury should sit on the fence, and it's a very uncomfortable place to sit. When it comes to giving a lead, it depends what people mean. If they want him to say a lot of clear sharp things it may not be very useful. It comes down to spirituality. What we need in an archbishop is deep spirituality, which means being courageous enough to be open to where the spirit may be leading. The Church is so frightened of that."[25]

Michael Ramsey's years as a professional theologian spanned 1940 to 1952, the first decade being spent in Durham, the last two years in Cambridge. Once he had been consecrated to Durham in 1952, and certainly after he had been translated to York only three and a half years later, he found it difficult to keep up with reading in a subject where the literature was proliferating. "He could not keep abreast in research," says Professsor Houlden, "but he went on reflecting on questions of belief and how you express them rationally. One of his strengths was not to specialize; he was a synthesizer. He liked to keep areas, which nowadays are often segregated in Church thought, in play together, so that, for instance, the way you state belief, ethics, biblical study and the way you pray he saw as a single whole, and he endeavoured to talk in a unified way about them. When he retired he hoped to make some substantial new contribution, but he quickly realized that for twenty years he had not read the monographs and journals and it really was too late to catch up. But he remained a theologian to his finger tips. He was a person whose whole being was cerebral. He was a thinking person and in that sense he remained a theologian to the end."[26]

Professor Macquarrie is also not surprised that no major book was written in retirement. "I think that rather than become a bishop he would have preferred the cloistered life of Cambridge or Oxford, but I don't know that he would ever have produced some great magnum opus. I can't imagine what it would have been."[27]

Ramsey was well aware of the conflicting demands on his time once he had become a bishop. In the Preface to his 1959 Hale Memorial Lectures, in which he discussed the development of Anglican Theology between 1889 and 1939, he wrote: "The inadequacies in this work may be explained, though I do not ask for them to be excused, by the plea that it is a sketch and not a treatise. Of one omission I am strongly conscious: that, apart from incidental references, I have not dealt with the doctrine of the Eucharist. On this, the literature within the period is considerable, but I have not had time for the full examination of it and the fresh assessment which I believe to be needed."[28]

Quite obviously Michael's headmaster, Geoffrey Fisher, had been watching his former pupil's career with interest, and in view of the uneasy relationship that was to develop between these two disparate clerics it is very interesting that in 1932, immediately he became bishop of Chester, Geoffrey Fisher appointed Michael Ramsey an examining chaplain, a post he held until 1939, the year that Fisher moved to London. Family events were also marching forward while Michael was at Lincoln. In 1933 his sister Bridget married Henry Barcroft, the boy who had so much enjoyed teasing Michael at King's College Choir School. Henry was now a lecturer at University College (in 1935 he became Professor of Physiology at Belfast) and Bridget was still training in medicine. They were married, on 17th February 1933, at Coton Parish Church, a few miles west of Cambridge, and a reception was held at Magdalene – without, according to their second son Michael, the benefit of any drink. Yet Arthur Ramsey could be very generous to his children in practical ways. In 1947 he bought a house for Henry and Bridget, who were to have four children, John, Michael, Sarah and Roger. Michael Ramsey stood as godfather to the two older boys, and regularly sent all four of them a Christmas present. "Being his godson didn't make the slightest difference", Michael Barcroft rather ruefully recalls. "Because he sent my sister and youngest brother a Christmas present I often wondered if he had got slightly confused as to which his godchildren were."[29] Ramsey signed his cards to his nephews and nieces "Uncle Mick". Asked whether he had been a good godfather to her sons, Dr Bridget Barcroft replied with an unequivocal No. "He didn't do anything for them *at all*. He couldn't be bothered. And perhaps he was a little jealous because he had no children of his own. I don't know. I think it was mostly because he couldn't be bothered. I'm not at all sure he even knew their names."[30]

This was an unhappy state of affairs echoed with some feeling by Ramsey's younger sister Margaret. She also had four children (all girls) and was widowed in straitened circumstances in 1962 when her husband, George Paul, a scholar of Trinity who read Moral Sciences and whom she had married in 1938, died tragically. He was being taught to sail by his brother-in-law, Henry Barcroft, when he suffered a heart attack, fell overboard and was drowned. "It was really sad", says Mrs Paul. "At the time that George died I was quite fond of Michael and I would have given anything for him to have been a proper uncle and to have supported me. It would have made all the difference. I was very isolated. The only time he came to stay with us as a family was really awful. The girls were aged from five to twelve. It was quite unprecedented for him to ask to come and stay, and it turned out he had only come at all because Aunt Lucy had given him a great dressing down and told him to visit us. But he behaved absolutely impossibly. He couldn't speak to the children. He couldn't even remember their names. He was at his most eccentric and withdrawn. For years he sent them each a £1 book token at Christmas. That made matters almost worse."[31]

Although he was once drawn to make a conventional reply on television when asked by Ludovic Kennedy whether he regretted not having children (he said he did), Michael Ramsey had no real rapport with children (patting their heads in a crowd does not amount to being able to relate to them as human beings), and much of the evident discomfort he felt when visiting Margaret and her children must also, surely, have stemmed from his inability to cope with bereavement. He would have been appalled by George's death, but quite unable to communicate his feelings about it. What he did do was provide Margaret with £500 a year. His stipend as archbishop of Canterbury in 1962 was £7,500, so if the money came from his personal income it was a generous gift.* He did have access to a discretionary fund, but it seems unlikely he would have thought it proper to use such a fund to assist a close relative.

Michael Barcroft's earliest memory of his uncle dates from about the age of twelve, for most of his early life was spent in Ireland. He remembers Michael Ramsey and

---

* The stipend of the archbishop of York in 1962 was £6,500, the bishop of London £4,500 and the average income of beneficed clergy £850. In Victorian times, before Anglican clergy stipends were pooled, discrepancies were enormous. Both the archbishop of Canterbury and the bishop of Durham had an income of £19,000 per annum, when most of the clergy had to manage on £400, some on as little as £50.

Arthur prancing up and down the garden at Howfield "doing a sort of dance. They were shouting together, 'Diddy-did, Diddy-da, Diddy-de, Diddy-day'. I think they had their legs tied together. I thought it was very jolly, but Grandpa sprained his ankle."[32] Michael Barcroft was born in 1938, so if he was twelve at the time, these japes took place in 1950, when Arthur Ramsey would have been eighty-three and Michael forty-five. Arthur Ramsey died on 31st December 1954, leaving £12,860 10s 1d, of which the rather mean sum of £50 went to a servant, and the even more extraordinary sum of £99 each to his executors, Henry Barcroft and Michael. A photograph of his father, wearing a skullcap, stood for years in pride of place on Michael's desk beside another of Pope John XXIII.

No one goes on holiday with their father when grown-up unless they want to, and on examination Michael's relationship with his father seems to have been closer than some people perhaps realized. In his last year at Lincoln Michael went on holiday with Arthur to Freiburg, where in the Black Forest he indulged his one physical passion, for walking, and he was to go walking with his father again, in the French Alps, in 1938, when he climbed Petit Mont Blanc. In August 1937 Michael also spent time walking in Antrim with his father.

But these holidays overseas were never resumed after the war, when year in, year out, Michael and his wife would retreat in August to the Church Inn at Holne in Devon – there to read and walk. Loss of contact with his family after marriage in 1942 may have been because Michael's wife found Arthur Ramsey intimidating and would therefore not have relished visits to Howfield. "I didn't get to know Michael's father very well," Lady Ramsey says, "because he was very fierce. By fierce, I mean not out-going. I imagine he had become like that because of the death of his wife and son. In those days people weren't helped to cope with that sort of thing. I think they had been a happy family but were rather driven into silence by catastrophe."[33] Joan Ramsey's own brand of "out-goingness" sometimes takes the form of amusing but astringent comments on other people, and one can sense the possibility of a clash of temperament between a family united by academic brilliance and traumatic bereavement, confronted by an aunt by marriage and a sister-in-law from a non-academic, military and hunting background less reticent in her approach to life, indeed often indiscreet, sharply observant and extremely funny. She came also to admire and respect an increasingly famous husband whose sisters retained memories not of a bushy-eyebrowed benevolent patriarch who could have people rocking with laughter, but of a very messy, unpredictable, withdrawn and distinctly odd little boy, who had contributed little to their childhood games and now could not even bother to remember their own children's names. Perhaps when Michael married they hoped that his wife would encourage him to take a closer interest in his nephews and nieces, but for a variety of no doubt complex reasons she does not seem to have done so. It is a myth that children invariably hold marriages together; if this were so, there would not be so many divorces, and childless couples often form particularly close relationships. Indeed, it seems that Michael and Joan Ramsey were to find their marriage entirely self-sufficient.

CHAPTER FIVE

PARISH PRIEST
AND BISHOP

Do not worry about status.   *The Christian Priest Today.*

It has been said that Michael Ramsey was never cut out to
be a parish priest, and it is true he could no more have
organized a garden fête than kept the parish accounts. He
was notoriously uninterested in the minutiae of ordinary
human existence. The way in which most people earned a
living was a closed book to him, and petty parish squabbles
over rotas for arranging the flowers were as alien to him as
making conventional small-talk prior to discussing the
state of someone's soul. But he had a stab at it. In 1936 he
was appointed to the oddly named Lectureship at St
Botolph Church* in Boston, Lincolnshire, famous for its
252 foot high tower known as the Boston Stump, the
dominant feature of the town since 1309. It is in fact
Britain's largest parish church, and in *The Buildings of
England* Sir Nikolaus Pevsner described the lantern-
topped tower as "the most prodigious of English parochial
steeples".

Since the nineteenth century the Lecturer of Boston

* Now St Botolph and St Christopher.

107

Parish Church has been the senior curate, or to be absolutely accurate, the senior assistant curate, for strictly speaking the incumbent of any parish, the vicar or rector, is the curate; it is he who has "the cure of souls" within the parish. But the post originally dates from the sixteenth century, when Boston Corporation annexed lands belonging to the church and undertook, in return, to pay the stipend of a "second presbyter" to assist the vicar, and most probably also to act as chaplain to the Corporation. Later in the seventeenth century the term "Lecturer" came to be used at a time when the Parish of Boston found itself under the sway of Puritan influences, and interestingly enough, in view of Michael Ramsey's Congregational background, the vicar in 1633, John Cotton, although considered "an eminently pious, learned, benevolent, energetic, consistent and conscientiously good man", resigned the living as a result of his nonconformist views, emigrated to Boston in Massachusetts and there became a Congregationalist minister. The first person actually recorded as "Lecturer" was John Naylor, who was appointed in 1645.

Michael Ramsey's parish priest, under whose guidance and direction he worked for rather less than two years, was Canon A. M. Cook, who was also rural dean. Mr William Brough, who sang in the choir, recalls Michael walking around with holes in his socks. "He seemed to be living in a different world. We did not find him very approachable, not in the way a normal parish priest would be."[1] Michael's duties as senior assistant curate would have been to celebrate Communion and to take all the other services in collaboration with the rest of the staff, to visit the sick and to teach scripture to senior boys in a local school. For a man who had spent six years training ordinands, and had just published a major book on theology, it was not very demanding work and perhaps even rather menial. To have undertaken an assistant curacy at all at this stage showed considerable humility. He managed during his short time in Boston to sow a number of apocryphal stories about himself, but one anecdote connected with Boston has a first-class pedigree; it was told to the present vicar, Canon Peter Fluck, by Lady Ramsey.[2] Apparently one day after Michael had been out visiting he returned to his house and rang the bell. "Mr Ramsey's out", his housekeeper shouted. "Oh, well, I'll come back later", Michael called back, and walked off up the road. As Ramsey would surely have had his own front door key, maybe even this story is apocryphal – unless of course he had mislaid or forgotten the key, which was perfectly possible.

In his memoirs, Michael's father says, "Michael rented a small house and engaged a housekeeper." Then he wrote a sentence which has been heavily scored out in black ink, but still remains legible, and reads, "The first was rather incapable but the second served him well and looked after his needs properly." It sounds as though it may have been the first of these good ladies who failed to recognize the unmistakable voice of her clerical employer. He also records that one of the parishioners on whom Michael called following a death in the family said to him, "We thought you would not mind if we buried her on the chapel side of the cemetery, because all her relations have been buried on that side, and if we put her on the other side it might make it so difficult for her if at any time she wanted to get across to them."[3]

After something like eighteen months Michael moved back to the city he loved and felt most at home in, Cambridge, for he had been offered, by the Master and Fellows of Corpus Christi College, his first and only living, that of St Benedict, in Benet Street in the heart of the city. In his entry in *Who's Who* Michael gave his years at St Benedict as 1939–40, but in fact he moved there late in 1938. The church was the oldest in Cambridge, with a Saxon tower, and a small parish parcelled into four separate areas; there were no parish organizations to bother running, and not even a vicarage, so that Arthur Ramsey came to the rescue by purchasing for his son 45 Owlstone Road, a small late-Victorian terraced house in a quiet suburban crescent some twenty minutes' walk away, near the Grantchester Meadows.

One of the most significant things that now happened was that Arthur Ramsey began to attend services at St Benedict instead of Emmanuel Congregational Church. He says he "felt unable to walk past the church in which my own son was ministering" and he offered to resign his office as a deacon at Emmanuel, but the offer was refused. Clearly, however, he was on the road to final reception by Michael into the Church of England, which presumably took place some time during the course of the next couple of years. Perhaps for romantic reasons it has often been believed that Arthur Ramsey's reception took place when Michael was bishop of Durham, but Lady Ramsey quite definitely has no recollection of the event occurring at any time after her marriage, which took place in 1942.[4] There was no choir at St Benedict, so although Michael would probably have liked to inaugurate a Sung Eucharist this was out of the question. In his day the Sacrament was not reserved, but although he heard confessions, the congregation, mainly middle-aged, middle-class academics and professional people, called him Mr Ramsey, not Father. There was of course an early celebration of Holy Communion, and then Matins, ending with what one of the parishioners, Miss Elizabeth Simons, a young girl in Ramsey's day, remembers was "a very long sermon" (although all sermons seem long to children), and continuing with a second Communion, for which Michael wore vestments.

The separated parish boundaries stretched to Barnwell

Bridge and Regent Street and took in the old Adden-
brookes Hospital, and Miss Simons says that Michael was
good at parish visiting. "My family thought he was a nice
man, but they didn't find him particularly easy to talk to.
It was his speech difficulty that hit you most."[5] His famous
manner of stammering over words seems to have been so
pronounced at this time that Miss Simons formed the
definite impression that he actually had a speech impedi-
ment, but this was not the case.

Ecumenically, he was fairly adventurous, inviting Pres-
byterian and Methodist ministers to preach as well as a
Lutheran from Germany, but there was no question of a
Roman Catholic occupying the pulpit. "The roof would
have blown off", says Miss Simons. "People would have
thought he'd gone mad." As far as his own sermons were
concerned, she found them "punctuated with paradoxes.
They were really aimed at theological students. As a
teenager, they were above my head, and I should think the
heads of a lot of other parishioners as well. But a lot of
university people came to hear him preach."

Apparently a cross that Michael had to bear at St
Benedict was the drawn-out playing of the organist of the
day, with interminable pauses between the verses. "Oh, I
endured tortures", he told a great friend of Aunt Lucy,
Mrs Rebecca Hurry, who became organist at St Benedict
sixteen years after Michael had left.[6]

It was while he was on holiday in the Lake District –
again with his father – that Michael heard Chamberlain's
lugubrious broadcast announcing the declaration of war,
listening to the wireless in the kitchen of the Royal Oak
Hotel at Rosthwaite. His churchwardens soon volunteered
to take in evacuees from the East End, and these children
helped to swell the small Sunday School. Miss Simons
remembers Michael's enormous frame wedged into a tiny
chair while he told the children about baptism. Some time

in 1939 he turned down the post of Warden of St Augustine's College, Canterbury, but obviously his days as a parish priest were numbered. Alwyn Williams, who had succeeded Herbert Hensley Henson as bishop of Durham in 1939, invited Michael to preach at his first ordination, and while Michael was debating whether to become an army chaplain (one can hardly visualize him in uniform, or conforming to the etiquette of mess life) a second offer arrived from Dr Williams, of the van Mildert Chair of Divinity in the University of Durham, and with it a post on the staff of the cathedral as a residentiary canon. Michael was thirty-five years old, and this was the kind of glittering academic prize he may hardly have dared to dream about. His decision to accept changed his life in almost every respect, for not only did it pave the way for the even more prestigious Regius Professorship of Divinity at Cambridge and an eventual return to Durham as its bishop, but, by heading north, he was also to meet his future wife.

Just before Michael left for Durham, a city soon to become a rival to Cambridge for his affections, yet another invitation arrived, this time from Geoffrey Fisher, to preach in St Paul's Cathedral at *his* first ordination service as bishop of London. Fisher's appreciation of Michael's early abilities certainly seems to have been in marked contrast to the doubts he later expressed about his suitability to succeed as archbishop of Canterbury. In the nave of St Paul's to hear the sermon was Michael's constantly proud and energetic father.

The possessions that had furnished the house in Owlstone Road hardly filled one room of the enormous and very beautiful battlemented house now assigned to Michael at Durham. It was in the area known as The College, situated to the south side of a cathedral which must rank as one of the architectural glories of Europe. The sitting room he now had to furnish was thirty feet long. There was no central heating, and the house needed decorating. This was hardly a time for lashing out on luxuries, however (Michael's move to Durham more or less coincided with Dunkirk), but he did go to an auction in Cambridge, where he bought a vestment box for £3.

When Michael Ramsey's warden at Lincoln, Leslie Owen, left the Theological College in 1936 he was appointed archdeacon of Durham (it may have been he who suggested to Dr Williams that he invite Michael to preach), and in 1939 Owen was consecrated suffragan bishop of Jarrow.* He employed as his secretary and driver a young woman called Joan Alice Chetwode Hamilton, who had no secretarial qualifications or academic pretensions but had a lively mind, an acute sense of the ridiculous and an often devastating wit. She was very close to the Owen family and actually lived with them in their house in The College. Michael's sermon having presumably met with approval, shortly before being offered a chair at the University he had received another invitation from the new bishop of Durham, to conduct an ordination retreat, and during the course of it he stayed as a guest of the Owens. This was when he and Joan Hamilton first briefly met. Once Michael had taken up residence in The College they found themselves living two doors away. After about eighteen months, in the Owens' drawing room, they became engaged.

"I was surprised", his sister Margaret recalls.[7] "I thought he wouldn't marry", a comment echoed by Bridget: "I was very surprised when he got married. I didn't think he was the marrying sort."[8] And Arthur Ramsey recorded in his memoirs: "I had begun to think of him as a confirmed

---

* In 1944 he became suffragan bishop of Maidstone and died in 1947, only a year after being enthroned as bishop of Lincoln.

bachelor, and was pleasantly surprised when he replied that he would marry when he found the right person." In Joan Hamilton Michael certainly found the right person, someone in whom he would encounter no intellectual competition, for she constantly under-played her mental powers, and someone with whom to share an identical sense of humour; someone, too, to look after as well as be looked after by, for while many observers believed it was Joan Ramsey who made sure the Archbishop had not got both legs in one trouser leg, he in turn kept a watchful eye on her mental and physical well-being in a way he never did with anyone else. He also found someone so sympathetic to his powerful personality and eccentric conduct that with her he was able to relax without feeling he was making demands. Sadly, this may have proved another reason why there was never any close bond between the Ramseys as a couple and Michael's family, for with Joan he discovered a compatability he never achieved elsewhere, and who could blame his own family if they harboured some resentment. "When you talked to him you couldn't feel he was attending", Margaret Paul recalls. "I remember lots of conversations with him in adult life when after about three minutes I realized he simply wasn't listening at all but was getting very agitated, making faces and fidgeting. He behaved to his family just as he did with other people. But he behaved much more normally with Joan."[9]

With Bridget, however, who was closer in age, Michael does seem, on one crucial occasion at any rate, to have established the kind of rapport rare between a brother and sister. "We were living in Belfast at the time," Bridget recalls, "and I went over to Liverpool, and on to Durham, especially to see what Joan looked like. I remember I went for a long walk with Michael, and he asked me about the facts of life. He was very ignorant. This was when he was thinking of getting engaged. I didn't find it embarrassing because I'd been a doctor working in that sort of area. I didn't find it embarrassing at all. I was flattered."[10]

Joan had ecclesiastical connections of her own. Her paternal grandfather, the Reverend C. Chetwode Hamilton, had been an Anglican clergyman – "the sort of parson", she says, "who left his parish and went to Canada for the summer".[11] Her father's younger brother, Eric Hamilton, had been suffragan bishop of Shrewsbury since 1940, and in 1944 was to be appointed dean of Windsor. But her father was an army officer, and she had one brother, who hunted, so that with his father-in-law and brother-in-law Michael could have had little in common. The marriage took place on 8th April 1942 (he was thirty-seven, she was thirty-two) at eleven o'clock in the morning in the Galilee Chapel at Durham Cathedral. Michael wore his cassock; Joan wore a very dignified bridal gown and carried a bouquet of enormous, rather funereal lilies tied together with a white bow. Aunt Lucy was there, with Arthur Ramsey. A clergyman escorted Joan through the cloisters to the chapel, where her father, Lieutenant Colonel F. A. C. Hamilton, who had lost a leg in the First World War, was waiting in front of the altar to give her away. They were married by the Bishop of Jarrow, and the Dean, Cyril Alington, gave an address. The Bishop's daughter was bridesmaid; Eric Abbott, who had succeeded Leslie Owen as Warden at Lincoln, and later was to become dean of Westminster Abbey and one of Michael Ramsey's closest friends, was best man.

There was a reception at the Owens' house, and then Joan and Michael slipped away to lunch alone at the County Hotel, where they walked slap into a friend of Joan's working for the Land Army who was doing the same thing. They took a train to the Lake District, where they stayed in a village inn, and on their return from honeymoon they were greeted by Michael's housekeeper, who had prepared the tea. "Well, sir," she said, "I hope you'll be as happy with her as you've been with me."

In 1943 Michael was joined in the Cathedral Chapter by Alan Richardson, beside whom in 1929 he had been made priest in Liverpool, and he and his wife Phyllis became firm friends of the newly married Ramseys. A church historian drawn at this time to the Chapter, and to a second chair of divinity at the University, was Stanley Greenslade, and other scholars in the faculty included H. F. D. Sparks and C. K. Barrett. The archdeacon of Durham was John Ramsbotham, later bishop of Wakefield. At St Mary's College Michael found a few women reading theology, two of whom, both former Methodists, he prepared for confirmation; one later became a Carmelite nun and remained in touch all her life. Teaching, preaching, reading and writing (in 1945 he published *The Resurrection of Christ* and in 1949 *The Glory of God and the Transfiguration of Christ*) became the settled pattern of Michael's life, but he began also to expand his active interest in ecumenical affairs. In 1948 he attended the First Assembly of the World Council of Churches, held in Amsterdam, where he held long discussions with the eminent Swiss theologian Karl Barth, a translation of whose book *Romans*, brought out by Sir Edwyn Hoskins, Ramsey had read in 1933.[*]

In 1950, after exactly a decade at Durham University, Michael Ramsey was offered one of the most exalted teaching appointments in any university, the Regius Professorship of Divinity at Cambridge, but only after a good

---

[*] When in 1968 Karl Barth died, Michael Ramsey was then archbishop of Canterbury, and he told the press that Barth was a brave Christian leader, fearless in his resistance to injustice, a theologian of immense influence "and a warm-hearted, humorous and most kind companion and friend . . . one of the great Christian figures of our time."

deal of argument had taken place among those responsible for the appointment. Despite the title of the chair, this is not a crown appointment,* and for ideological reasons several members of the faculty committee were very much opposed to Michael. Although he had no vote, Michael's Liverpool mentor and immediate predecessor as Regius Professor, Charles Raven, did not consider him a good enough Classical scholar, and attempts were made to enlist opposition from the dean of St Paul's, W. R. Matthews, who was so at sea about the election he had not even grasped the candidates' names, and asked one day in the Athenaeum, "Who is this Michael Foster who must not be Regius Professor?" Michael was very much aware of a frosty reception from the faculty when he eventually arrived. For his first lecture he was given one of the smallest rooms in the Divinity School, and began by saying to the undergraduates, "The caretaker tells me you are only attending out of curiosity."

"But there was tremendous rejoicing among the catholics", Harry Williams recalls.[12] Most of those attending Michael's lectures were men reading for the Theological Tripos, but Father Williams, who in 1969 became a member of the Community of the Resurrection, went across from Westcott House, where he was chaplain, to hear what Michael Ramsey had to say. "He went down very well. The undergraduates loved his lectures. He had not progressed at all from the theology enshrined in *The Gospel and the Catholic Church*, and he gave them a positive theology that could easily be linked to their religion." One of Michael's duties as Regius Professor was

---

* Following a dispute between the Fellows of Trinity College and Queen Mary I and by a subsequent reconciliation with Queen Elizabeth I, the Fellows of Trinity assumed responsibility for the appointment, which was eventually taken over by the University.

to act as ex-officio chairman of the Governors of Westcott House, and before the first meeting he attended, the Principal, Kenneth Carey, showed him the agenda consisting of about a dozen items, and asked him to close the meeting with the Grace. As soon as he had completed Item No 1 Michael stood up and said, "The Grace of our Lord Jesus Christ . . ."

Back for a second time in his alma mater, Michael Ramsey was elected a Professorial Fellow of Magdalene (in 1952 he was elected an honorary Fellow), and a year later he became examining chaplain to the bishop of Lincoln (he had been examining chaplain to the bishop of Durham from 1940 to 1950) and a canon and prebendary of Lincoln Cathedral. Michael and Joan now began what seems to have been a restless search for a home, a search that continued even in retirement. Because in The College they had become accustomed to a large house, they moved in October 1950 into another big property, 14 Latham Road, to the far south of the city on the way to Trumpington and adjacent to the Leys School playing fields. No sooner was that more or less ship-shape than they decided they needed a smaller house after all, and a year later they moved nearer to the University, to 3 Wordsworth Grove, a quiet *cul-de-sac*. (The house has since been demolished.) In 1952 they moved again, to a house in Fitzwilliam Street, across the road from the Fitzwilliam Museum.

As Michael had no church of his own when he became Regius Professor, he celebrated Holy Communion in the chapel at Magdalene, where there happened to be no chaplain at the time, and returned to St Benedict to hear confessions.* Much of his time as professor would have been taken up with supervising doctoral candidates, but he

---

* Since 1945 the parish of St Benedict has been run by the Society of St Francis.

found time to produce his fourth book, *F. D. Maurice and the Conflicts of Modern Theology*, published in 1951. In essence this contained the text of the Maurice memorial lectures he had delivered at King's College, London during the Lent term of 1948, when he was still a Professor of Divinity at Durham. In 1853 Maurice had been dismissed from his chair at King's College for heresy, but ended his career as a professor at Cambridge, and as a theologian Michael Ramsey had for long found him a kindred spirit. He told his audience that Maurice was one of "the greatest figures in the history of Christianity in our land", and his aim in the lectures was to evaluate Maurice's teaching on Atonement and Sacrifice, and to examine "his methods of biblical exegesis in relation to the subsequent trends of biblical study."

After *F. D. Maurice and the Conflicts of Modern Theology* there was only to be one more original book devoted exclusively to theology, *God, Christ and the World*, subtitled A Study in Contemporary Theology, published in 1969. Most of the later, often quite substantial, works were (like the Maurice memorial lectures) reprinted lectures or miscellaneous collections of essays and addresses. But by now Michael must have fulfilled many of the dreams Arthur Ramsey had entertained for Frank. He had held two professorial chairs, he was a Fellow of his own old college, and in 1952 he received from Winston Churchill a letter to say that he would like to nominate him for the see of Durham, made vacant because Alwyn Williams had unexpectedly been translated to Winchester.

There was a typically Anglican Alice-in-Wonderland aspect to the appointment of diocesan bishops until matters were brought more under the proper control of the Church towards the end of Ramsey's own time at Canterbury. Although the voice of the Church is now made known to Downing Street through the deliberations of an

appropriately constructed selection committee, known as
the Crown Appointments Committee, the Church of
England remains the only Church in the Anglican Communion to have its bishops ultimately selected by the State,
for they are still appointed by the sovereign on the advice
of the prime minister. This is a direct consequence of the
Establishment, because since the reign of Henry VIII the
sovereign has been Supreme Governor of the Church of
England. But back in 1952 there was still an official called
the Archbishops' Appointments Secretary,* whose
responsibility was to "take soundings", as the Tory party
used to do when they needed a new prime minister, to
dine at the Athenaeum, lunch in deaneries, occasionally
venture into the gastronomically less appealing environs of
a vicarage, note "promising material" and place a lethal
black mark against the names of those who had blotted
their copy-book, or were just not considered "quite right".
On the matter of all diocesan bishops and deans, and on
any other Crown Appointment within the ecclesiastic fold,
the Archbishops' Appointments Secretary would confer
with the prime minister's Appointments Secretary. Eventually, in the case of a bishopric, two names would emerge,
which was part of the fantasy that the sovereign was going
to make a choice. What the monarch actually did was
automatically tick the first name of the two, and this name
was sent to the appropriate dean and chapter for the even
more farcical ceremony of "election".

It has long been a cause for incredulous comment (some
have even based their belief in miracles on the strength of
it) that under all these unpredictable circumstances some
very remarkable bishops went forward to their consecration as direct successors to the Apostles. Few were more

* For much of the relevant period covered by this book, Mr William
Saumarez Smith, formerly a member of the Indian Civil Service.

remarkable than Arthur Michael Richard Ramsey, whose choice for the senior see of Durham at the age of forty-seven can now be seen, taking into account the likely chain of succession and the current ages and abilities of the other contenders, to have borne all the hallmarks of a carefully laid Establishment plan to place him in position to succeed, in due course, his old headmaster, Geoffrey Fisher, as archbishop of Canterbury. If this was not the case, then there was, also on the part of the Establishment, an almighty blunder. For by the time he did succeed, in 1961, as archbishop of York he was the senior bishop on the bench, at the age of fifty-six at the peak of his powers and likely to remain in the job a reasonable length of time, and intellectually he was quite obviously head and shoulders in front of his peers. It is not by any means a *fait accompli* that the archbishop of York will succeed to Canterbury (Donald Coggan, who succeeded Michael Ramsey in 1974 by default, Ian Ramsey of Durham having died two years before, was only the ninth archbishop of York ever to do so), but in 1961, when Geoffrey Fisher retired, there was no one so obviously superior to Michael Ramsey in ability that anyone even seriously thought of making a bet on the matter. But on the day that Michael Ramsey announced his impending retirement in 1974, Ladbroke's did "open a book". Times had changed. However, in 1952 Ramsey's appointment to Durham was an event which really set the seal on the leadership of the Church of England for the next twenty years.

Did Michael Ramsey hesitate about accepting the see of Durham? "He went about on a bicycle consulting with two or three people", according to Lady Ramsey. "It was quite a decision. If you are an academic and you become Regius Professor you tend to think, that's it, don't you? I don't think he ever regretted the decision to become a bishop, but it took a lot of settling. I should think a week or two. I had only just gone out to get pansies for the window boxes and that sort of thing. I think if he'd been offered any other bishopric he wouldn't have gone. But the pull of Durham was terrific."[13]

There are several accounts of Michael saying to people in the street, "They've made me Bishop of Durham. Oh hell!" It must actually have been a difficult decision to make, because to accept any bishopric meant an end to his academic career, and the question was whether to contribute his theological training and insights to his episcopacy. This eventually is what he decided to do, and it is hard not to believe it was the right decision. "He was very much a Church theologian", in the opinion of Father Harry Williams. "He was impressive as a theologian but he was not a pioneer thinker and he would never really have got beyond *The Gospel and the Catholic Church*."[14] But Lady Ramsey is surely right too in suggesting that Michael was not tempted by the idea of being a bishop *per se*; two factors that would have swayed him were the respect he felt for the theological traditions of Durham – Joseph Lightfoot (1879 to 1889), Brooke Westcott (1890 to 1901) and Herbert Hensley Henson (1921 to 1939) had all made their individual mark on the Church as well as the diocese – and the knowledge that in large measure it was because many of his former colleagues in the diocese wanted him back as their bishop that the offer had been made in the first place. It is today *de rigueur* for the diocese involved to be consulted about its future bishop, and although this was not always the case in the past, certainly in 1952 the Chapter of Durham Cathedral, with most of whom Michael Ramsey had worked for ten years, made their opinion plain. The dean, John Wild, had been appointed after Michael's departure for Cambridge, but Alan Richardson, who now knew him very well indeed, made no secret of his belief that Michael Ramsey should return to Durham as bishop.

Durham is known as a palatine diocese, for in the past it enjoyed truly royal privileges, accruing from the prestige of St Cuthbert and the wealth which gathered around his shrine; this had enabled the bishops of Durham to become both civil and military rulers of the north-east. Much of the princely power of the bishop was reduced by Henry VIII, and the last prince-bishop was William van Mildert, in whose name Michael Ramsey's chair at the University had been founded, for on his death in 1836 the regal authority of the palatine reverted to the crown. It was Bishop van Mildert who had founded the University, in 1832, by making over to it his town house, adjacent to the cathedral, and moving permanently into Auckland Castle, eleven miles away at Bishop Auckland – in the Middle Ages only one of a string of castles and manors throughout the north inhabited on progress by the bishops. But so influential had the bishops of Durham been in secular affairs that the bishopric still ranks immediately after London in seniority (then comes Winchester; after that bishops rank in seniority according to the date of their consecration). So it was an appointment to the fourth most senior bishopric in the Church of England, one that automatically carries a seat in the House of Lords,* to which Churchill had been asked to address his mind. But unless someone had greatly displeased him he was little interested in Church appointments, and almost certainly accepted without question the advice of his appointments' secretary, who in turn would have heard from the Archbishops' Appointments Secretary that serious and

---

* The archbishops of Canterbury and York, and the bishops of London, Durham and Winchester, sit in the Lords as of right. The remaining twenty-one seats are taken by bishops according to seniority by date of consecration.

informed church people believed the Northern Province, with its enfeebled and autocratic archbishop, Cyril Garbett, could do with another scholar and ecumenist in its midst. At all events, those who did not personally choose Michael Ramsey came to welcome him.*

Michael already knew most of the cathedral and university staff, and a good many of the diocesan clergy in the three hundred or so parishes. From the bishop's point of view it is an easy diocese to get around and therefore – a distinct advantage in Michael Ramsey's case – not too difficult to administer. When Michael became bishop the diocesan offices still remained in Durham, but they have since been transferred to Auckland Castle. The eight-hundred-acre park, once roamed by deer, is now owned by the Church Commissioners, and contains picnic areas and a golf course. Dour, gaunt and rather forbidding, the castle itself contains a prized collection of portraits, some fine furniture, beautifully proportioned seventeenth-century state rooms, and a chapel consecrated in 1665 which is so large that for nearly five hundred years it served as a banqueting hall. The most notable modernizer to get his hands on the house, in the eighteenth century, was George III's architect, James Wyatt.

Michael Ramsey regretted there was a scarcity of books about the office and work of a bishop,[15] and spent the week before his consecration, on Michaelmas Day, reading Pope Gregory the Great's *Regula Pastoralis*. "The bishop is still a priest," he reminded himself and the clergy, "and unless he retains the heart and mind of a priest he will be a bad bishop."[16] He was enthroned in the Cathedral Church

---

* One of the strongest arguments in favour of Disestablishment is the fact that the prime minister may not even be an Anglican, but two prime ministers responsible for some of the more inspired episcopal appointments in modern times were Neville Chamberlain, a Unitarian, and Harold Wilson, a Congregationalist.

of Christ and Blessed Mary the Virgin, Durham on 18th October, St Luke's Day, 1952, the cathedral where the Venerable Bede, author of the *Ecclesiastical History of the British People* and the greatest scholar of the eighth century, lies buried. Along with him lies St Cuthbert, who died in 687, for whom the original Benedictine abbey had been built as a shrine. Here, in addition to Westcott and Lightfoot, hovered the shades of many men whose memory Michael held precious, including the seventeenth-century bishop of Durham, John Cosin, who had contributed Collects for the 1662 Prayer Book. The Ramseys acquired a cat, which they named Pudsey in honour of the twelfth-century bishop of Durham, Hugh Pudsey. Pudsey went on to lord it over both Bishopthorpe and the Old Palace at Canterbury, where on her first night in residence, in 1961, Joan Ramsey was discovered on her hands and knees stuffing newspapers up a chimney so that Pudsey should not escape.

In his enthronement sermon, Michael recalled the names of some of his distinguished predecessors, and he told the congregation, "I want only so to rule, so to teach, so to minister the mysteries of grace, that the love of Christ may be not hindered but spread abroad." Some people – but not perhaps as many as should, for the popular image of a bishop is of someone who makes world-shattering pronouncements on every possible public occasion – believe the first duty of a bishop is to be a father-in-God to his clergy. "He was very much a clergyman's bishop", says a Durham clergyman, Canon John Turnbull. "He had an episcopal presence, although most afternoons he would wander round Bishop Auckland and talk to people in the town. But essentially it was his concern for the clergy I remember. The clergy would certainly go to him with their problems."[17]*

* Michael Ramsey's ability to talk informally to strangers out of doors

It was partly because some of the diocesan clergy had been so impressed by Michael Ramsey's pastoral abilities before he became their bishop that they welcomed his appointment so warmly. Canon Ray Knell, vicar of St Mary's, Heworth, recalls: "When I was at Ridley Hall and Michael was Regius Professor in Cambridge he delivered a series of lectures on the Atonement, and I had always been in a right muddle over the subject, having been brought up as a conservative evangelical. But he sorted me out, and the thing I remember most vividly was that he was able to present the most profound ideas in the most magnificently simple language. His talks were luminously clear and beautifully done."

At the ordination retreat conducted by Michael Ramsey for Bishop Williams in 1939, the occasion of his visit to the Owens when he first met Joan, he had preached on the text from Ephesians 4: 11: "And some, pastors and teachers", and the first student to be ordained by Williams, Frank Chase, now retired in the Durham diocese after serving under Michael, remembers the retreat and the sermon to this day. Many years later, Michael told Canon Chase, "It was a kind of vetting before I was invited to come up here to the University. They wanted to see what I could do."[18] Canon Chase claims that as soon as Bishop Williams's move to Winchester was announced he had said, "The next bishop will be Michael Ramsey. The retreat had been marvellous. In 1980, when Michael was retired and living in Durham again, I invited him to preach at the fortieth anniversary of my ordination, and the first thing he did was produce his notes for that ordination retreat sermon."*

---

was in marked contrast to his inability to make small talk with guests at home. After paying a private call for tea on a member of his household in Hove one day he wandered off up the road to chat to startled neighbours in their front gardens.

* This ordination charge was published in *Durham Essays and Addresses*.

Michael had told the ordinands that "Inevitably parochial work brings many friendships, and we need not fear these. But beware of the domination over you of any parochial friendships: you can hardly guess at the outset the dangers to which this, *instigante diabolo*, can lead. Beware also of thinking too much about being liked, approved, and admired by the people." He also advised the students to begin by writing out all their sermons. "They require", he said, "order, shape, coherence, literary form." He told them, also, to read "some of the great books of timeless value, and not waste time on ephemeral books with their self-conscious attempts to be 'relevant'."

He gave, in this particular address, evidence of his cautious liberal ideology, an example of how he tended always to believe in the possibility of change without undermining fundamentals. "Be ready for new experiments," he told the ordinands, but "do not, by sophisticated attempts to be contemporary at all costs, blunt the force which lies in the universal imagery of the Bible: bread, water, light, darkness, wind, fire, hunger, thirst, eat, drink, walk." Canon Chase became one of hundreds – possibly thousands – of clergy who came to value Michael's pastoral concern for them, and to remain astonished by his memory. Ten years after Michael had left Durham, Canon Chase met him on the stairs at Lambeth Palace, and Michael knew exactly which parish he was in, and asked whether his wife was still teaching.

Both Michael and Joan Ramsey exhibited a phenomenal memory for people and places, in this country and overseas, a memory that encompassed whole families, and was often pinned to hilarious events or mishaps on journeys. As they eschewed snobbery, and often poked fun at rather grand people, they struck up an easy and unaffected rapport with north country folk. Their love of the north of England, particularly of Durham, went very deep and was totally sincere. One day after a visit to Newcastle – as Ramsey walked on to the platform at Newcastle Station an elderly lady said to a friend, "'E, I've never seen him in the flesh before!" – the Archbishop was travelling south again by train, and he recalled how happy he had been in the north, adding how nice it would be if the Church of England, like many other Churches in the Anglican Communion, allowed their senior primate to remain in his diocese. "Yes," he said, "if I could have been archbishop of Durham I should have been perfectly happy, perfectly happy." When the time came to bid farewell to the north for ever, after spending twenty-two years of his ministry in dioceses in the Northern Province, Michael wrote in the *York Quarterly*, "of some of my feelings at this time I could not trust myself to speak."[19]

Canon Chase says that Ramsey kept a photograph of every priest he ordained and remembered each one in his prayers. "His spirituality was the real thing about him. Even in retirement when he attended Communion in the cathedral you knew that it was he who was really praying the Eucharist. You could tell."[20]

Canon Turnbull believes that Ramsey "always preached in parishes at parish level, not as though to an academic audience. And each sermon was geared to the occasion."[21] This certainly seems to have been the case in 1953, when, according to Canon Knell, "Michael instituted a priest to an Anglo-Catholic parish where the previous parish priest had fathered two illegitimate children, and I remember the brilliance with which he spoke, so that those of us who knew what had been going on were able to understand that he was saying to the parish, 'You must put the past behind you and go forward', and yet anybody who didn't know would have been able to get a good message from his sermon anyway. It was a masterly performance. It really was."[22]

Owing to Michael Ramsey's alarming propensity for involving himself in mishaps, not every diocesan occasion went so smoothly. When Canon Turnbull was inducted in 1953, Michael robed in the vicarage and was walking to the church when his mitre got entangled in a rose trellis, fell off and had to be retrieved by a choir boy.

Ramsey's influence on the young could bear surprising results. In 1947 a young teenager, David Webster, thought he might be able to endure the first hour of the Three Hours Devotion on Good Friday at St James's, West Hartlepool. It was being taken by Professor Michael Ramsey of Durham University. David remained for the whole three hours and is now vicar of Belmont, in Durham. "This experience", he has written, "made it impossible for me to justify a shorter Good Friday observance in subsequent years with less enthralling preachers."

When Michael Ramsey was archbishop of Canterbury, David Webster had his own experience of that extraordinary memory. He was told to sit by the Archbishop at tea at Lincoln Theological College, and reminded Ramsey that he had been "curate at Billingham St Cuthbert's to Canon Tymms". Ramsey asked what he had done during the iterregnum.

" 'Nothing that caught the headlines, sir.'

"For a moment or two he searched his memory and then gave up and resumed conversation with the others. Then he turned back to me.

" 'You wrote the Vicar's Letter in the parish magazine.'

"I admitted that during the interregnum I had done so.

" 'Yes,' he said, 'January 1960, an exhortation to Christian Unity.'

"I said that was probably the case, and added that it wasn't remarkable.

" 'Well,' he said, 'I remarked it!'

"I was flabbergasted. To be able to recall, several years later, an article written by a curate in a parish magazine, out of all his reading. It still stuns me to recall that feat of memory."[23]

It was while he was bishop of Durham that Michael Ramsey began to express serious doubts about the move to place greater emphasis on Communion in parishes which did not already celebrate, as a matter of course, a Sung Mass at 11 o'clock, doubts and concerns which highlighted his own spiritual attitude towards the Eucharist. He noted "in a growing number of parishes a celebration of Holy Communion at 9 or 9.30, with a large congregation, a general communion, music and a sermon, and ceremonial varying from the elaborate to the simple." But, he asked, "is it possible to regard this movement with enthusiasm as providing the solution to our problems? I cannot think so. There is much that makes me uneasy . . . The awe in the individual's approach to Holy Communion, which characterized both the Tractarians and the Evangelicals of old, stands in contrast to the ease with which our congregations come tripping to the altar week by week." He thought it was a mistake to exaggerate the place of the physical togetherness of a congregarion. "If you have one celebration of Holy Communion at 9 and suppress the services at 7 and 8 so that all the people are present at 9, is there necessarily more 'fellowship' in the Christian sense? I doubt it." He thought the "wide and rapid growth" of the Parish Communion Movement had been accompanied by a "lack of teaching, bringing in its train a lack of meaningfulness and reverent understanding." And he brought this argument to a climax by revealing the source of his own spiritual strength. "There was, and is, much to be learnt from the quiet, early celebration. It keeps alive, and gives real place to, the meditative element in religion. It is the meditative element which is desperately needed, and so often imperilled."[24]*

Durham was to prove a tug of war between the meditative and the pomp and circumstance of the palatine. Michael Ramsey was thoroughly at home tramping across the sands barefoot on pilgrimage to Lindisfarne, not quite so comfortable before the television cameras in Westminster Abbey. The bishops of Durham and Bath & Wells traditionally support the sovereign at the coronation, the bishop of Durham on the monarch's right hand, the bishop of Bath & Wells on the left, and within six months of his enthronement Michael found himself summoned to a series of rehearsals for the Queen's coronation. According to Michael's story, the Queen unexpectedly decided to call an extra rehearsal, but her right-hand supporter was nowhere to be found. Eventually he was located shopping in Cambridge. "Well, and suddenly this police car pulled up and they said, 'Are you the Bishop of Durham?' and I said, 'Yes, I'm the Bishop of Durham', so they said, 'We're going to take you away. The Queen wants you.' So myself and a shopping bag, we all went to Westminster Abbey and we had another rehearsal."

In order to appreciate the flavour of Michael Ramsey's idiosyncratic conversation it is necessary to realize that unlike most people these days, he gave full emphasis to every syllable. So that, for instance, he would not have made the word "police" sound like "pleece" but "pol-ese". And "You" in the phrase "Are *you* the Bishop of

---

* "Christian people are often shy of contemplation, thinking it to be an exercise which is beyond them or a practice suitable for monks and nuns or an escape from the practical needs of the world", he wrote in a Foreword to *Encounter the Depths* by Mother Mary Clare (Darton, Longman & Todd, 1981). "Contemplation is none of these things. It is a liberation from our restless brain-activity into the depth of the love of God in our souls, a love which brings us nearer to the needs of the world around us."

Durham?", and "I'm" in "Yes, *I'm* the Bishop of Durham" would both have been emphasized, which was the way in which his speech acquired its rhythmical tone, like a sailing boat bobbing up and down. And he would conclude a story or anecdote with a final rush of words, like a pianist taking a grand trill up the scale. Those who heard him speak, particularly in private, never forgot the unique delivery, but very few have ever been able faithfully to reproduce it, though many thought they could. Part of the secret is to recapture the precise timing. Canon James Owen of Little St Mary's in Cambridge, who happens in any event to be an exceptionally accurate and clever mimic, is one of the very few people (possibly the only person still alive) who has ever mastered to perfection both the pitch of voice and the intonation, with the stammers and repetitions in precisely the right place. However, he was run a close second by the late Dennis Russell, a parish priest in the diocese of Worcester, who taped a lecture given in the diocese by Michael Ramsey, and then re-recorded the lecture in his own voice and sent the faked tape to the bishop, Robin Woods, pretending it was the original. Apparently Bishop Woods was completely taken in.[25]

In 1955 the eighty-year-old Cyril Garbett was eventually persuaded to retire as archbishop of York (he died very shortly afterwards), and it became Sir Anthony Eden's responsibility as prime minister to advise the Queen on a successor. This must have been a matter of close concern to Fisher, for it is important that the two archbishops should get on well, but he does not seem to have voiced any opinion one way or the other. Clergy in the Durham diocese have said they were sorry Michael Ramsey was chosen but not surprised, for they had all thought he was the obvious choice for York, yet the fact remains that Michael had only been a bishop three-and-a-half years, and his translation to the primacy of the Northern Province was an astonishingly swift promotion. When the letter from Eden arrived, a strong inducement to accept was the fact that Michael's childhood scripture teacher, Eric Milner-White, was still dean. "But," says Lady Ramsey, "it was a great bore to go to York. We were loving it at Durham."[26] Some people even believe that Milner-White canvassed for Michael; he would almost certainly have been consulted, and would have been only too anxious to have his star pupil with him again.

While in Cambridge, probably on a visit to Aunt Lucy, Michael met Cecil Hurry of Trinity College on the Backs, and said to him *apropos* his translation to York, "I wish the Lord would leave me alone."[27] Nevertheless to Bishopthorpe he went, in 1956. Michael was automatically sworn a member of the Privy Council,* and although as bishop of Durham, the senior bishop in the province after the archbishop, he had, when necessary, been obliged to chair the Convocation of York, he now found himself full-time occupant of the chair, and increasingly preoccupied with Church administration and committees, tasks for which he had little aptitude and less inclination. He much preferred to lecture than to listen to speeches in Convocation or the General Assembly, and in 1959 he accepted an invitation to give the Hale Memorial Lectures, established in 1900 under the will of Bishop Charles Hale, at one time bishop of Cairo, at Seabury-Western Theological Seminary in the USA. These were published the following year as *From Gore to Temple*. In 1961, while still archbishop of York, Michael also worked up from notes some of the addresses he had delivered during a mission to Oxford in

---

* The archbishops of Canterbury and York and the bishop of London always become members of the Privy Council.

1960, and these were incorporated in his 1961 publication, *Introducing the Christian Faith*. His theme at Oxford had been to show "that the Christian faith has its own congruity with reason, and calls for the vigorous use of the mind, and yet it can be grasped only by the personal response of faith and repentance to Christ as the Way, the Truth and the Life."

He was given another opportunity to escape from the administrative round inseparable from the archbishopric of York when the Community of the Resurrection asked him to become their Visitor, a post he held until his retirement from Canterbury. (The Visitor has to be a diocesan bishop.) He was obliged every five years to visit the Community's mother house at Mirfield in West Yorkshire, and there to see every member of the Community for fifteen minutes and then to deliver a charge. "He was very good as Visitor", Father Harry Williams recalls. "I heard two of his charges and they were theologically apposite, particularly at a time when morale in the Community was low after one of our members had resigned.* His spirituality was so sane and deep. Michael Ramsey thought that Mirfield was what an Anglican religious community ought to be. He had a kind of Eastern Orthodox theology, and had he not married I could easily have envisaged him as a religious."[28] Ramsey's attachment to Mirfield was such that in his Will he designated the Community as his residuary beneficiary in the event of Joan not surviving him for twenty-eight days.

When William Temple was archbishop of York he had founded a magazine called the *York Quarterly*. It ceased publication in the war, but as soon as Michael arrived at Bishopthorpe he relaunched the publication as a private venture, with himself as editor and chief contributor. He

---

* Father Hugh Bishop, at one time Superior, who died in 1989.

intended the *York Quarterly* "to be an organ of his teaching ministry", and the nineteen issues he produced before departing for Canterbury display a wide range of concerns and involved him in a good deal of the kind of work he thoroughly enjoyed. He wrote at length on theological matters, and almost always contributed the lead book review, which sometimes ran to 2,500 words, as well as shorter reviews and occasional notes and comments. Writing about a visit to Moscow in July 1956 he extolled the virtues of "some excellent light wines from Georgia"; in February 1957 he rehearsed the pros and cons of proposals to replace the "matrimonial offence" in divorce proceedings with the general concept of a marriage having "broken down". And he noted that "The revival of Fundamentalism is doing great harm", a theme to which he returned, when archbishop of Canterbury, during a dinner party given by Tim Beaumont,* when he complained of the growing numbers of evangelical fundamentalists who were being ordained. He did not trust those who took up extreme positions at either end of the ecclesiastical spectrum, and with good reason; they were eventually to combine to destroy one of his most cherished ecumenical dreams.

* In 1967 created Lord Beaumont of Whitley.

CHAPTER SIX

CANTERBURY

Establishment has never been one of my enthusiasms.
Canterbury Pilgrim.

One has to think back to a member of the Salisbury family, Lord William Gascoyne-Cecil, appointed bishop of Exeter in 1916, to recall a bishop of the Church of England as genuinely eccentric as Michael Ramsey, and it is impossible to conceive of any former archbishop in the same league. Yet after only five years as archbishop of York, and scarcely nine in the episcopate, he was appointed Archbishop of Canterbury and Primate of All England, the hundredth successor to St Augustine.* He was fifty-six, and barring accidents he could expect a tenure of office of at least fourteen years, which indeed was to be the case. In view of the absurdly heavy workload the Church imposed upon him, exacerbated by his own chaotic notions of administration, it was quite long enough.

"Baldock", Michael Ramsey once remarked out loud while driving home the morning after he had dined with the Cambridge Union and taken part in a debate. "Baldock. Baldock." He had raised his eyes from *The Times* and spotted the signpost as he entered this spectacularly uninteresting Hertfordshire town. "Baldock. Baldock."

---

* Augustine landed in Kent in 597.

Again and again, in monotonous tones, the word "Baldock" was repeated. Had it triggered some childhood memory? Was it just the sound of the word he found mesmeric? Was he perhaps a little mad? He must have repeated the word "Baldock" thirteen or fourteen times. Even for someone in his company who knew him well, the experience was strangely unnerving.[1]

Then there were, for those unattuned to them, the equally unnerving silences. "Ramsey was a dear. He really was a dear man. But you could tell him something and suddenly his mind would go completely somewhere else. He would just sit, and you'd think, what *have* I said? Oh, what *shall* I say!" That was the experience of Mrs Rebecca Hurry, Aunt Lucy's friend,[2] and it was not uncommon. Ramsey once asked Sir Kenneth Grubb, chairman of the House of Laity of the General Assembly, to stay behind after a meeting at Lambeth Palace. He and the Archbishop sat down in the study. Nothing was said. After a long and embarrassing silence, Sir Kenneth left. In the morning he received a letter from the Archbishop, who wrote: "I much appreciated your companionate silence." On the evening before his consecration in 1968, Simon Phipps stayed the night at Lambeth, as was the custom, and after dinner he was invited into the study. He assumed that Michael Ramsey would proffer some sage advice. But Bishop Phipps recalls, "It was all rather stilted, and I could hear Big Ben banging away across the Thames every fifteen minutes, and it was getting later and later, and there was no sign of the Archbishop moving at all, and in the end I said, 'Archbishop, don't you think you ought to go to bed?' and off he went. The only advice he had given me about being a bishop was to take every fifth Sunday off, and always to leave a space in my diary every week for the crisis which was likely to emerge. I thought it was wonderfully characteristic of him to say two completely mundane things and to leave the rest to God."[3]

Not only was Michael Ramsey eccentric in the sense of being totally unworldly and accident prone, for ever tripping over or walking into doors, he was eccentric in the truly "absentminded professor" sense. While archbishop of York he was once interviewed for television by Ludovic Kennedy, whom the Archbishop liked enormously, and after the recording, as Ramsey had time to spare before catching his train to return north, Kennedy suggested dinner. They repaired to Brooks's in St James's Street.

"How about a glass of sherry?" Ludovic Kennedy asked as they studied the menu.

"A glass of sherry. That would be lovely."

"And what would you like to eat, Archbishop? Lamb cutlets, perhaps?"

"Lamb cutlets. That would be lovely, simply lovely."

"And perhaps a bottle of claret?"

"A bottle of claret. Simply lovely, simply lovely."

After dinner they withdrew for coffee.

"Perhaps, Your Grace," said Ludovic Kennedy, "you would care for a glass of port?"

"A glass of port", said Ramsey. "That would be lovely, perfectly lovely."

So the waiter produced two glasses of port, both of which, before Kennedy had been given a chance to take a sip, Ramsey drank.

Denied his own glass of port and still hoping he might enjoy one, Ludovic Kennedy enquired, "Would you like another glass of port, Archbishop?"

"Oh, dear me no", said the Archbishop. "Two glasses would be far too much."[4]

So how did a man with few social graces, no small-talk at all, practically no affinity with women, children, or men of his own generation unless they were very brilliant, who never read a novel, never watched television or went to the theatre, cinema or a concert, who was incapable not only of mending a fuse but even of finding the light switch, whose clothes needed permanently brushing down, whose shoe laces were seldom done up (the prime minister of Honduras himself, a devout Roman Catholic, one day went down on his knees in the dust to tie up Michael Ramsey's shoe lace), acquire precedence immediately after the Sovereign's sons?* Needless to say, Michael Ramsey had his own peculiar version of events.

"Well," he used to say, "I can tell you how it happened. In 1961, when Fisher was archbishop of Canterbury, and Macmillan was prime minister, Fisher went to see Macmillan, and he said, 'Oh, Prime Minister, I shall be retiring shortly, and I don't think the Archbishop of York, Dr Ramsey, would be entirely suitable as my successor.' And Macmillan asked, 'Why is that?' So Fisher said, 'He was a boy under me at Repton, and I don't think he'd be very suitable.' So Macmillan said, 'Oh, Dr Ramsey *would* be suitable.' And Fisher said, 'Dr Coggan, the Bishop of Bradford, now the Bishop of Bradford would be *very* suitable.' So Macmillan said, 'Well, Archbishop, you may have been Michael Ramsey's headmaster but you're not mine, and I intend to appoint Dr Ramsey, good afternoon.'"

Presumably Harold Macmillan had not objected to Michael Ramsey preaching on 2nd October 1960 at the Labour Party Conference in Scarborough, nor to him describing Ernest Bevin, in a book review in the *York Quarterly* in November that year, as a great Englishman, for in 1958 he had invited Mervyn Stockwood, an avowed socialist, to become bishop of Southwark. And of course

---

* "Small talk was not his strong point, and he appeared frequently to be frightened by women": Bishop Cuthbert Bardsley in a letter to the author, 25th April 1989.

the story is partly fanciful. But there has never been any secret that when it came to Ramsey achieving the highest office, Fisher was extremely dubious, partly, no doubt, because he distrusted or disliked his churchmanship, partly (and with better reason) because he did not believe him to be whole-heartedly in favour of the Church of England remaining established. Ramsey set so little intrinsic store by the Church of England's established links with the State that when serious plans (aborted in 1968 by Harold Wilson in a fit of pique) for reform of the Upper Chamber were drawn up he was perfectly content for the numbers of bishops with seats in the House of Lords to be reduced from twenty-six to sixteen. Yet while Fisher was certainly prone to interfere (in retirement he became a thorn in Michael Ramsey's flesh by rallying opposition to the Scheme for Anglican-Methodist Reunion), and his modesty was not always in evidence (when he retired he asked that people should continue to call him Archbishop Fisher and address him as Your Grace),* it seems unlikely that he would have gone so far as to offer advice regarding his successor unless he had been invited to do so. However, there has never been any secret of the fact that Fisher did at that moment favour the almost inconceivable promotion to Canterbury of Donald Coggan, who had been a bishop for scarcely five years. In the event Dr Coggan succeeded Michael at York, perhaps because the Northern Province wanted one of their own diocesan bishops translated, perhaps also to strike what is often fallaciously seen as a subtle balance arrived at by having one high and one low archbishop, but on this occasion it did not make for

---

* There is no such thing in the Church of England as an emeritus archbishop, and anyone holding an appointment as an archbishop should automatically revert on retirement to the rank and status of a bishop, as Michael Ramsey did himself.

harmonious relations, as Michael seldom consulted Dr Coggan, of whose particular abilities, admired by some of the other bishops, he had little understanding or appreciation.

Over the appointment of anyone to Canterbury, few people would have been likely to get their own way confronted by a genuine churchman like Harold Macmillan, whose commitment to the Church of England was very real. Macmillan's resident tutor had been Ronald Knox, and Knox's youthful influence, combined with the marked development of Macmillan's Trollopean view of the political and social scene, ensured that he took a close personal interest in Church appointments. With his government tottering about his ears in 1959 he had spent the best part of a morning at the height of the Profumo Scandal discussing who was to be the new dean of Wells.* And the truth about his recommendation of Ramsey to the Queen in 1961 was that Macmillan believed the country needed a religious leader in the truest sense; he also recognized without any difficulty that intellectually and theologically Ramsey was way out in front. On three criteria put together – personal holiness, spirituality and Godliness; intellectual ability; and theological scholarship – there was no serious rival.

On his retirement, Fisher accepted a life peerage, and was immediately dubbed by Ramsey "the Baron". After an exhausting day in Portsmouth, where the Ramseys were staying in a house bequeathed to the town by Lady Astor for the use of distinguished guests, Ramsey was once asked if he too planned to accept a peerage on his retirement. Not only did he flatly deny that he would, but while half-hidden behind the crumpled pages of *The Times* he

* Christopher Woodforde, a Fellow and Chaplain of New College, Oxford, was appointed.

dictated an imaginary letter to the prime minister declining the honour. In 1974 he did accept a peerage. He was rather adept at dictating imaginary and extremely amusing letters. During a lull in conversation at a luncheon party at the Old Palace in Canterbury, a member of his household remarked, in flippant vein, that he would not mind being offered the bishopric of St Albans (vacant at the time following the resignation of Michael Gresford Jones) simply because he liked the Abbey. Ramsey jumped at the opportunity for improvization, and promptly pretended to dictate a letter to the prime minister: "Dear Mr Wilson, I am writing to you about the bishopric of St Albans. You may think my request a little unusual, but I should be grateful if you would give your serious consideration to the appointment of my press officer . . ."

The Ramseys enjoyed attaching nicknames to people, and in honour of the legendary giants, Dr Coggan became the Cog, and Mrs Coggan Ma Cog. Many of his anecdotes were retailed about Cog and Ma Cog, but it is important to disentangle from Ramsey's own stories those which are literally true, and those which are apocryphal, both of equal value however, for those which are clearly apocryphal tell us what he would have liked to believe about someone. He got in a very early dig about Lord Fisher, in a story that has two settings, Lambeth Palace and Bishopthorpe. He is supposed to have been seen getting out of his tiny Ford at Lambeth in 1961 on his return from a modelling session at Madame Tussauds – although the Ford was not in fact purchased until about 1968 – and to have explained to Eric Kemp, now Bishop of Chichester, "They ran out of wax and had to melt down Geoffrey Fisher!" But Tony Hart, the last priest ordained by Ramsey while archbishop of York, and now a Canon at Durham Cathedral, says that Ramsey made his joke about Fisher being melted down to provide enough wax for his own effigy during a visit Canon Hart paid to Bishopthorpe in 1961.[5] What matters is that Ramsey was tickled pink at the thought of his old headmaster giving way in such an undignified manner, and many of the stories he invented were polished and kept in reserve for the appropriate occasion and an appreciative audience.

It is typical of the modest side of Michael Ramsey's nature that in 1964, when he came to publish a miscellaneous collection called *Canterbury Essays and Addresses*, he placed his enthronement sermon in Canterbury Cathedral (preached at the first enthronement of an archbishop of Canterbury ever televised) at the very end of the book. It was on 27th June 1961 that he entered in temporal splendour the cathedral where today his ashes lie buried in the cloisters, and swore to preserve the rights of "this Cathedral and Metropolitan Church of Christ, Canterbury" on a book of the Gospels brought to England, it is believed, by St Augustine, the first Archbishop of Canterbury, in 601. Michael Ramsey seldom preached in order to gain the headlines; indeed, in purely secular terms his sermons were usually quite without interest, and even judged theologically, his enthronement sermon of 1961 might have been addressed to a congregation in 1931, decked out as it was in old-fashioned paternalist language, with reference to himself as a shepherd. But it was remarkable for the gauntlet he flung down to parliament. "Here in England," he said, "the Church and the State are linked together, and we use that link in serving the community. But in that service, and in rendering to God the things that are God's, we ask for a greater freedom in the ordering and in the urgent revising of our forms of worship. If the link of Church and State were broken, it would not be we who ask for this freedom who broke it, but those – if there be such – who denied that freedom to us."

He always realized that Disestablishment would be an "immense administrative operation" and he never advocated it for its own sake; he merely stood by ready to face the disadvantages that Disestablishment would bring in its wake if on balance a break with the State became morally imperative. When he retired in 1974 he summarized his personal feelings about the Establishment with admirable clarity:

> My own Nonconformist ancestry on my father's side gives me a feeling for that tradition of religion in this country which has for three centuries witnessed to Christ without the protection of privilege and can say "at a great price obtained I this freedom" ... it seems that in the world as a whole Christianity is passing into a post-Constantinian phase in which the buttressing of Churches by privilege may hinder rather than commend their witness and claim. It would not be a grief to me to wake up and find that the English Establishment was no more.[6]

The liturgy was indeed to be revised – some believe to its detriment – during Ramsey's time at Canterbury, and the Church of England achieved a far greater say, although not a final one, in the appointment of its bishops. But this was not the only area for which, in his sermon, he provided an agenda. "Our Church must reach out in the quest for unity," he said, "for Christ is longing that there will go with him not separated bands of followers but, as one band, all those whose hearts God has touched." In the search for organic unity, Ramsey was, as he saw it, to lay his reputation on the line, and to retire a sad and disillusioned exponent of the ultimate form of ecumenism.

A greater measure of freedom for the Church and real strides forward in the search for Christian unity were Ramsey's two priorities, but much of his time and energy were diverted to dealing with other issues, some, like administration, almost inevitable, others, relating to the

144

ethical, social and theological upheavals of the 1960s, far less easy to foresee or to avoid. But whatever the particular interests or gifts of any archbishop of Canterbury, he enters into an office already circumscribed. Although largely indifferent to the existence or will of God until some national calamity befalls, the nation sees the arch-bishop of Canterbury as its personal guru, and tends to expect instant judgements from him on both major and minor matters. The present Archbishop of Canterbury, Dr Robert Runcie, neatly summed up the situation when he said, "The Church of England remains the focus of vague religious expectations on the part of the great majority of the English people and therefore the archbishop of Canter-bury always has an audience by reason of his office."[7] The archbishop is automatically at the centre of much national pageantry, in itself a form of worship, and most conspicu-ously he has the honour of crowning the sovereign. He stands therefore in a close personal relationship to the royal family although he is not in fact their "parish priest"; chief pastor to the royal family is the dean of Windsor, whose appointment is solely in the gift of the monarch.

Until the establishment of synodical government the archbishop of Canterbury, if present, always chaired meet-ings of the General Assembly, and the time of any archbishop is much taken up with Assembly – now Synod – business, reading reports, preparing speeches and attend-ing meetings of the standing committee. Michael Ramsey also spent a morning once a month as chairman of the Board of Governors of the Church Commissioners. Much of their work is involved with finance (in his day they spent £23 millions a year), about which he understood very little, but Dame Betty Ridley, the first ever woman Estates Commissioner, says he did it "awfully faithfully".[8] As Metropolitan he exercised an overall responsibility for the diocesan bishops in the Southern Province, and inherited responsibility for some half-dozen extra-provincial dioceses overseas. As senior bishop of the senior Church of the Anglican Communion he chaired the 1968 Lambeth Conference (the conference, for bishops of the Anglican Communion, is held every ten years), and although only first among equals, without jurisdiction of any sort in any Church other than his own, he was expected to keep abreast of developments and problems throughout the Communion.* In his capacity either as a president of the World Council of Churches (from 1961 to 1968), on behalf of the ecumenical movement, in order to lecture, or as president of the Lambeth Conference, Michael Ramsey travelled to Moscow, Constantinople, Athens, Louvain, Rumania, Rome, Belgrade, Geneva, Paris, Canada, Nigeria, New Zealand, Australia, Honolulu, Fiji, Mauritius, Madagascar, Bermuda, the West Indies, West Germany, Puerto Rico, the United States of America, Sweden, India, South Africa and Uganda, and also to Normandy, to the Abbey of Bec, which sent to England two archbishops of Canterbury, Lanfranc, its first Prior, and Anselm, its second Abbot.

A long-serving member of the House of Laity of the General Assembly, the Duke of Richmond & Gordon,† recalls that Michael Ramsey "wasn't a terribly good chairman, because he was uninterested in that sort of thing. He was interested in a certain number of the issues that came before the Assembly or the Synod, and on some of those he spoke of course, and often spoke very well, but when he was just in the chair he was bored. I remember him best in the chair at the Church Commissioners, and he was

---

* In Michael Ramsey's time there were nineteen separate Churches or Provinces in the Anglican Communion, all in communion with the Church of England but all autonomous.
† He inherited the title in 1989 and sat in the House of Laity as Earl of March & Kinrara.

completely bored there, because the Church Commissioners never addressed a question of any interest to him. I was sitting next to him one day and I could see he was just drawing pictures of bishops and their mitres.

"But when it came to coping with radical measures before the Assembly, he let it rip, so to speak. He allowed the spirit to move. Fisher would have stopped many of the radical proposals that came up in Michael Ramsey's time, or tried to stop them. But because Michael Ramsey agreed with quite a lot of it, he let it all happen. I think that's one of the most significant things he did. When Church and State came up, somebody somewhere, it may have been Michael, said, 'Let's see what happens'. Obviously he always wanted to see a change in the way bishops were appointed and parliament controlled worship, and this was his opportunity."[9]

"His Victorian liberalism was one of the things that I find fascinating", Dr Runcie says. "I'm more conservative than Michael Ramsey was. He had a feeling that it was the task of the archbishop to let good things happen, not to initiate but to remove obstacles, and this was the way in which he released a new sort of Anglican Communion, a new sort of Church of England with a newly translated Bible, a new form of synodical government, new forms of liturgy, new ways of training the clergy, a new Church–State relationship. A lot of things happened because he let them happen. It was his holiness and his learning that enabled him to be respected and to stand a bit above the tumult of the sixties."[10]

Ramsey gave evidence to the Archbishops' Commission on Church and State, and the Duke of Richmond says, "I remember thinking, when he left the room, there wasn't a single thing he'd said that the more radical of us wouldn't believe in. If 'radical' means going to the root, and he often did go to the roots, he was a radical. He was certainly very liberal for an archbishop – in the context of his time probably more liberal than Runcie. I never heard him make an establishment remark. There was a big divide between bishops ordained before and after the war, and it was awfully significant that Ramsey should have sided with the younger radicals."*

Mervyn Stockwood remembers that at Church Assembly Michael Ramsey used to draw up cricket teams composed of those whom he regarded as the greatest bores who spoke. "The captain of one team was frequently Graham Leonard.† For every five minutes they spoke, they got a run. 'He's got a boundary today!' Michael would exclaim with glee if one of his pet bores went on at exorbitant length."[11] Another bishop, Cuthbert Bardsley, for twenty years bishop of Coventry, confirms that Michael Ramsey was "often bored by committees and appeared on occasions to have gone to sleep at critical moments in a long debate", but he adds that "the appearance of sleepiness belied the fact that his brain was still very active, and at the end of a long debate he was often enabled to sum up the whole argument concisely and to the point, frequently giving utterance to some profound remark, putting everyone at their ease and saying what many of his audience wanted to hear."[12]

In some important areas of his life Michael Ramsey found himself inevitably following in his predecessor's footsteps. Fisher's visit to Pope John had only constituted

---

* A Commission was appointed under the terms of a resolution passed by the General Assembly on 10th November 1965 "to make recommendations as to the modifications in the constitutional relationship between Church and State which are desirable and practicable and in so doing to take account of current and future steps to promote greater unity between the Churches." Their report, *Church and State*, was published in 1970. The Duke of Richmond, then Lord March, was the vice-chairman.

† Suffragan bishop of Willesden, later bishop of Truro and now Bishop of London.

a courtesy call, but because it had happened at all Ramsey's official visit to Rome could not be counted a "first". Fisher's 1946 Cambridge sermon had been an ecumenical initiative Michael found himself capitalizing upon. And because Fisher had been a president of the World Council of Churches, formed in 1948, Michael felt he had to accept an invitation to be a president too, which added considerably to his workload without producing any very startling results. He was present at the Assembly in New Delhi in November 1961, only months after assuming office as archbishop of Canterbury, when he spoke on the need to seek holiness and truth in the general search for unity, and he attended the Fourth Assembly, in July 1968, at the Swedish university town of Uppsala. On this occasion a number of Orthodox bishops decided to give a dinner in his honour. The occasion was held in a pavilion in a park, and was paid for by a wealthy Greek lady. The first course consisted of a large plate of unpeeled prawns. Ramsey proceeded to attack the prawns with a knife and fork, consuming not only the prawns but every scrap of shell.

"He made no great impact on the World Council" in the opinion of the Duke of Richmond. "He wasn't given the opportunity. He wasn't made head of a section, and he didn't grasp the opportunity at Uppsala of making a major speech."[13] One reason for this may have been that he believed there was a "naive Conference mentality" which was a "growing evil in the Church". Thus, at any rate, he had written on his return to Durham from a meeting of the World Council of Churches at Evanston in 1954, a meeting he had thoroughly disliked, believing it too large ("I have rarely known such stultifying of the personal touch between speaker and audience"), "accompanied from first to last by the sort of publicity which can only be called vulgar 'boosting'", and overloaded. "For over a fortnight the whirl of oratory, discussions, committees and typed documents continued without pause." He doubted, he wrote, whether such a medium was one through which the Holy Spirit was likely to speak to the Church.[14] Another reason he made little impact at the World Council of Churches may have been because he was anxious, when treading the world stage, not to pull rank and parade as an archbishop among delegates, many of whom did not even have episcopacy in their system. At Uppsala he declined to have a special car sent for him to the airport or to be received by the ambassador, and he mingled during the day in a cassock with a label attached explaining who he was. Part of the reason for Ramsey's lack of active participation in the World Council of Churches was also because he felt he was on holiday – a busman's holiday, perhaps, but certainly on holiday from the Church of England, and he positively enjoyed not feeling under pressure to "make an impact". In the British Council of Churches, according to Dame Betty Ridley, "because of his sheer goodness and capacity they all became absolutely devoted to him – more than the Anglicans."[15] In his relations with Christians of other denominations, Ramsey very much epitomized the adage about no man being a prophet in his own land; there was an ambivalence in the relationship between himself and the Church of England, but overseas, and with Christians from other traditions, there was none, and in the informal atmosphere of the World Council of Churches he felt too relaxed to need to impose his views in a major series of set speeches.

Indeed, Michael Ramsey was never happier than when he was travelling. The actual process of travel held no terrors for him, but then he did not have to pack or struggle through the customs. While Archbishop, he invariably flew first class, if only because this provided greater privacy and an opportunity to rest during what were often exhausting journeys, and whenever he possibly could, although it sometimes drew criticism, he flew with Pan Am, for they made an enormous fuss of him, sending a fleet of cars to Lambeth Palace for the luggage and providing hospitality on a thoughtful and generous scale. He seemed entirely oblivious of danger, real or imaginary. As soon as he was aboard an airplane he burrowed into a book, and he had no idea when the 'plane was taking off or landing; his concentration or rest was only ever disturbed by the ministrations of an air hostess. Once, while the Archbishop was having a drink, a member of his household said to him, "I thought you were asleep, Father."

"I was", replied the Archbishop. "And then I heard the word 'champagne', and I woke up!"

The overseas visit which attracted most publicity was of course his visit to the Vatican in March 1966, to be received by Pope Paul VI. This visit came in the wake of the Second Vatican Council, and while the importance of much that had occurred to make the visit possible, and much that later flowed from it, should not be underestimated, perhaps the actual historical edge had been slightly blunted by Archbishop Fisher's inspired initiative in making a private visit to Pope John XXIII in 1960. Indeed, many observers felt that circumstances might have been better arranged had Fisher met the tall and rather austere Pope Paul, and Michael had met his saintly and well-rounded counterpart, Pope John. As it was, however, Michael always looked back upon his meeting with the Pope as a highlight of his life. He never doubted that one day, if unity had any meaning at all, an accommodation of gigantic proportions would have to be made between Rome and Canterbury, and on the controversial issue of Papal Supremacy he quite easily envisaged a form of collegiality wherein the archbishop of Canterbury and the pope would officiate as episcopal partners. It was during that visit that the Pope made an imaginative gesture that was to ensure that further progress would be impossible to halt. In 1896 a papal encyclical, *Apostolicae Curae*, had declared Anglican orders invalid. It has not yet been revoked. But the Pope did a remarkable thing, and Ramsey's own version of events placed an extra symbolic gloss upon the Pope's actions.

"As we walked down St Peter-without-the-Walls," he used to explain, "he took off his ring, he took off his ring and he put it on my finger, just like a wedding, very nice, and we got in to our two big black cars, and we drove off in opposite directions."

The ring was set with a cross of diamonds and emeralds, and from that day it permanently displaced Ramsey's own episcopal ring, given to him in 1952 by Magdalene. He wore the Pope's ring until the day he died. To whom did the Pope imagine he was giving an episcopal ring? To some over-dressed layman? In one swift and brilliant gesture he had in effect revoked the wretched encyclical of Leo XIII, and made conditions possible for the setting up in 1969 of the Anglican-Roman Catholic International Commission, whose Agreed Statement on the Ministry, issued in 1973, prompted Michael Ramsey to write in the *Guardian* on the day of publication, "if priesthood is understood to be what the learned Roman Catholic, as well as Anglican, authors of the document say it is, then Pope Leo XIII will seem less right or wrong than irrelevant. Let that, however, be said in humility rather than in any 'I told you so' spirit, for we may all one day wake up to the painful irrelevance of some of our polemical positions."

There was an amusing insight into Ramsey's relations with Cardinal Heenan, archbishop of Westminster, when, in 1971 the Commission produced an Agreed Statement on the Doctrine of the Eucharist. Shortly beforehand, Ramsey had been asked by the *Tablet*, the weekly Roman

Catholic review of politics and the arts, for his views about proposals to canonize the Forty Martyrs. Ramsey expressed himself very forcefully on the subject, and revealed that he had written to the Cardinal protesting. He appeared not only happy but anxious that his views should be more widely known, and extracted from a filing cabinet a memorandum he had sent the Cardinal on the subject. This he gave to the *Tablet*, who acquired a scoop.

As it had transpired that the two religious leaders were at loggerheads, it was thought a good plan to have a conciliatory photograph taken at St George's House, Windsor Castle, where the Archbishop and Cardinal Heenan were due to lunch with the Commission. Both archbishops agreed, and the firm condition was that no press statement would be made, there would merely be a photo call. Ramsey kept to the bargain; Heenan lost no time in surrounding himself with a posse of reporters. "Look at him! Look at him!" Ramsey expostulated, clapping his hands together as he did when agitated, and pointing an accusing finger at the errant Cardinal. "What did I tell you! What did I tell you! He's giving a press conference!" Ramsey's own press officer could only politely prise the Cardinal away by saying the Archbishop of Canterbury was ready to leave when he was, for Ramsey was to give Heenan a lift back to London. Ramsey duly dropped the Cardinal off at his house in Victoria, and when he got out of the car at Lambeth Palace he said, "You know, Cardinal Heenan's an awfully nice man, but I don't believe he understands a word I'm saying!"

Generally, however, the public consummation of private ecumenical discussions gave Michael Ramsey visible and vital pleasure. When he was invited to preach at Westminster Cathedral and entered the west door, with Cardinal Heenan waiting in front of the altar to greet him, the congregation burst into thunderous applause, and Michael almost ran up the nave to embrace his host. But the ecumenical occasions that warmed him most were the visits he paid and received from the Orthodox, for whom his respect was often further increased by the knowledge that they had, only in recent years, been tortured for their faith, and whose religious tradition was at heart so akin to his own concept of spirituality. He saw too, long before he became a bishop, that the root of divisions lay in the original schism between East and West, and wrote, "I shall not shrink from making some very big claims: . . . that in unity with the East there lies a remedy for many of the problems and perplexities of the whole Church, that the Church of England has a special debt and obligation in this matter, and that the present crisis in Church and world summons our thoughts *Eastwards*."[16]

It was Michael Ramsey who recalled that "From the time of the first English Prayer Book of 1549 we see the Church of England looking Eastwards. There was in the Liturgy of 1549 the *Epiklesis* or invocation of the Holy Spirit upon the bread and wine, recovered from the Eastern usage. There was, and still is, the 'Prayer of St Chrysostom' at the close of Matins and Evensong. There was the renewed study of the Greek Fathers by the Anglican divines."[17] He loved participating in the Liturgy at the Greek Orthodox Cathedral in London, and the Orthodox bishops and priests who came to Lambeth and Canterbury knew that Michael Ramsey had studied their tradition and was devoutly in sympathy with it. They particularly appreciated his emphasis on holiness. "What is wrong with Christendom is not only that we are divided," he told the annual conference of the Fellowship of St Alban and St Sergius in 1962, "it is also that we lack holiness, and that we monkeyed about with truth. And that being so, it seems to me entirely insufficient to think and talk about reunion unless in the same breath we are thinking and talking about reconstruction and recovery of the fullness of truth."

Using equally colloquial language – not many archbishops speak of monkeying about with the truth – he had written sixteen years before in such a way as to place the tasks of the ecumenical movement in clear perspective:

> We have long been confronted in our own land with the problems of Church and Chapel, Anglican and Roman. These divisions arose, of course, from lopsided presentations of Christianity, one sort of lopsidedness often leading to other sorts of lopsidedness by way of reaction. Thus the lopsidedness of Rome in the later Middle Ages led to the lopsidedness of Luther and Calvin, and the lopsidedness of the Church of England in the eighteenth century encouraged the separation of the Methodists. But before and behind all the familiar tragedies of division there was the initial tragedy of the schism between East and West, a tragedy which meant that thenceforth all Christendom was maimed. East and West sorely needed one another, and ever since they went their separate ways neither has been able to present the wholeness of Christian and Church life.[18]

As an ordinand at Cuddesdon Michael Ramsey had made the acquaintance of a prophetic figure in Anglican-Orthodox relations, Derwas Chitty, and it was due to his influence that an appreciation of Orthodoxy developed so early. And his contacts with the Fellowship of St Alban and St Sergius dated back to his years at Lincoln, when he sought out Father George Florovsky, in the opinion of a former canon of Canterbury Cathedral, A. M. Allchin, "certainly the greatest scholar and one of the outstanding theologians of the Russian emigration".[19] Unlike so many members of the Church of England who have always feared that ecumenical progress in one direction would hinder progress in another (the classical example is objections to the ordination of women for fear that such a move would hinder reunion with Rome, ignoring the fact that one day the Holy Spirit may will that Rome should have women priests), Michael Ramsey believed that every quest for unity was potentially valid. "We have in ecumenical work all found ourselves to be all so much wrapped up in a bundle," he said during a lecture in Oxford in 1962, "that any genuine and sincere action in the service of Christ and Christ's unity will be helpful in other directions as well."[20]

Unlike the Church of Rome, the Orthodox Church is not a united body, but there is much uniformity between its branches, and when in 1922 the Patriarch of Constantinople affirmed his recognition of the validity of Anglican orders, Jerusalem, Cyprus and Alexandria followed suit. Davidson, Lang and Temple had all fostered Anglican-Orthodox relations, and it was on this firm foundation, buttressed by his own study of Orthodoxy, that Michael Ramsey paid visits to the Patriarchates of Constantinople, Moscow, Bucharest, Sofia and Belgrade, and to the Archbishopric of Athens. While leading a delegation of Anglican theologians to Moscow in July 1956, for the first discussions ever held between representatives of the Church of England and the Russian Orthodox Church, Michael preached one sermon with such eloquence that a woman in the congregation became hysterical with emotion and had to be carried out. When writing about the visit in the *York Quarterly* in November 1956, Michael noted that the "Holy Orthodox Church of Russia worships in only fifty churches in Moscow" and that "The godless state has come". Only fifty churches? There are certainly more in London, but would Michael have found them "crowded with worshippers, standing very closely packed"? The measure of freedom accorded to the Church in Russia in 1956 was surely very considerable for a Communist and "godless" state, which was godless only in the sense that the President was not, like the Queen, Supreme Governor of the State Church. It was a quixotic sleight of eye that often tempted Church leaders of Michael's generation to claim that England remained a Christian country despite half-empty churches (Dr Fisher once described them as half-full) while Russia was a "godless state" despite the fervour of those who worshipped in fewer but "closely packed" buildings.

In 1964 Alexis of Moscow, consecrated in 1913 (before the Revolution), came to Lambeth, and this was the first visit of any Patriarch of Moscow to the British Isles. The eventual outcome, in 1973, of all Michael Ramsey's contacts with the Orthodox Churches was the creation of the Anglican-Orthodox Theological Commission. There is a solemnity and dignity about the Orthodox Liturgy that mirrors the good manners and courtesy of the Slavonic races, and the atmosphere of Alexis's visit was well caught by an expert on the Orthodox Church, Sir John Lawrence, when he wrote that the four days of the Patriarch's visit seemed like a liturgy. "Both Patriarch and Archbishop seemed to know exactly what was required of them and to find perfectly fitting words and gestures for every moment. One could see something of that liturgical quality of Russian life before Peter the Great, when every meal, every journey, every going out and coming in, all the relations of family and social life were given form by set words and actions which seemed to incarnate worship in life."[21]

Justinian, Patriarch of Rumania, returned Michael Ramsey's visit of 1965 the following year, when services were held at Canterbury and Westminster Abbey, and permanent links were forged between the Rumanian Orthodox Church and the Benedictine nuns of St Mary's Abbey at West Malling. But although other Orthodox bishops were to be entertained for a weekend at the Old Palace in Canterbury, the climax to Michael Ramsey's love affair with Orthodoxy came in 1967 with a visit to Lambeth Palace from the Ecumenical Patriarch himself,

His All Holiness Athenagorus I, Archbishop of Constantinople and, in the Orthodox world, a figure *primus inter pares*, holding a position comparable to the archbishop of Canterbury's in relation to the Anglican Communion. Athenagorus was a tall, imposing figure, with a long, flowing grey beard and a deep, rich voice in which he spoke good English. For him the visit was the climax to a remarkable life lived simply and with great courage; he had in fact been making a pilgrimage, to Serbia, Rumania and Bulgaria, to Geneva, to Rome, and finally to London. At Heathrow Airport Michael Ramsey went aboard the Patriarch's airplane to greet him in private, and when the time came for his departure, the Patriarch broke with tradition in two respects. Normally no woman would be expected to accompany him to the airport, but Mrs Ramsey went to Heathrow to say farewell, with a curtsey, and although the Archbishop's press officer was a layman, at the foot of the steps, as he made to kiss the Patriarch's hand, Athenagorus enfolded him in his beard and gave him a warm embrace.

Ramsey's view of ecumenism was a very broad one indeed. In New York in 1970 he told a seminar of bishops, "The ecumenical task is never rightly to be described as if it were like the reconstitution of a toy once made in its completeness and subsequently broken. Had there been no quarrels in the Church of Corinth, no schisms in the Church, no great schisms between East and West, there would still be the growth through years of spiritual and intellectual struggle into the fullness of the unity which Christ once gave."

If Michael Ramsey was happy hobnobbing (hobnobbing was one of his favourite expressions) with Church leaders from other denominations, he was equally at home chairing the 1968 Lambeth Conference, where his innate understanding of the position of honour – nothing more –

accorded by the rest of the Anglican Communion to the archbishop of Canterbury was so obviously apparent. The sense of missionary zeal and adventure imported by many of the bishops from poor African dioceses excited him (the bishop of Gambia and the Rio Pongas, for example, had a diocese with six million people and six clergy), and he felt keenly the contrast between the conditions of Anglicans living as minorities in, say, a Muslim country, and the privileged situation of Anglicans in England, whose Church was by law established and whose Queen was also their Supreme Governor. Simon Phipps recalls that the Conference began each day with the *Veni Creator*, "Michael leading it. It was very impressive. He really was talking to the Holy Spirit."[22] Michael declined a suggestion, not, in 1968, put very forcefully, when perhaps it should have been, that television cameras should be admitted, and this was a splendid opportunity lost to communicate the powerfully spiritual side to Michael Ramsey's nature, seldom apparent when he was facing a television interviewer. "I think ordinary people are impressed by holiness when they meet it", Bishop Phipps has commented. "The television camera very much picks up the truth of a person, whether holy or insincere."[23]

The bishops enjoyed Michael Ramsey's sense of humour and lucidity, but there were subdued criticisms of a few of his comments made during the Conference. Although theoretically opposed to the practice of receiving Communion from a Church with which one's own Church is not in communion, he did suggest at Lambeth that where two Churches had engaged in serious conversations with the aim of coming together into a more visible unity based on catholic principles a point might be reached short of full agreement when intercommunion would be a natural step to take. "I should say that quite a few bishops at the Conference disagreed with Dr Ramsey on this point",

159

Professor John Macquarrie said while lecturing in New York in 1988. "But it does provide a possible compromise between those of a conservative mentality who want to see everything finalized before taking any practical steps, and those whose impatience hurries them into actions for which there has not been enough thought, consultation and preparation."

Although one side of Michael Ramsey's personality stood aloof from establishment values there was no denying that he was steeped, as are most middle-class Englishmen, in English ways of doing things, and he tended to conduct meetings attended by people from overseas, who often have very different concepts of time and protocol, as though he were an umpire at Lords, everybody playing was "a gentleman" and they all understood standing orders. "There was a certain amount of grumbling among the bishops at the 1968 Lambeth Conference", according to Professor Macquarrie. "They felt perhaps he was sometimes pushing the business on."[24] There was also an unfortunate occasion when Ramsey was asked by the World Council of Churches to chair a session at a conference on race relations in Notting Hill. Mr Shar, at the time a leader of the Black Power movement, wanted to intervene, and although strictly speaking he was out of order, it was obvious the conference wanted to hear him. But the Archbishop refused to allow him to speak, so Mr Shar promptly left the room and gave an interview to the press. The Archbishop later made a handsome apology.

But once away from England Michael Ramsey was truly in his element. He thrived on the spontaneity of Christian worship in African countries, and he was genuinely amazed at the crowds of school children who turned out in a nation like Trinidad to wave to him from the roadside. He never fussed over or even seemed to notice the often muddled arrangements, nor did he flinch when faced with

Left Francis Dodd's preliminary study for his 1927 portrait of Michael Ramsey's father, Arthur Stanley Ramsey (which hangs in the Combination room at Magdalene College, Cambridge). Reproduced by courtesy of Dr Bridget Barcroft.

Below Michael's mother, Mary Agnes Ramsey.

Below A family holiday at Little Holland, Norfolk. Michael is fourth from the left. His brother Frank and his mother are on the right.

Frank Ramsey by the Cam, with his wife Lettice on the left and his mistress, Elizabeth Denby, on the right. Photograph by courtesy Frances Partridge.

Left The Mitre House photograph, taken at Repton when Michael, seated third from the left, was 18. On his right is a boy who arrived the same day, Hampton Gervis. The boy at the extreme left of the back row is now Sir Desmond Lee. Alan Thornhill, who sang duets from Gilbert and Sullivan with Michael, is fourth from the left in the second row.

Below Michael's aunt, Lucy Ramsey, in the garden of her house in Mount Pleasant, Cambridge.

Michael's elder sister, Bridget, photographed by her sister-in-law, Lettice Ramsey.

Michael's younger sister, Margaret.

Michael and Joan on their wedding day in 1942.

Michael Ramsey, Archbishop of Canterbury, in episcopal evening dress with the Queen. The orders he is wearing were presented by the Orthodox Church. Photograph the *Sun*.

Above On 18 November 1967 the Archbishop was the guest at the Greek Orthodox Cathedral in London of His All Holiness the Ecumenical Patriarch, Athenagorus 1, Archbishop of Constantinople, seated. On the left is Mrs Ramsey. Behind the Archbishop is the general secretary of the Council for Foreign Relations, John Satterthwaite, now Bishop of Gibralta in Europe. Photograph *Guardian*.

Left On 6 February 1969 the Archbishop spoke at a press conference at Lambeth Palace conducted by his press officer, Michael De-la-Noy, seated beside him, on the results of voting in Diocesan Conferences on the Scheme for Anglican-Methodist Reunion. Photograph *Sport & General*.

bove In the garden at Lambeth Palace, in
ll flight from Jane Bown, preparatory to
alking back towards her up the garden
th.

ight In the study at Lambeth. Photograph
aily Express.

A portrait study of Michael Ramsey by Jane Bown.

a punishing schedule, in exhausting heat, of airplane journeys, car rides, speeches, sermons, sometimes rather boring
lunches and the protocol attached to staying in Government Houses. Above all, he felt free of the irksome round
of administrative chores and the constant interruptions to
his mind occasioned by Assembly reports and attendance
at committee meetings. Secretly he longed to be primate of
a non-established Church, and one reason for this was
because the laity overseas reacted to him not as a remote
figurehead of the State but as a priest. In New York in
1970, when Ramsey was lecturing to a seminar of bishops
at the Trinity Institute, a photographer asked, not to be
admitted to what was in fact a private session, or even to
be allowed to take a photograph, but simply for the
Archbishop's blessing. As soon as the Archbishop stepped
down from the rostrum, the photographer was introduced,
and although the bishops were applauding, Ramsey
immediately switched off from the lecture and gave his full
attention to the photographer, and of course gave him his
blessing. Such an occurrence in Fleet Street would have
been unimaginable.

It was also in New York, after a particularly tiring day,
that the Archbishop was disrobing after a service late at
night when a young woman went up to him in the vestry
and asked if he would bless her crucifix. Without a
moment's hesitation Ramsey again became totally
absorbed in the woman and his priestly function. After he
had prayed with her and blessed her crucifix, she stepped
back and exclaimed, "Truly, you are a child of God!"

At the conclusion of one visit overseas the Archbishop's
return to England seemed likely to be delayed indefinitely
owing to an impending strike at Heathrow Airport, and
last-minute changes of plan had to be made, necessitating
a switch to an Australian aircraft due to land about ten
minutes before the strike was timed to begin. The only

person unperturbed was the Archbishop, who sometimes gave the impression that, given half a chance, he would never have returned to England at all. In order to report on the progress of events, his press officer entered the Archbishop's bedroom to find him stretched out on the bed, his hands clasped behind his head, repeating again and again, "I hate the Church of England! I hate the Church of England!"

"It's a good job there's no one but me to hear you saying that!", his press officer said.

"Oh, but it's true", was Ramsey's reply. "I do hate the Church of England. Indeed I do."

The fact is often overlooked that any archbishop of Canterbury is a diocesan bishop as well as Primate of All England, and that he has his own diocese to run on top of all his other tasks. But much of the pastoral work in the Canterbury diocese was of necessity delegated to the suffragan bishops of Croydon and Dover. John Hughes, consecrated in 1956, very probably had the unique distinction of serving as bishop of Croydon under three archbishops of Canterbury – Fisher, Ramsey and Coggan.

"There was a staff meeting every month," Bishop Hughes recalls.[25] "Fisher began at eleven and went on after lunch until four, because he liked to discuss matters other than those purely concerned with the diocese. Ramsey finished at lunch time. He said very little at staff meetings. He had a way, of course, of looking as if he wasn't listening, but the extraordinary thing was that he would come in at the end of a discussion and say, 'My guess is this . . .' and he was normally dead right. He had a marvellous way of settling the matter. Whenever Fisher had anything to do with Croydon and he thought I ought to know about it I would get a letter. I remember one vicar had complained about me, and Fisher sent me a resumé of the conversation. He gave you all the time you wanted.

He was fascinating. He treated me as a bright sixth-former and I enjoyed it. It was absolutely the reverse with Michael Ramsey. At the end of a staff meeting with Fisher everything had been decided, appointments to livings and so on. Not with Ramsey! I would discover from the newspaper that someone I'd never heard of was coming as vicar to a parish. It never occurred to Ramsey to say, 'Let so and so know'.

"I was here five years before he asked me to go and see him. We had met, and he did know me in a funny way. But did he ever know anybody, as a friend? He never asked me a single thing about Croydon. He would learn bits and pieces at staff meetings. One or two of the clergy said to me, 'How does the Archbishop seem to know so much about the parish when he's never asked me a single question?' But he was passionately devoted to getting round his diocese. He liked to as much as he could, in order to take institutions and confirmations. But what he would have done when visiting the vicarages without Joan I can't think. People liked her very much indeed."

The lack of liaison between Lambeth Palace and the suffragan bishops was at times nothing less than a disgrace. Bishop Hughes was diocesan director of ordinands for Croydon. "On two or three occasions," he says, "Michael Ramsey had all the ordinands to Lambeth and the directors were not invited. It caused wonder!" In 1966, while still bishop of Croydon, John Hughes had also been appointed Bishop to the Forces, a post first created by William Temple and during the war delegated to the suffragan bishop of Maidstone. "I could never quite understand his way of not letting me know what was going on. For example – and you can hardly believe this – on two occasions Michael invited all the service chaplains to Lambeth Palace for the day, and I was not invited. I was quite hurt."

Bishop Hughes unwittingly found himself involved in

one of the most frightful muddles Michael Ramsey ever got into as father-in-God to his clergy. The bishop of Bermuda, John Armstrong, was due to retire. Bermuda is a tiny diocese in the Atlantic Ocean, off the east coast of the United States and north of the Church of the Province of the West Indies, whose colonial clergy and laity still clung to the apron strings of England. It was what was called an extra-provincial diocese, with the archbishop of Canterbury retaining ultimate responsibility. A certain amount of racial tension was brewing up on the island, there was deep discord within the miniature synod, and Ramsey believed the best solution was for the diocese to cut its links with Canterbury and be ceded to a diocese of the American Episcopal Church, a plan hotly contested by the clergy. He paid an eight-day visit to an island you can drive round in a morning, staying at Government House with Lord and Lady Martonmere, and generally assessing the situation and trying to boost the morale of the parishes. During the visit, he attended a meeting of the synod, and he came away with the clear (and almost certainly accurate) impression that the synod had asked him to nominate a new bishop, the implication being that his choice would automatically be ratified.

The first person Ramsey approached with an offer of the see was John Hughes, who in about 1962 had already been invited to allow his name to go forward as archbishop of Perth, and it had only been when Hughes went to Lambeth to discuss the matter with Ramsey that he discovered it was Ramsey who had nominated him; he also discovered that Ramsey knew next to nothing about Perth and was quite unable to offer any sensible advice. Believing himself in any case unsuited to the task, with due modesty Hughes withdrew. Now he felt that Ramsey was making a second attempt to get rid of him, for by this time he was Bishop to the Forces, responsible for 350 chaplains. "The job was fascinating, and then he asked me to be bishop of Bermuda! I could not believe it. I should have been dean of the cathedral as well, but with only about nine clergy. I could not think why he should want me to switch from a major job to one like that, and I declined it. I remember discussing it with Eric Abbott, and he was as astonished as I was."

So Ramsey now offered the diocese of Bermuda to the provost of St Edmundsbury & Ipswich, who accepted with alacrity, and began to make preparations to resign his post, purchase episcopal garments, collect congratulations and say his farewells. Alas, the synod declined to have him. Ramsey was speechless, and told the synod to choose their own bishop, washing his hands of the whole affair and at the same time of any responsibility for the provost's disappointment or embarrassment. No alternative appointment was ever offered.

Apparently Ramsey said one day to Bishop Hughes, " 'There are two kinds of suffragan bishop, there are the contented ones and the discontented ones. You are one of the contented ones.' The fact is, he had never asked me! He found it extremely difficult to make a personal approach, he had to write letters. I came to believe that Michael was very, very afraid of his own emotions, and he could best deal with them in a letter. He didn't take umbrage at all over my not going to Bermuda, and when I said No he wrote a very kind letter indeed."

After fourteen years of loyal service, Bishop Hughes was remembered at the end. About three weeks before Michael Ramsey retired he was guest of honour at the tri-annual dinner of the naval chaplains at Greenwich. In his speech he said, "Now, there are those people who think they represent the Archbishop of Canterbury. They think they do. But they don't. But there is one person who does officially represent the Archbishop of Canterbury [as

Bishop to the Forces], and that is the Bishop of Croydon, and he has done it superlatively well." Geoffrey Tiarks, suffragan bishop of Maidstone and the Archbishop's senior chaplain, turned to Hughes and said, "He's saying thank-you."

One of the most important tasks to which any arch-bishop of Canterbury can address himself is the building up of a strong bench of bishops, and it was not only in the misjudging of John Hughes's suitability for Perth and Bermuda that Michael Ramsey conspicuously failed to take an intelligent interest in the episcopate. At home his disinterest in patronage was notorious. A member of the House of Lords who is also a priest, the Reverend Lord Beaumont of Whitley, who regards Michael Ramsey as one of his heroes, says, "Michael Ramsey was a very great archbishop, but his chief fault was an inability to do anything about appointments at all. This was a great sadness for the Church. Robert Mortimer of Exeter, Launcelot Fleming of Norwich and Ian Ramsey of Durham stood out, but by and large the episcopate in Michael Ramsey's time was of a low standard. And of course neither Mortimer nor Fleming were appointed under Ramsey." But Lord Beaumont thinks that Michael Ramsey was "very good" in the House of Lords. "There was never a time when I thought that he failed the forces of good. He lived up to the image of saintliness that we projected on to him. And in standing up to the Tory peers, who thought he was out of his depth, he showed a good deal of moral courage. In some ways he was what one would describe as lazy – in my view, a profound theologi-cal virtue."[26]

Lord Beaumont, prominent during the 1960s as a radical Christian journalist, supplies his own explanation for Ramsey's disinterest in patronage. "He knew nothing about people. Indeed, he was a bad judge of people, and he had no interest in the kind of wheeling and dealing of ecclesiastical politics that so many members of the Church establishment enjoy."

So far as Ian Ramsey's consecration was concerned, it seems to have been the exception to the rule, for in 1966 Michael is said to have come up to Eric James, at that time director of Parish and People, saying, "I've had a brainwave, I've had a brainwave, Ian Ramsey for Durham!" It was while attending a conference on Spirituality for Today, run by Parish and People (a ginger group concerned with reorganization and reform of the liturgy) at Durham University in 1967, that Ramsey was driven back to the station by a taxi driver whom he had ordained, but who was no longer a priest. The driver had no wish for Ramsey to be embarrassed by the situation, but Canon James thought the Archbishop ought to know who the man was, and told him. On getting out of the taxi Ramsey went round to the driver's window and said, "I'm not supposed to know who you are, but I should like to give you my blessing." His arrival at the conference had been equally typical. He asked Eric James to take him to the bar, and entering, held up his arms and said, "I'm a very shy man, come and talk to me."[27]

"He's an awful ass", Michael Ramsey would sometimes say of a bishop whose actions had not met with his approval, and he could not have been expected to have much in common with some of them, with a conservative evangelical, for example, like Maurice Wood, appointed bishop of Norwich in 1971, who said things like, "Let us remember that we're marked men on the Devil's list ... Those who stand near the captain are targets for the archer's arrows."[28] He was fond of the taciturn bishop of Ely, Edward Roberts, much admired Edward Wickham, suffragan bishop of Middleton, and had a good deal of respect for John Moorman, the bishop of Ripon, despite his opposition to Anglican-Methodist Reunion, and for Harry Carpenter, bishop of Oxford, because of his support for the Scheme. But his friendships with his fellow bishops were highly selective; it really seems extraordinary that someone like Cuthbert Bardsley, bishop of Coventry from 1956 to 1976, should write, "Alas, I never knew him well."[29] But with the present Archbishop of Canterbury, whom Michael consecrated as bishop of St Albans in 1970, he had a good deal in common; Dr Runcie had been Principal of Cuddesdon from 1960 to 1969, he was a theologian and an intellectual, and shared many of Michael's ecumenical aspirations and his impatience with State interference in Church affairs.

Dr Runcie believes that Michael Ramsey was "very dependent upon friendship, but it was the friendship of those who gathered round a table and prayed with him in chapel rather than a consultation with informed minds. He was a fatherly figure. For residential bishops' meetings he gathered us all together at Cuddesdon and we accepted it. I loved it, of course, but others were not so keen on this rather Victorian retreat, which wasn't very comfortable. But it was dear to him. And on those occasions he was always very ready to listen and to have a prayer with you. But he had a low threshold of boredom, and he was, I suppose, inclined to listen to some when they spoke rather than to others. And he was pretty discriminating in knowing when it was worthwhile! But I don't think anyone could deny he was the most loved archbishop among the bishops. He would talk to me because we had so much in common and he could relax, but I suppose he didn't talk to very many bishops in the way he talked to people like me, with whom he had common ground. Oddly enough, I don't think the other bishops resented this."[30]

Whatever his personal relationship with the bishops,

Michael Ramsey always seems to have retained a rather sceptical view of their general usefulness as a species. Of a new appointment in 1979 he remarked, "He can do far less damage as bishop of ****** than he can as vicar of ******!" His attitude to the bishops was very much that of a senior member of the common room; he expected them to behave well, and when they didn't he was deeply shocked, hurt and nonplussed. Some of the blame for an accumulation of less than inspired diocesan bishops can fairly be laid at Michael Ramsey's door, but some at Churchill's, too. So far as the Church was concerned, when Temple died in 1944 he ought to have been succeeded by George Bell of Chichester, and had that happened, a very different bench of bishops would have emerged under his leadership. But Bell had spoken out strongly against Churchill's war aims, particularly the bombing of civilian targets in Germany, and he never had any chance of being nominated by Churchill for Canterbury.

Ramsey's indolence in the matter of appointments was compounded by a woeful lack of imagination. Ralph Dean, an Englishman who in 1957 had been elected bishop of Cariboo in the Canadian Province of British Columbia, was episcopal secretary to the 1968 Lambeth Conference and Executive Officer of the Anglican Communion. The way in which he administered the Conference and appeared daily for a month at press briefings was widely admired, and his knowledge of the Anglican Communion vastly exceeded that of anyone else (he had travelled round the world five times). When the Conference was over Michael Ramsey allowed him to return to Cariboo, where his duties as bishop could scarcely have begun to match his abilities. He ought of course to have been offered an English diocese, but in his own quiet way he was something of a radical, and he could see very clearly the

169

parochial nature of the Church of England in relation to the missionary nature of so many Churches overseas. It was surely that element of uncertainty in Ralph Dean's make-up, the possibility that he might shake the Church of England out of its complacency as an established Church, which failed to endear him to Ramsey, who was all for rocking the boat occasionally himself but tended to panic if someone else, particularly a bishop, gave a shove.

Part of Michael Ramsey's almost wilful refusal to exercise patronage was born of an unworldliness that blocked from his mind the need most people have for a helping hand up the ladder. There was a secretary of one of the councils of the General Assembly who, like Ralph Dean, had acquired very considerable experience in his own field, had great gifts, should have been offered a deanery, and on whose behalf approaches were made to Ramsey by at least one bishop. Ramsey said the man should live by faith, and when the natural time came for him to move on, nothing whatever was done for him; to the detriment of the Church he was put out to grass in a rural parish. Ramsey made no enterprising use of the Lambeth doctorates and M.A.s at his disposal, for it never occurred to him that a pat on the head or a word of thanks is often what makes the world go round. He could have engineered a life peerage without any trouble at all for William Temple's widow, a most admirable and able woman, but perhaps the most notorious occasion of his failure to exercise patronage in the secular realm took place when his Lay Secretary, Robert Beloe, retired. Again, a life peerage would have ensured that his gifts were placed at the disposal of parliament, but Ramsey had always felt threatened by Beloe's presence at Lambeth, with his quiet insistence that Ramsey give his mind to matters that bored him, and Beloe's accumulated wisdom was allowed to go to waste.

The imminent demise of the Church of England has

been predicted at regular intervals for the past fifty years, and certainly during Ramsey's time at Canterbury church attendances fell, ordinations fell and church buildings were declared redundant. In 1960 there were 190,713 confirmations, a figure which represented 34.1 per thousand of the estimated population aged between twelve and twenty. By 1970 annual confirmations had fallen to 113,005, or 19.7 per thousand. In 1961, 605 men were ordained into the Church of England. In 1970 the figure was a mere 185, a number of theological colleges having been closed or merged in the meantime. In 1857, out of a population of just under eighteen millions, Horace Mann estimated that nearly eleven million people attended church or chapel in England and Wales. On Easter Sunday 1970, out of a population of 46 million, only 1,600,000 Anglicans received Communion. A falling off in regular church-going has been a phenomenon certainly since the First World War, which saw the dissolution of the squirearchy and with it the collapse of virtually compulsory parish worship in the countryside, but loss of allegiance to the parish church is not necessarily a reliable yardstick of fundamental Christian belief, as the way in which cathedral churches are packed out for memorial services following any national disaster clearly demonstrates. And no one person, certainly not an archbishop, can ever be held responsible if a nation decides to adopt a secular attitude to life. Whole waves of historical and social issues combine to bring about patterns in human conduct, and these patterns are seldom confined to one country. In times of affluence people have traditionally abandoned dependence upon prayer, and the period in which Michael Ramsey presided as archbishop of Canterbury was one of inexpensive housing, cheap food and a choice of jobs. While clergymen like Nicolas Stacey, rector of Woolwich, became so disillusioned with small congregations despite their best endeavours to care for parishioners and enliven services that they left the Church's employ for better paid secular jobs, Michael Ramsey always played down the quantitive aspect of organized religion, preferring instead, in so far as anyone can, to measure the depth of the personal commitment of those in search of religious experience. He was not unsympathetic to people who sought alternatives to organized religion, and his fatherly appearance often encouraged them to seek him out. When an American singing group called The Temptations asked to meet him, Ramsey promised twenty minutes, saying he was sure he would soon be bored. In the event, he questioned them closely for forty minutes and gave them his blessing, and they left his study in a kind of collective trance.

While still bishop of Durham, Michael suggested that "perhaps the paucity of the ordained" was a divine judgement, "calling us to put certain things right and to do certain things differently."[31] He did actually believe that sometimes God judged his Church "for grevious failings by not giving to it what it seems most to need". By the end of the 1960s the clergy were in no doubt what they most needed. Between October 1966 and July 1968 clergy attending conferences at St George's House, Windsor Castle were invited to fill in a questionnaire. Asked what they considered should be the top priority of a bishop they voted for the pastoral oversight of his clergy. But by 1968 they, like their archbishop, had lived through nearly a decade of social and theological upheaval which had left many of them no longer sure why they were ordained, or even Christians.

CHAPTER SEVEN

FERMENT

Be ready to accept humiliations. They can hurt terribly, but they help you to be humble.   *The Christian Priest Today.*

When he came to sum up some of his most vivid impressions of his years as archbishop of Canterbury, Michael Ramsey wrote:

> In the world there has been the increase of violence, the polarizing of racial conflict, the confusion of morals, and the sharpened awareness of the contrast between the affluent and the hungry peoples. In Christendom there has been the theological malaise associated with the phrase "Death of God", the decline of church allegiance, the revivals of a charismatic kind, the involvement of Christianity with the problems of social revolution, and the growing feeling in the West for prayer and contemplation as essential to the life of Man. Who would have foreseen the renewal within the Roman Catholic Church during and after the Second Vatican Council,* or the startling advances and frustrations in the ecumenical scene?[1]

Essentially what happened both in Church and State during Michael Ramsey's years at Canterbury was a sudden overthrow of paternalism. The young did not simply refuse to obey orders; what they did was to question them. But friction between the generations was

* 1962–65.

nothing new, and the rash of satire that broke out was akin to a vicarage tea party in comparison to the eighteenth-century lampooning of royalty and politicians. Yet the so-called and largely misnamed Permissive Society did come as a shock to many, with nudity on the stage and swearing on television. It is necessary to remember, when assessing how Michael Ramsey's generation dealt with all this, that he had been born in 1904, when there was no television and the cinema was silent, Edward VII was still on the throne, the British Empire was intact, and parental education had been formed and administered according to the mores of Victorian England.

A degree of "permissiveness" was of course long over-due. Between the ages of eighteen and twenty-one, young lads could still be shot on active service but denied the vote. Both men and women as young as eighteen could be hanged. Male homosexuals who were discovered to have made love were sent to prison. A trade in back-street abortions flourished, and lies and deception were essential if you wanted a divorce. The degree of reaction among conservative cabinets after the war led to sickening judgements on social issues. Many of the Anglican bishops (Ronald Williams of Leicester and Stretton Reeve of Lichfield were prime examples), products of the same public schools and universities as most of the Conservative politicians, were equally outmoded in their social and moral attitudes, as were whole swathes of the laity; letters received by John Robinson, suffragan bishop of Woolwich, when he preached against capital punishment, made horrifying reading. It was fortunate for those likely to benefit from reform that Michael Ramsey was far from typical of an Establishment leader of his generation. A liberal by instinct, the son of a Liberal father and a Socialist mother, brought up in a middle-class home, educated at a public school not known for producing bishops, he had not mixed with Eton and Harrow boys nor mingled in London clubs. His mind, although sometimes slow to grasp an issue, would never refuse to address itself to a question once it had been raised, and it is almost impossible to think of any other bishop at the time who would have put a braver face on his appearances in the House of Lords to argue for reform, for the Lords was his least favourite debating chamber.

But to the Lords he went, to speak on divorce, abortion, hanging, immigration and homosexual law reform. Often he reacted instinctively to moral issues, issues he could not have avoided had he wished, for if he was ever to be interviewed, on television or by the press, he was going to be asked about them. Before leaving for a visit to the USA in 1967 he knew he would have to commit himself to a view on the Vietnam War, and he decided to say that while he revered those who had given their lives in what they regarded as a just cause, he felt bound to say that the war was one which neither side could win, and that America should pull out. He was accompanied by the chief information officer from Church House, a retired major general with an unfortunate penchant for serving South African sherry to journalists, who began to offer Ramsey gratuitous military advice. The Archbishop told the general he was not concerned with military strategy but with ethics, and that if he did not like publicizing the line Ramsey had decided to take the general could go and run the Boys' Brigade. Ramsey thought this sally so amusing that he repeated the story many times on his return to Lambeth.

Michael Ramsey became involved with matters concerned with immigration long before it was fashionable to adopt a moral stance on race. He was already chairman of the National Committee for Commonwealth Immigrants when late in 1967 the Labour Government produced plans for a Commonwealth Immigrants Bill, and when Ramsey went to see the Home Secretary, James Callaghan, to discuss the Bill, his visit resulted in over eighty telephone enquiries from the press. The Bill was eventually rushed through parliament in six days. Its purpose was to restrict the entrance into Britain of Kenya Asians who possessed United Kingdom passports, and on 29th February 1968 the Archbishop of Canterbury told the House of Lords what he thought of it. He complained that no advice had been sought from the National Committee, and, more importantly, that the Bill virtually distinguished United Kingdom citizens on the score of race and involved the country in breaking its word. The Bill became law the following day.

"It is more and more apparent that Christians are incredible unless they stand with the underprivileged in the world, and that the Church is incredible if it is not clearly on the side of justice in the world's conflicts", Ramsey was to say during a lecture in Cambridge in 1972. By that time he had come to be seen by black and Asian people around the world as a standard-bearer on their behalf, crowning his concern in this direction with a visit to South Africa in 1973. At St Mary's Cathedral in Johannesburg he described an industrial system "which forcibly separates wage-earning men from their families for nearly all the year" as "utterly at variance with the sacredness of the family and the true character of human community". He asked: "Ought the Christian conscience to tolerate this?" And he summed up his opposition to apartheid by saying, "If we exclude a man because he is of another race or colour are we not excluding Christ himself?"

In Pretoria in 1970 he had already experienced an uncomfortable meeting with President Vorster, leaving him in no doubt about his views on apartheid, and before going to see the President he had done something he often did, he had practised making an appropriate face. "I practised making one unpleasant face after another, while shaving," he explained afterwards, and press photographs showed him with one of the most unsociable faces he had ever tried putting on. "I did it so that I should get a sort of continuity of unpleasant faces." It was far more usual for Michael to emerge from a courtesy call wreathed in smiles, but on this occasion he was afraid it might appear as though he and Vorster had hit it off, and Ramsey took the view that there was little point in going all the way to Pretoria to enjoy a glass of chilled South African hock; while there he might as well tell the President his mind. He had a collection of faces, some of which appeared on the covers of his books. "That's the pious one", he used to say, pointing to one photograph. "That's the who-the-hell-are-you face."

Bishop John Hughes noticed how Ramsey's mind seemed to have compartments. "He had a compassionate compartment which might move into a funny compart-ment, and his face reflected this. At lunch at Canterbury after a staff meeting, Mrs Ramsey once said, 'Look at Michael, he's got his ecumenical face on.'"[2] There was a common fallacy that because Ramsey's face was so mobile he would be easy to paint, but it is questionable whether any portrait done of him was successful. Only a photogra-pher could capture in a flash any truly characteristic expression, for when he sat to be painted he tended to nod off instead of giving something of himself to the painter. After taking advice from Roy Strong, at that time director of the National Portrait Gallery, he sat for Guy Roddon some six years before retirement for his official portrait for Lambeth Palace, but after being hung in the corridor for a few years the painting was discreetly stored away.

While still at York, Michael Ramsey had listed for students[3] what in 1960 he believed to be "three outstanding moral issues on a world scale": the urgency of radical disarmament, the need for a radical change in the attitude of races, white and black, towards one another, and the need for rich countries to give resources to help those in terrible poverty. "It is outrageous," he said, "that some countries enjoy a high standard of living while others are dangerously near the famine line." He knew next to nothing about international banking, but to him, the moral issue was perfectly clear. He also saw quite clearly – for a glance at the diverse lives and times of Becket, Cranmer, Laud and William Temple told him so – that "the problem of the priest and politics" was unavoidable, even though it might take different forms in different ages. "The selfish motive in all affairs is always wrong," he would tell ordinands, "and the altruistic motive is always right. Wealth is always dangerous to its possessor, and the rich man can only with difficulty be saved. There is no discrimination between races in God's eyes, and there must be no discrimination in man's eyes."[4]

When Michael Ramsey became archbishop of Canterbury there existed a totally irrational discrimination, in law as well as in man's eyes, between men who were homosexual and those who were heterosexual. A heterosexual man could indulge in sexual intercourse with a girl of sixteen if she consented; all homosexual men were barred, on penalty of fines and imprisonment, from ever under any circumstances giving physical expression to their sexual and emotional nature. Blackmail and police harrassment were rife (police harrassment still is), but as a result of proposals put forward in 1957 by a committee chaired by Sir John Wolfenden,* parliament passed legislation in 1967 making homosexual activity in private between consenting men over the age of twenty-one legal. Clearly there

* In 1974 created Baron Wolfenden.

were both ethical and legal issues at stake, and in the House of Lords on 12th May 1965, when the Earl of Arran, a rather dotty and endearing peer (now dead) who contributed wildly controversial and eccentric articles to the *Evening News*, first introduced a Motion based on the Wolfenden Proposals, Michael Ramsey said he wished to support him. But in making clear the moral standpoint from which he approached the question he said, "I believe that homosexual acts are always wrong in the sense that they use in a wrong way human organs for which the right use is intercourse between men and women within marriage. Amidst the modern talk about the 'new morality' I would uphold the belief that just as fornication is always wrong so homosexual acts are always wrong. At the same time, wrong acts in this case as in others can have various degrees of culpability attached to them. In this case there are not only degrees of culpability but also varieties of causes of the trouble and categories of the trouble, psychological and sociological."

These remarks were scarcely exceptional, coming from an archbishop of Canterbury in 1965, and at this stage no one in the Church had seriously begun to differentiate between a vocation to celibacy and the consequence of a blanket condemnation of all homosexual activity. But having established his moral position (the House of Lords was jam-packed with rabid reactionaries, and it was part of Ramsey's task at least to try to get enough peers to vote for the eventual Bill on rational grounds), he went on to say: "The case for altering the law in respect of homosexual acts in private rests, I believe, on reason and justice, and on considerations of the good of the community. As to the first, I think that there is real cogency in the plea of the Wolfenden Report that not all sins are properly given the status of crimes, not even such sins as the adulterous conduct of a man or woman, which can smash up the life

179

of a family and bring misery to a whole family of children. If the line can reasonably be drawn anywhere, homosexual acts in private between consenting adults fall properly on the same side of the line as fornication. To say this is not to condone the wrongness of the acts, but to put them in the realm of private moral responsibility. I believe that the present location of the line gives a sense of injustice and bitterness, which helps morality no more than would a law which made fornication a crime." He also told the Lords, "It can hardly be argued that the law in this matter has been successful as a deterrent or a means of eradicating the practices."

By 21st June, when the House conducted a committee debate on what had now become The Sexual Offences Bill, passions were so enflamed that Ramsey felt it necessary to breathe traditional Christian brimstone, for public consumption at any rate, to prove that although he wanted homosexual acts to be legalized he remained firmly on the side of the angels. "Let me say, not for the first time, that I regard homosexual behaviour as abominable, utterly abominable. I am a supporter of this Bill in the belief that this Bill will help and not hinder the forces making for morality in this respect." He had also been challenged over his own comparisons between homosexuality and fornication. "I think", he said, "it is extraordinarily hard for any of us to assess the relative seriousness of sins. When we start doing that we get into questions to which the Almighty Himself knows the answer and we do not."

Ramsey was back in the Lords on 28th October for the Third Reading, when he made much plainer than before the moral requirement for removing from the statute book a crime that among other things so often led to blackmail. He believed the law already protected young people, but he made the astute observation that "if the law is to protect and help young people, it must be a law which wins their respect as being just. I think that the respect of young people for the law, and the morality which it tries to uphold, is at present hindered by the feeling of young people that the law is really unjust." And he went on to say, "My support of this Bill has been increased by hearing, among those who have opposed it during these debates, what I can only call a really lopsided presentation of morality – a presentation which quotes the Old Testament, which takes the line that sexual sins are apparently the worst of all sins, and that homosexual sins are invariably the worst sort of sins among sexual sins. I think that such a presentation of morality is lopsided and is going to be rejected by the people of the new generation, who need a better presentation of morality to win their respect and admiration."

On Ramsey's support in principle for the 1967 Sexual Offences Act he could not be faulted. The interesting question is the extent to which his public and official pronouncements on homosexuality itself agreed with or were at variance with his private views. He evinced a genuine interest in the work of the Homosexual Law Reform Society and its umbrella charity the Albany Trust, and never shunned the company of homosexual men; at one time no fewer than five out of seven members of his household were homosexual.

During the decade or so following the change in the law a considerable shift in opinion occurred among individual members of the Church of England. A number of clergy began to hold services of blessing for homosexual couples, and the argument was developed that for homosexuals, homosexuality was as normal as heterosexuality was for heterosexuals. It would have been too much to expect any archbishop of Canterbury at the time to have given public utterance to such a basic over-turning of Church teaching, but if Michael Ramsey secretly believed there was a good deal of truth in these propositions – and many who knew him well believe that he did – the way he saw himself helping most usefully was probably by offering quiet non-judgemental encouragement behind the scenes.

Michael Ramsey was fastidious but not puritanical. During an address he gave in Central Hall, Westminster in 1972 he said, "I hope we welcome the greater openness about sex, as I am sure the old puritanical idea that sex should always be hushed up was unwholesome and did harm. We must avoid a kind of backlash towards puritanism. But sex is the bond of a union between two persons in their totality as persons; that is its true meaning. And today we have to witness against all those influences which separate sex from human personality and treat it as an excitement on a sub-human plane. The commercial exploitation of sex is horrible, yes horrible." The most interesting phrase in this passage is Ramsey's seemingly quite deliberate use of the words "two persons". Had he wished to say "between a man and a woman" he would have done so.

While abortion is not strictly speaking a sexual matter, more a medical one, it was another ethical subject with bearings on the most fundamental aspects of human life to which Ramsey had to give his mind. In 1966 the Church of England's Board for Social Responsibility produced a report called *Abortion – An Ethical Discussion*, debated by the General Assembly[5] at a time when two successive Bills concerned with abortion were also being debated in parliament. Michael Ramsey felt that "first principles" had been "somewhat obscured by the sheer mass of detailed discussion", and when addressing the Convocation of Canterbury on 17th January 1967 he drew a distinction between abortion and infanticide although, like the authors of the report, he laid stress on the sanctity of the human foetus. He thought the "absolutist position against abortion" was strained to absurdity when it could be seen that in certain circumstances it might condemn both mother and foetus to death, and in the measure of support he gave to an attempt to clear the air about abortion, Michael Ramsey knew he would be condemned by his Roman Catholic friends. Ramsey was not a moral theologian; Robert Mortimer, the bishop of Exeter, was, but it seems that almost no matter what the subject under discussion, the Church and the nation only ever wished to hear from the archbishop of Canterbury. At least when Ian Ramsey became bishop of Durham he took on the novel problems thrown up by transplant operations, but when one reviews the range of social and ethical issues Michael Ramsey had to brief himself about on top of his routine work, the reliance on virtually only one man's judgement at such a time of ethical upheaval was a bit absurd.

If there were certain issues – homosexuality was obviously one – where Michael Ramsey tended to hold back in line with public opinion, there were others – and hanging was an equally obvious example – where he was perfectly prepared to give a lead in opposition to the majority view. Even today, twenty years after hanging was finally abolished, in a referendum the public would almost certainly vote to bring back the death penalty, but in the House of Lords on 20th July 1965, when parliament was proposing to abolish hanging for a five-year trial period, Michael Ramsey tempered the drama of the occasion by spelling out some basic moral premises. "There ought", he said, "to be a recognition of the fact that the taking of life as a penalty does devalue human life", and he denied that there was any convincing evidence that any penalty acted as a unique deterrent. He saw, too, an absurdity in the attempt to differentiate between "capital" and "non-capital" murder, and he told the Lords, "where the penalty is sometimes to kill the murderer, and sometimes not, it seems that law and morality have gone apart on the very point where it is imperative for them to go together." He did not lecture or hector the House, nor pander to emotion on a highly emotive topic, he offered carefully weighed moral advice. The Murder (Abolition of Death Penalty) Bill passed its second reading by 204 votes to 104, and on 18th December 1969, to Ramsey's infinite relief and satisfaction, the death penalty was abolished once and for all.

Abortion, capital punishment, divorce, these were matters on which Michael Ramsey had time to reflect, and to draft speeches or lectures in his often almost illegible handwriting. But sometimes, usually on political matters, he was caught on the hop. One such occasion concerned Rhodesia, and the press coverage that ensued he later described as "crucifying".[6] On 26th October 1965 Ramsey was in the chair at a meeting of the British Council of Churches in Aberdeen. The chief information officer was not in Aberdeen, but at his country house in Hampshire. And the prime minister, Harold Wilson, was in Salisbury, Rhodesia, negotiating with Ian Smith. During a debate on Rhodesia, Ramsey decided to intervene, in order to try to clarify the issues he thought lay before the Council. He had not previously intended speaking, and in the event he did so without notes. What he said, *inter alia*, was this: "If the British Government thought it practicable to use force for the protection of the rights of the Rhodesian people then I think that as Christians we have to say that it would be right to use force to that end."

The press exploded. In editorials and cartoons outrage was expressed. Letters condemning Ramsey flooded into *The Times* and Lambeth Palace. There was even talk of a motion of censure in the House of Commons. Generally speaking, Ramsey was depicted as politically inept and a warmonger. He had certainly been politically naïve, as he later privately admitted,[7] and he should have called a press conference the next morning in order to limit the damage by explaining far more fully what he had in mind, but there was no one on hand to advise him. Exactly a year later Ramsey was in Canada, and got into trouble by making comments on the effectiveness of Billy Graham's crusades, comments he later claimed had been misreported. This got so badly out of hand that first his Secretary had to defend him in the press and then Ramsey himself felt it necessary to write a letter to *The Times*, explaining that what he had said was, "We need an evangelism which gives more space to the social content of Christianity and to the intellectual difficulties of belief". This, while perfectly true, had been a rather donnish thing to say when answering questions about an old-fashioned (and some at the time believed very dangerous)* evangelist like Billy Graham, out for instant conversion and no questions asked, and this got translated by newspaper headline writers into "Ramsey Attacks Billy Graham", "Church 'does not need Billy Graham'", "Ramsey hits at Billy Graham", and, in the *Sun* (predictably), "Come off it, Archbishop".

The fracas over Billy Graham soon died down, but the taste engendered by Rhodesia lingered for a very long time, and was seen by Ramsey as a litmus test for his future relations with the press and public: were they better or worse than Rhodesia? Almost always thereafter, they were infinitely better. He was highly amused in 1969 when he read, in a review in *The Times* of J. C. C. Davidson's memoirs, "We learn for instance that Lloyd George's Press Secretary, William Sutherland, boasted of countering gusts of unpopularity for his chief by hiring fifty or sixty people

---

* In 1954 the writer and literary editor J. R. Ackerley, accompanied by Rose Macaulay, went to hear Billy Graham at Haringey. "They were duly appalled by the vulgarity of the proceedings, though Macaulay thought Graham 'sincere'. Ackerley thought him a 'dreadful creature' and reported that the atmosphere of the rally was fascist." *Ackerley* by Peter Parker (Constable, 1989).

to cheer outside 10 Downing Street 'at a bob a head'." He sent a cutting to his press officer, with the words under-lined and a note that read, "When are you going to try this?" Fortunately, there was no need.

Disturbing though contretemps like Ramsey's interven-tion over Rhodesia may have been, and time-consuming though his mastery of social and ethical issues undoubt-edly was, they can be seen to have been peripheral to two major concerns, one ecumenical and one theological, which really dominated "the Canterbury years", and in varying degrees left indelible scars and impressions. Both lay at the heart of his concerns, at the centre of his life and mission. The ecumenical catastrophe – as he saw it – was the failure of the Church of England to agree to reunion with the Methodist Church. The theological crisis which took him by surprise (although heralded in 1962 by a Cambridge collection of essays called *Soundings*) was enshrined in a book written – and this was what shocked him – by a bishop, *Honest to God*. Published in March 1963, this was the product of another transparently honest and painstaking theologian, John Robinson, suffragan bishop of Woolwich, and it threw Michael Ramsey into a fit.

What seems so strange a quarter of a century later, when assessing Ramsey's reaction, is that *Honest to God* was only part of a continuing attempt to demythologize the gospels; as far back as 1954, when an English translation of essays entitled *Kerygma and Myth* was published,* Ramsey had been fully aware of the debate in Germany originated by Rudolf Bultmann's preliminary efforts to demythologize. In 1956 he devoted a chapter of *Durham Essays and Addresses* to the subject. "Anyone who sets out to present the Christian faith today is up against the

* SPCK

problem of religious language", he wrote in the Preface to his 1960 collection of essays, *Introducing the Christian Faith*. But perhaps an awareness of the need to address a modern congregation in "modern language" was not the same thing as dispensing with topographical concepts of heaven and hell, and trying, after two thousand years of Christian art, to redefine the familiar imagery of theism. In 1969 he blamed his own slowness to grasp what was happening on "the insularity of theology in England",[8] and in *Canterbury Pilgrim*, compiled in 1974, he reiterated this excuse by saying, "At the beginning of the sixties there was in the Church of England little awareness that a theological upheaval was on its way." He went on:

> For my own part, I was aware that the "biblical theology" within whose stream most of my own theological work had been done was in danger of talking in a vacuum unrelated to the world around. But the lack of a common "universe of discourse" made impossible that Christian "map" of the world, with the Incarnation at the centre, of which William Temple had dreamed in his earlier writings. Not believing that a logical or philosophical synthesis of Christianity and contemporary modes of thought was possible, I none the less believed, as I still do, that the death and resurrection of Jesus Christ give through faith some shape and clue to the meaning of existence. As one whose theology had been almost entirely "historical" in discipline, I thought that the Christian tradition had within itself resources of supernatural faith and spirituality equal to whatever shocks might come.
>
> The storm over *Honest to God* broke in March 1963. I was at the time, after eighteen strenuous months in finding my feet in a new office, scarcely prepared for a theological crisis. The initial error in reaction, in which I myself shared, was to think that the trouble was only that the author of the book was missing some of the profundities of the Christian faith and was being unnecessarily negative in expression. I think that was true. But I was soon to grasp how many were the contemporary gropings and quests which lay behind *Honest to God*. Again, I rather supposed

that the need was to reaffirm the coherence of the faith on familiar lines, albeit with greater sensitivity and persuasion. If that was my initial mistake, I saw after a little further reflection that there was in the background a widespread crisis of faith which cried out for another kind of spirit in meeting it.

Michael Ramsey's ambivalent relations with John Robinson went back to 1951 when, as Regius Professor, he had warmly recommended Robinson's appointment, at the age of only thirty-one, as dean of Clare College, Cambridge. Eight years later, when Robinson was still only thirty-nine, Mervyn Stockwood asked for him to be appointed suffragan bishop of Woolwich, in the diocese of Southwark. Fisher, who was against the idea, for some reason consulted Michael, by now archbishop of York, and after talking over the matter with John Robinson, Michael Ramsey seems to have agreed with Fisher that his consecration should at least be postponed until he was older.[9] But Mervyn Stockwood persisted in his request, and Fisher eventually gave way with a good grace. John Robinson was duly consecrated, and within months he had probably become the best-known bishop in the Church of England, for in 1960 he appeared as a witness for the defence when Penguin Books stood trial over publication of *Lady Chatterley's Lover*.

By the time John Robinson came to write *Honest to God*, Ramsey was archbishop of Canterbury. Robinson sent a copy of the manuscript to Ramsey, and asked him to a supper party on 29th June 1962 at which those invited had been requested to say whether in their opinion the book should be published, and if so, whether they had any amendments to suggest. Ramsey was too busy to attend but sent "warm good wishes". Publication was agreed upon, with a modest six thousand print run. The book sold out on publication day, went into seventeen languages, eventually sold over one million copies and induced four thousand letters, to most of which (some were too mad or abusive to warrant an answer) John Robinson sent a personal reply.

On 17th March 1963, two days before publication of *Honest to God*, Robinson summarized his book in an article in the *Observer* which carried the headline "Our Image of God Must Go". Eric James, Robinson's biographer, has said that the headline suggested he was an atheist, but surely the crucial word, "Image", was a very precise choice of word in relation to the point *Honest to God* was making, and it is hard to see how the headline could fairly be criticized either on the grounds of inaccuracy or journalistic sensationalism. But as things turned out, it was very much the publicity that worried Ramsey, allied to the quaint notion that the ideas within the book should have been discussed genteelly in common rooms rather than committed to paper.

Not only had John Robinson sent a copy of the manuscript to Ramsey, inviting his comments prior to publication, but he now sent an advance copy of the book to Lambeth Palace. Somewhere in the administrative maze, it got lost, and a message was sent to Robinson asking for a second copy. This was duly dispatched, but never acknowledged. "John", says Eric James, "was not hurt, just puzzled."[10] It seems pretty certain Ramsey had not read the manuscript. Now he certainly read the book – not the easiest book, even for a trained theologian, to follow. But did he discuss the book, or his worries about it, with anybody? What he too often did when under stress was to bottle up his emotions until they boiled over in some rash and uncharitable act. Under the avalanche of publicity he probably felt his authority as archbishop under threat, and on 1st April, without warning Robinson that he planned to criticize him in public, he went on television to say that the book "caricatured" the ordinary Christian's view of God. "It is utterly wrong and misleading," Ramsey said, "to denounce the imagery of God held by Christian men, women and children, imagery they have got from Jesus himself, the image of God the Father in Heaven, and to say that we can't have any new thought until it is all swept away."

These were not the carefully considered words of a former Regius Professor of Divinity in response to a fellow theologian's attempts to synthesize the work of such great contemporary Christian thinkers as Bonhoeffer, Bultmann and Tillich. They were rather the facile, conservative reflexes of a public figure trying to steady a rocking boat, and did not begin fairly to reflect either the truth about religious imagery or what John Robinson was trying to say. Ramsey now returned to his study, to produce an instant critique, a short pamphlet he called *Image Old and New*, rushed out by SPCK ostensibly as a reasoned contribution to the debate let loose by *Honest to God*. Although it directly criticized certain passages in *Honest to God* it showed some understanding of John Robinson's approach, and Ramsey would have been well advised to let his reactions, reasonably balanced in *Image Old and New*, rest there. But he now informed the Bishop of Southwark that he intended to make a statement about *Honest to God* when he addressed the Convocation of Canterbury on 7th May. The Bishop wrote a courteous and carefully argued letter to Ramsey, warning him of the danger should he state publicly that the doctrines of God and the deity of Christ as stated in John Robinson's book were incompatible with the doctrine of the Church, a danger that might "lead to estrangement between my Diocese and the Province with the possibility of the Archbishop and the Diocesan Bishop on different sides, and perhaps open conflict."

But Ramsey had the bit between his teeth, and remained

determined to reiterate in front of the clergy in Convocation the criticism he had made of Robinson on television. He did not even see fit to send the Bishop of Southwark advance warning of what he planned to say, and in protest, Stockwood absented himself from the meeting. "I was very cross with him and hurt when he never consulted me", Bishop Stockwood has recalled. "Apart from anything else, common courtesy demanded that he spoke to me before publicly rebuking one of my suffragans."[11]

On his own eightieth birthday party in 1984, Michael Ramsey said to Mervyn Stockwood, "I made two major mistakes in my primacy. One was the way I reacted to John Robinson."[12] But what is undeniably reprehensible, looking back on events, is that Ramsey had ample time and opportunity in which to collect his thoughts and wits, to take advice, to weigh up the most constructive, creative and helpful method of encouraging those whose faith was said to have been shaken, and of helping to reconcile conservatives and liberals, radicals and reactionaries. This is the task of an archbishop. The worst thing he could have done was undermine the spiritual and teaching authority of a fellow bishop by failing to support him in public, no matter what he might have felt it necessary to say to him in private. To fail to support a colleague in public is always perceived as a means of pandering to popular prejudice. But Ramsey never had the courage to discuss *Honest to God* and the consequences of its publication with the author face to face, and Canon Max Warren of Westminster Abbey even had to act as a go-between between Ramsey and Stockwood.

When he came to address the Convocation, Michael Ramsey acknowledged that the questions discussed in *Honest to God* were real questions, but he went out of his way to criticize "the method chosen by the Bishop for presenting his ideas to the public", specifically the

Observer article, which he believed had done much damage and caused "public sensation". More seriously, he said the book appeared to reject the concept of a personal God as expressed in the Bible and the Creed, so John Robinson felt obliged to issue a statement saying, "some of His Grace's statements appear to me to misrepresent what I believe". And so the row inevitably rumbled on. There was, however, a personal reconciliation on 21st May when Mervyn Stockwood invited both Michael Ramsey and John Robinson to a party to celebrate his fiftieth birthday. Sitting in a corner was a veteran of public rows who had never allowed them to disturb his sleep, Earl Attlee. "Never read the book" was his typically crisp comment on the controversy.*

John Robinson came to be regarded by those who knew him as a man of outstanding moral courage, utter sincerity, without rancour of any kind, possessed of simplicity in the true sense (he was exceedingly naïve and in his own way nearly as eccentric as Michael Ramsey; his nervous laugh and contagious shyness could be quite unnerving) and, as an original thinker and "explorer" theologian, in the front rank. But the rumpus caused by *Honest to God* so unsettled the Establishment that after the age of thirty-nine he was never offered another job by the Church. There are those who believe that this was a scandal, but what jobs had the Church to offer him? A deanery perhaps. As a diocesan bishop he might have been out of his element, but Bristol is the diocese he is believed to have had his eye on. On 1st January 1969 Michael Ramsey

---

* Attlee was sometimes a welcome guest at Lambeth Palace. He was there in 1967, at the age of eighty-four, and a few days later at luncheon the Archbishop mentioned the fact. "Yes," said Ramsey, hunched over the table, hacking away at a pair of recalcitrant lamb cutlets, aged sixty-two and looking like Methuselah, "he's become a poor, decrepit old thing, a poor, decrepit old thing."

wrote a letter recommending John Robinson as Dean of
Trinity College, Cambridge.

"I have no doubt that your Committee will feel that Dr
Robinson is a somewhat controversial figure", he told Dr
Keith Moffatt, a Fellow of the College. "Having seen a
good deal of him and watched his development, I believe
that he could do very well in the post of Dean of Chapel
at Trinity if the opportunity came to him. He is an
adventurous thinker and went through a phase of being
somewhat confusing in his efforts to grapple with the
difficulties of the people right outside the Christian fold. I
believe that he has been increasingly finding a grasp of
things which is far more positive than negative and that
this would be very apparent in his influence on the young
men." Robinson became Dean of Trinity, and no doubt
Ramsey relaxed, for once again he had succeeded in one of
the tasks he most enjoyed, "fixing Cambridge", and an
"adventurous thinker" had been safely removed from the
mainstream of Church life.[13] Although Michael Ramsey
told Eric James he had thought it best "if after a few years
at Trinity, JR should go and be a Diocesan Bishop",[14]
there is no evidence that Ramsey ever lifted a finger to put
that hope into practice, and Robinson remained at Trinity
until in 1983 he developed inoperable cancer, from which
he died six months to the day after being told by his
surgeon that he had six months to live. Those six months
were heroic, and in his dying John Robinson provided a
spiritual inspiration to match the prolific creativity of his
life.

The publication of *Honest to God*, with its staggering
sales, was not an isolated event. It exploded into a world
already alive with hope and expectation. There was, among
academics, theologians and radical clergy and laity, a real
feeling that the Church was on the verge of a renewal of
energy and enthusiasm. Religious publishing, of both

books and magazines, was thriving. The Church of England had a theologian at its helm, and its roll call of intellectual excellence has only the palest counterpart today. In the opinion of Don Cupitt, *Honest to God* "represented a major upheaval in the Church by struggling to make religion more contemporary, so that you didn't have to be a time traveller to be a Christian. So I think the hopes and aspirations of that period, 1963 to 1965, were much the most important thing that happened in Michael Ramsey's life time, and the failure and disappointment of those hopes the most important event in modern Church history.

"To discover why they failed you have to look both at the Roman Catholic Church since Vatican II, which was happening at the same time, and at the Anglican Church since. One factor in England was that John Robinson's position was difficult to understand because it rested on a personalized philosophy, which not many reviewers could make sense of, and I suspect that ordinary people, on gathering that the experts didn't know what to make of Robinson, became confused. Also, establishments always close ranks. People don't get made bishop if they are likely to be converted by a new idea. In dealing with all this, I think Michael Ramsey did rather well by the standards normally applied.

"But hopes were so high for a short period, and it all came to nothing, and we need to understand why. It has been suggested that the new theology of that period was too shallow. The religious humanism expressed in John Robinson's work was too thin and middle-class, too much like the humanism of the caring professions, without enough cutting edge in politics and social ethics, while on the philosophical side the enormous changes taking place in European thought had not yet reached Britain. We were very provincial back in the sixties.

"The excitement between 1963 and 1965 didn't have sufficiently strong intellectual roots. Support from the establishment would have helped, but the establishment wasn't persuaded that a modernization of faith was needed. The crucial thing was that in Michael Ramsey's preaching, traditional biblical imagery and language was simply reaffirmed. He did not see it as essential in preaching to bridge the gap between the biblical world and the modern world. That's to say, he saw exposition as the main task of the theologian. He did not think reinterpretation essential. He didn't acknowledge that historical and cultural change called for drastic reinterpretation.

"Ramsey was a subjective symbolist. That's to say, when pressed he would admit that religious language was symbolic but he would claim that the symbols referred to something. However, since it can't be said *what* the symbols refer to, I would claim that that view is empty. I think objective symbolism is an untenable position. But it's probably the majority view in the Church.

"I was impressed by many of Ramsey's stands on social issues; in social ethics he was ahead of his time. But in theology he was very much of his generation. Theology is creative religious thought, and it is no longer enough to defend the given faith. The interpreter is also a creative artist, and the theologian must be an inventor, which Ramsey wasn't."[15]

Those are the views of a relatively young and very radical theologian who nevertheless invited Michael Ramsey to preach for him. Yet a number of Cupitt's points were likewise made, in 1974, by an older theologian of a far more traditional complexion, John Macquarrie, when he wrote: "I have elsewhere dubbed the sixties 'the decade of the dilettantes' as far as theology is concerned. It was an age of rapidly changing fashions, represented by such popular catch phrases as 'death of God', 'religionless

Christianity', 'secular man' and so on. Unfortunately, although all of these phrases do conceal in themselves genuine and highly complex issues, the mood was such that they were rarely treated in any depth. Already some new fashion had arrived and the old problem was discarded."[16] As far as the theological crisis of Michael Ramsey's time was concerned, criticism of his handling of it is in fact fairly evenly distributed across the theological spectrum and the years. Harry Williams, a generation older than Cupitt, says, "He dealt with it very badly. *Honest to God* was not a scandalous book at all, it was a ragbag of various theologies, a resumé of personalities and views. John Robinson was quite conservative in many ways and *Honest to God* was not an original book. Michael Ramsey ought to have seen it coming and seen it more clearly. He had deep spirituality but he was not a great scholar."[17]

Looking back to a time when he was himself training a new generation of clergy, including Don Cupitt, Dr Robert Runcie says, "Michael Ramsey was out of sympathy with the unhistorical approach of theologians in the sixties, and he would number John Robinson among them. He was out of sympathy with the lack of poetry in the soul of people like Robinson, and with their cavalier treatment of history. There are historical characteristics of the Christian religion you just can't dismiss."[18] Of course, had Michael Ramsey remained at Cambridge as Regius Professor he might have reacted very differently. The publication of *Honest to God* was his first real test of leadership, and in trying to come to the rescue of orthodoxy he erred on the cautious side. Perhaps that was what an archbishop ought to do, and if he was correct in his approach then perhaps it is pointless to expect archbishops to be leaders in any conventional sense. What it really boiled down to was Ramsey's fear of any publicity that tended to give the impression that things were not under control, that the faith was under attack, not from secular forces – that was to be expected – but from a bishop. Despite his Noncon-formist background, of which he was so proud, he held the episcopate in deep esteem, and as far as he was concerned, anyone might lay their head on a block if they wished, except a bishop. So now that he was archbishop of Canterbury he felt it quite impossible to side publicly with a bishop who had broken all the common room rules by thinking out loud instead of waiting until his thoughts were totally arranged before publishing them in a book. The whole episode tells us something about Michael Ramsey but also something about the role of the arch-bishop of Canterbury. It is not too fanciful to imagine that "Professor Michael Ramsey" might well have leapt to John Robinson's defence.

It is extremely easy for those on the radical frontiers of any organization to overestimate their strength and the degree of support they can rely on when it comes to the crunch. Just a year after the publication of *Honest to God*, in April 1964 in fact, Eric James, at that time vicar of St George's, Camberwell, rather bravely resigned his living to stump the country in the cause of the renewal and reform of the Church. Looking back, in a sermon he preached at Gray's Inn Chapel on 17th April 1988, Canon James said, "Alas, as I went from place to place what became immediately obvious to me was how few commit-ted and convinced supporters there were for such a renewal movement ... Meetings which I had expected to be meetings of supporters turned out often to be gatherings in which forces of the opposition, Catholic and Protestant, were strong. But they were not the only opposition. Unthinking conservative ecclesiastics, of no fixed abode of churchmanship except the C of E, especially in the more rural areas, were no less strongly represented.

"In fact," he went on to say, "those years turned out to be some of the most painful of my ministry. It was all too clear that my friends and I were simply part of an enthusiastic, if voluble, minority."

Whether a Scheme to reunite the Church of England and the Methodist Church actually came under the heading of renewal or reform is a matter of opinion, but during this period it certainly became a contentious issue, over which attitudes polarized, and often in a very strange way. This was not simply a matter of Anglicans being asked to be nice to Christians of another denomination; they were actually being invited to take positive steps to merge with another Church, and it was widely believed that if they could not bring themselves to merge with the Methodists, whose founder had been an Anglican priest and for whom episcopacy was no great stumbling block (Methodists in America and elsewhere actually have bishops as adminis-trative officers, although they are not consecrated to a specific order of ministry), there was little future for any attempts at organic union elsewhere. But the Scheme was beset with opposition, and just as *Honest to God* had put to the test specifically Michael Ramsey's leadership in the theological field, so the Scheme for Anglican-Methodist Reunion was to prove a crucial test of his leadership in the ecumenical sphere – although, like *Honest to God*, the Scheme also contained matters of profound theological concern, as do most issues of an ecumenical nature.

What the Scheme embodied was a two-stage plan to unite the Churches, first through intercommunion and an exchange of ordained ministries and finally through a total "organic" merger. And at the heart of the Scheme, drawn up by leading theologians from both Churches, lay a proposed Service of Reconciliation, during which it was intended that Anglican and Methodist ministers would accept one another's ministries, the Service being worded in such a way as to offer a "studied ambiguity". But what was at issue was the validity of orders, and staunch Anglo-Catholics like Cyril Easthaugh, bishop of Peterborough, thought that "catholic order" was in jeopardy. Were Methodist ministers already validly ordained or did they need to be ordained by Anglican bishops in order that they might unequivocally be regarded as ordained in the direct Apostolic succession? Was what would occur during the service "ordination", or was it not? Michael Ramsey said only God knew what each Church's ministry needed, God would supply that need and a healthy ambiguity on the issue was theologically justified. As a theologian, he took the pragmatic view that theology was not always a matter of certifiable knowledge but of perceiving and reacting to the will and movement of the Holy Spirit, and he had long since rejected extreme fundamentalist views in theological matters. Most of his fellow bishops, a large majority of whom were always in favour of the Scheme, were also "central" in their attitudes.* Until the introduction of synodical government the laity, although consulted through the diocesan conferences, had no ultimate say, and the bulk of opposition to the Scheme within the Church of England came from a seemingly unlikely coalition of high and low church clergy, the high church party saying the Service of Reconciliation was not ordination and ought to be, the low church party saying it was ordination (and a slur on the Methodists) and ought not to be. Never mind that the Methodist Church was overwhelmingly in favour of the Scheme, including the Service of Reconciliation, those in the Church of England who

---

* Cyril Easthaugh of Peterborough, John Moorman of Ripon and Ronald Williams of Leicester were notable opponents of the Scheme in the House of Bishops. The present bishop of London, Graham Leonard, as suffragan bishop of Willesden, had been perhaps the strongest episcopal opponent of all.

opposed the Scheme were determined to have their own way.

Although Lord Fisher had been largely instrumental in initiating dialogue between Anglicans and Methodists, it was he, from his retirement home at Trent in Dorset, who fired some of the earliest and – because of his prestigious position as a former primate – noisiest broadsides. Indeed, as a former archbishop he behaved very badly indeed. There was an intellectually arrogant aspect to his mind that never permitted him to sit down and shut up, and retirement imposed unbearable restraints on his nimble brain. Over Anglican-Methodist Reunion he was diametrically opposed to his successor, and did not trust him to give the Church the right advice. Instead of exercising his gifts by settling down to some serious academic work (he never wrote a single book), he continued in public to let off verbal fireworks, and in private to dispatch reams of letters to all and sundry when, as they frequently did, they incurred his displeasure.*

"The Trent postmark; now, the Trent postmark always filled me with a feeling of doom", Michael Ramsey used to lament at Lambeth Palace. "It always filled me with a feeling of doom." But he claimed that the Baron's letters "went into the wastepaper basket. They simply went into the wastepaper basket. She tried to stop him posting them", he would add, referring to Lady Fisher's pretended efforts on behalf of good relations between Lambeth and Trent. "Yes, she tried to stop him. She used to run after him down the street, but all to no avail!"

Michael Ramsey had always believed John Wesley to

---

* In an interview he gave to the author for *Church Illustrated*, April 1966, Lord Fisher said he thought the ecumenical movement had been carried away with the idea that "unity" must be a constitutional union. In the same interview he said, "I'm always itching to write to *The Times*. I only write when I can't refrain any longer."

have been a great Christian, and when speaking to a gathering of Methodists in Darlington in 1953, when he was bishop of Durham, he referred to Wesley's "passion for holiness". It had always been his good fortune, he said, "to have Methodist friends to whom my debt is great, chiefly scholars, whose books and persons have meant much to me." He regarded his presence among Methodists on this occasion as a symbol "of that unity which we hope to have when the shame of denominationalism has been conquered." At the York Convocation he had previously made his own theological position about Methodism crystal clear when he said, "all who are baptized in the name of the Blessed Trinity and worship the Lord Jesus are fellow members with us in the Catholic Church which is the Body of Christ. Methodists and Congregationalists lie within the Catholic Church." No wonder that if this was what he believed he was opposed to any overt form of ordination for Methodist ministers merging into a united Anglican-Methodist Church. He went on in 1953 to say, "My own longing is this: the Methodists in England as a society, with traditions and methods of their own and with their own ample use of lay evangelists and yet linked with the Church of England through Bishops. Would John Wesley have said 'No' to this?"

The Scheme for Reunion was a plan in which Michael Ramsey came to believe quite passionately, but he almost certainly failed to make clear his position, and his reasons for it, until too late. "One can never be certain," the Bishop of Durham has said, "but if he had given a firm lead earlier it might have gone differently. Like William Temple, he may have been too optimistic, not fully appreciative of how difficult it is for some people to see things which seem obvious to others. Because he was not essentially a partisan person he could sympathize with all sorts of people."[19]

The present Archbishop of Canterbury makes an even more telling point to explain Ramsey's chosen course of action. "If you are a theologian and a scholar you are bound to see more than one side of a question, and that doesn't make you into the kind of dynamic leader that some people want. It was the same with Archbishop Cranmer. My impression was that he made his position clear at the right moment. If he had made his views better known earlier it might have been counterproductive on such an evenly balanced issue."[20]

The Duke of Richmond & Gordon says, "He might have given a lead earlier than he did, but he was probably afraid of dividing the Church, which of course was divided anyway. I thought he did give a strong lead but it might have been too late."[21] One of Ramsey's suffragans, Bishop John Hughes, agrees. "I rather think it would be true to say he didn't make his approval of Anglican-Methodist Reunion clear enough soon enough. He was too ready to be completely open and to let everyone have their say before coming down in favour."[22]

Michael Ramsey thought that in theological matters he could lead from his study. But this was a theological issue on which the diocesan conferences were going to be invited to vote, in a sort of advisory capacity, before the fate of the Scheme was decided in the Convocations, and if he believed, as he almost certainly did, that this was the most important ecclesiastical issue of his time (for if it failed there could be little hope for schemes of organic union between Churches with far less in common than the Anglicans and the Methodists) he could at least have asked permission to address the diocesan conferences of those half dozen bishops opposed to the Scheme. As it was, he made two brilliantly reasoned speeches in favour of the Scheme to two Convocations who had already made up their minds. When the Anglican vote went against the

Scheme in the Convocations on 8th July 1969 there was an unseemly burst of applause from the public gallery, instantly silenced by an outraged Bishop of Leicester, who had just voted against the Scheme. Ramsey went out of his way, behind the scenes, to put his arm round the Bishop of Ely to console him, but very shortly came to see the decision as a personal affront, as a rejection by the Church of his powers of persuasion in, of all things, a matter of theology, and for several weeks he moped around Lambeth Palace in a state of paranoid depression. He even contemplated retiring. One day Mrs Ramsey, almost in despair, said, "Just look at him slumped on the settee. What *are* we going to do? This simply can't go on."

But like many depressives, Michael Ramsey possessed remarkably quick powers of recovery, and one day he suddenly burst out of his study on to the landing and said, "I'm on the up! I'm on the up!" He had a way of rationalizing disasters because he could not bear to be on the losing side, and he had decided to comfort himself with the belief that all was for the best in the worst of all possible worlds, that good would eventually come out of evil, and that the way forward should be through greater co-operation at local level. But this was a policy that evidently he felt he could not go along with indefinitely, and forgetting, perhaps, the indignity that befell the Church in 1928 when it brought Prayer Book revision back to parliament a second time, he agreed, after the introduction of synodical government in November 1970, to the Scheme being debated and voted on a second time.*

---

* Had the Archbishop not wanted the Scheme reintroduced it is inconceivable that the Standing Committee of the General Synod would have placed it on the agenda. Under synodical government, the laity were to have an equal say with the clergy in matters of doctrine, and Michael Ramsey may have been relying on decisive support from the House of Laity, even though the Scheme needed to be carried in all three Houses individually as well as in the Synod overall.

The Duke of Richmond (at this time still Lord March), who was chairman of what was called the New Synod Group, a loosely knit body of radical church men and women not aligned to any Church party, felt it right to inform the Archbishop of the results of a survey carried out by his Group into possible voting intentions. They were not very encouraging. "He was unclear when I came into the room why I had come to see him, and I said I had come to tell him what the New Synod Group thought would be the result of the vote on the Anglican-Methodist Scheme. And he said, 'I must find a piece of paper'. He did several circuits of his desk and came up with a quarter of an envelope. He sat down and said, 'Now tell me'. And then he said, 'I must find a pen'. And he did a few more circuits."[23]

Although Lord March – and probably others – warned Ramsey that the Scheme would almost certainly be lost, he could hardly back off once it was on the agenda, but at least he could have been under few remaining illusions. He began his speech to the General Synod on 3rd May 1972 by saying, "I am told that if this resolution passes with sufficient authority it will be a miracle. I pray for this miracle." His prayer was not answered, even though on any impartial reckoning he made the most accomplished speech of the day, was listened to with the closest attention and respect, and received the loudest and longest applause. Perhaps with a classic sense of British fair play they were applauding someone they already recognized as a popular and plucky loser. He pitched his speech deliberately, and wisely, in a low key, and it was full of humour. He ended by warning it was a mistake to think that if the Scheme was rejected "something else will be cooked up". On the contrary, the outcome would be unpredictable, and a vacuum would exist "in the divine theological sense". It had been decided that a two-thirds majority in each House would be required for acceptance, and a seventy-five per cent majority overall. Rather than risk a dive into uncharted theological waters, the Synod, largely middle-aged and middle-class, voted not against Methodism so much as in favour of retaining the status quo, and one young member who had the courage to make a speech after changing his mind had to endure the insult of being called a turncoat. The House of Bishops voted thirty-four for, six against; the House of Clergy 152 for, 80 against; the House of Laity 117 for, 87 against. Only the bishops had voted in favour of the Scheme: eighty-five per cent. The clergy voted 65.52, the laity 62.82, and the overall figure for the Synod was 65.81. It was not even a near miss, and at the conclusion of a four-hour debate and fifteen years of preliminary discussion the Scheme was dead.*

At a rather dull and pointless press conference held by the Archbishop afterwards, he simply said he was sad, and he certainly looked it. No suggestion had ever been made that he might resign if the vote was lost (his previous threats had been made entirely privately and no whisper had ever got out), but so sad and tired was he now that he even fell into the trap of denying a non-existent rumour. He seemed drained of all his usual humour, and said he felt that life had ceased to have surprises for him in any direction; it was one long series of mysteries. He still believed it was the will of Christ that there should be one Church in England, and the best approach might now be through local efforts rather than schemes.

One of the journalists present, Philip Crowe, has commented: "To bring the Scheme back a second time was a

* In 1972 only about sixty-eight per cent of the lay and clerical members of the diocesan synods had expressed approval of the Scheme, another indication that it would fail to find approval in the General Synod.

grave mistake. Even worse, there were no contingency plans for what to do if it did fail. Personally I thought the Scheme was a piece of ecclesiastical joinery and dodged the theological issues, and I was always against it, but I don't think Ramsey's leadership, from his own point of view, was very good. He never campaigned or made persuasive speeches other than in the Convocations or the Synod."[24]

Speaking in Cambridge almost six months later, at the federation of three theological colleges, Michael Ramsey bluntly referred to the decision of the Synod taken on 3rd May as a blunder. "If", he said, "old friends in Cambridge ask what I think of this I might be tempted to reply in the words of Aeneas to Dido: *infandum, regina, iubes renovare dolorem.** Yet there is a strange postscript to all this. In 1974 a dinner was held in New College, Oxford to honour Ramsey on his impending retirement, during the course of which Professor Macquarrie confessed that he had not felt able to support the Scheme for Anglican-Methodist Reunion. Apparently Ramsey turned to Macquarrie and said, "very decisively, 'Oh, that was a bad scheme!'"[25] Perhaps he had eventually recalled his own words when speaking to the World Council of Churches in New Delhi in 1961. "Patience includes the will to see that an apparent set-back in some scheme may be our call to go into things more deeply than before. Patience includes, above all, the will to expect that God's blessing upon our own cherished plans may not in his wisdom be separated from his disciplining us in holiness and in truth."

It was also at the dinner at New College that Ramsey delivered one of his most brilliantly witty after-dinner speeches. He said he had recently dreamed that he was in heaven, attending a sherry party given for former archbishops of Canterbury. One by one they came up to speak to

* This, dear Queen, brings back your ancient sorrows.

him, and as Ramsey mentioned his predecessors by name – not all ninety-nine but a fair number – he amused the guests by inventing some apposite conversation he was supposed to have enjoyed. Cranmer, for example, said to Michael, "Ramsey, I don't think much of Series 3."

"Eventually," Michael continued, "I saw a little man whom I immediately recognized as Anselm. When we met we embraced one another because here, I felt, was a man who was primarily a don, who tried to say his prayers, and who cared nothing for the pomp and glory of his position." It was perfectly apparent that Ramsey was drafting his own obituary. Suddenly he punctured the solemnity he had wrought by summoning up his *tour de force*. "And just as Anselm and I seemed to be getting on so well together, who should come up to us but the Baron. 'Now then, boys,' said Fisher, 'time to get back to work!'"

CHAPTER EIGHT

THE ARCHBISHOP AT HOME

The more the Church knows, the more it is aware of the great
unknown that lies ahead.

A speech at the 1968 Lambeth Conference.

As archbishop of Canterbury, Michael Ramsey had two
official homes, Lambeth Palace on the south bank of the
Thames, almost opposite the Houses of Parliament, from
where, during the week, he discharged his responsibilities
to the Church at large and to the State, and the Old Palace
in Canterbury, close by the cathedral where in 1170
Thomas à Becket was murdered. Here he generally spent
the weekends, engaged in the normal duties of a diocesan
bishop. The Old Palace is a rambling, stone-flagged,
homely house, whereas Lambeth Palace, although of
intrinsic historical interest, has been heavily restored and
cannot be held to be one of the most beautiful buildings in
the world. But when Joan Ramsey was chatelaine both
homes radiated hospitality and a kind of modest, middle-
class comfort. Spring flowers, potpourri, sherry before
lunch, drinks in the bedrooms for guests, a workaday
muddle of books and papers strewn around the Archbishop's study, above all a lack of pomposity were the immediate if superficial impressions gained. The first thing

Michael Ramsey did on becoming archbishop of Canterbury was to discard his gaiters and apron. He travelled in a suit but at home he always wore his purple cassock. The only time he ever struggled into gaiters was when he had to dress for a state banquet or evening reception at Buckingham Palace.

Although in public the Archbishop's chaplains and press officer addressed him as "Your Grace", at home they called him "Father". Depending on their own preference, visitors addressed him as "Archbishop" or "Your Grace", and those who felt inclined, including, on one occasion, a Roman Catholic journalist, genuflected and kissed his ring. He generally received visitors who had come to Lambeth on business in his study, off a landing reached after climbing a wide sweep of stairs from the front door,* but before luncheon he and Mrs Ramsey would dispense sherry and conversation in the drawing room next door, and on informal occasions they lunched in a small dining room on the left hand side of the corridor.† Also on the first floor is the chapel, and at the far end the Guard Room, hung with some notable Tudor portraits, where large, formal luncheons were held. Michael Ramsey's taste in food and drink was essentially unsophisticated: soup or melon, lamb cutlets or a beef stew, and cheese (he detested sweet puddings) constituted his ideal meal, and if guests were present, white wine was usually served. But although he did not greatly care for red wine himself (he said it gave him a headache), when he had journalists to lunch they were usually treated to claret. "You can't do these things absolutely sober", he said, surveying with approval the arrangements for the first press lunch he gave in 1967,

* Michael Ramsey had declined to make use of Archbishop Fisher's study, at the east end of the house, which was turned into a conference room.
† This now serves as an additional sitting room.

which included several bottles of wine on the sideboard. After a special dinner at night Michael might have a glass or two of port, but he never drank spirits or liqueurs. When alone, the Ramseys dined at seven, and after one cup of coffee the Archbishop would scamper back to the study, to work.

The archbishop of Canterbury, like the Sovereign, has a household in addition to a staff. The staff consisted of cleaners, typists, a housekeeper (Joan Ramsey was not in the normal sense domesticated and did no cooking), and, as with all bishops, a chauffeur and a gardener. For the first seven or eight years the household consisted of two chaplains, two clergy who ran the Council for Foreign Relations, a Secretary, a Registrar, and a press officer. From Fisher, Michael inherited his Secretary, Mr Robert Beloe, formerly an education officer, and Colonel Robert Hornby, who before arriving at Church House to create the Church Information Office more or less from scratch had been director of public relations for the Far East Land Forces. Hornby left in 1965 and was succeeded as chief information officer by Major General Adam Block, who relinquished responsibility for the Archbishop's public relations in 1967, the year that Ramsey appointed a journalist as his press officer. When Robert Beloe – who handled matters concerning Buckingham Palace, the House of Lords and Government Departments like the Home Office – retired in 1969 he was succeeded, as "lay assistant", by a former civil servant, Mr Hugh Whitworth.

Ramsey's Registrar, Mr David Carey, brother of Kenneth Carey, who became bishop of Edinburgh, advised him on legal matters, and was said to exercise more influence than the Archbishop over the appointment of bishops. He worked in Dean's Yard, next door to Westminster Abbey. The Council for Foreign Relations, with offices in the grounds of Lambeth Palace, advised the

Archbishop on relations with overseas governments and Churches outside the Anglican Communion. For example, it organized visits from or to leaders of the Roman Catholic and Orthodox Churches, those from the Orthodox Church often being conducted in an amazing spirit of cloak and dagger secrecy. The general secretary of the Council from 1959 to 1970 was the Reverend John Satterthwaite, now Bishop of Gibraltar in Europe.

It is usual for an archbishop to have a senior chaplain, a man of reasonable age, experience and gravitas who can act as a trusted liaison between the archbishop and other senior clergy, especially the bishops, as well as a domestic chaplain, a kind of youthful *aide-de-camp*, who lives more intimately with the family, deals with routine correspondence concerning the diocese, has breakfast and lunch with the archbishop, travels with him, meets visitors and generally takes care of domestic arrangements. Michael Ramsey brought with him from York a young domestic chaplain, John Andrew, whom he had ordained. Although never formally appointed senior chaplain (he was known as the senior domestic chaplain), for eight years he served in many ways as the most influential member of Ramsey's household, for he enjoyed the total confidence and affection of the Ramseys and allowed himself to become something of a buffer rather than a stepping-stone between Ramsey and the bishops. This the bishops came to resent, as well as his somewhat extravagant life-style, which was strangely at variance with the simple life led by the Ramseys. It was generally felt that John Andrew was too young and inexperienced to act in such a senior capacity (a senior chaplain to an archbishop is more usually someone virtually in training himself for the episcopate), and the lack of a senior chaplain for much of Ramsey's time at Canterbury was believed by many to be the major cause of much indifferent administration and lack of communication.

"We always wondered who John Andrew was", the former bishop of Croydon recalls. "Once when I tried to make personal contact with Michael Ramsey, John simply said, 'You must remember, the Archbishop always discusses things very thoroughly with *me*.'"[1]

"John Andrew's influence was one that was not appreciated by most of the bishops", says the former bishop of Southwark. "They thought he had much too much influence, and that Michael left far too much in his hands. One reason the bishops kept away from Lambeth was because they were not going to be palmed off on to John. That was a very serious defect, a very serious weakness of the Ramsey regime."[2]

Eventually so much dissatisfaction was expressed that steps were taken to appoint a senior chaplain both in name and function. The man chosen by David Carey for this unenviable role was the Reverend Geoffrey Tiarks, who was duly consecrated and appointed suffragan bishop of Maidstone. He thus had equal rank with those he had to deal with, but it did him little good, for while Tiarks got on all right with the other bishops, he was virtually ignored by Michael Ramsey. The last thing Michael wanted was another bishop in the house, breathing advice down his neck and generally posing what Ramsey saw as a threat to his own sometimes rather haphazard methods of conducting business. In any event, they had little in common, and the choice of Tiarks, even if the idea of appointing a bishop as senior chaplain had been a sensible one in itself, was less than inspired. Tiarks was soon expressing distress because the Archbishop never consulted him, and on one painful occasion he was half-way through a rather long joke in the drawing room when Ramsey simply turned round and walked away.

Tiarks complained that the press were "like a pack of ravening wolves seeking whom they might devour", though they were certainly not in pursuit of the Archbishop, whose relations with the press had never been better, and who, unlike most bishops, enjoyed the company of journalists, often inviting them to lunch. Ramsey was an avid reader of newspapers, and any morning following some major event in which he had taken part he would be found enfolded in pages of newsprint, often chuckling over cartoons or editorial comments. He greatly admired such writers as Ivan Yates of the *Observer* and Geoffrey Moorhouse of the *Guardian*, whom he honoured by reviewing his book about monastic life, *Beyond All Reason*, for the *Spectator* when Nigel Lawson, later a Tory Chancellor of the Exchequer, was editor. Another future cabinet minister Ramsey first met as a journalist, at lunch at Lambeth Palace, was Norman Fowler, when he was home affairs correspondent for *The Times*. He had great sympathy with journalists. He seldom accepted private invitations to lunch or to dine out, but he did not hesitate to go to lunch with the staff of the *Observer* when they invited him. When a journalist still on trial on a newspaper made a serious blunder concerning the Archbishop, he waived the chance of a correction, because the journalist seemed in fear of losing his job, and entirely on his own initiative wrote the young man a letter in his own hand telling him not to worry.*

* He seems however to have been more at ease with secular journalists than religious. The editor of the *Church Times*, Dr Bernard Palmer, wrote to the author on 31 January 1989: "Although his reign coincided with my first few years as Editor here I don't recall that we had a great deal of contact – certainly far less than has been the case with either of his successors. The only occasion when I had any prolonged conversation with him was at our centenary dinner in 1963, when he was the guest of honour. My chief memory of that occasion was how difficult it was to make small talk with him!"

If a reporter was patently professional, like Douglas Brown of the BBC, Ramsey respected his judgement and never tried to impose conditions about interviews, and his standing among journalists, many of whom seem today to be looking back to Ramsey's time as to a golden age, was high. "He was very powerful", in the opinion of Philip Crowe, an evangelical clergyman far from biased in Ramsey's favour, who covered many of his most important appearances for a religious weekly. "He didn't speak all that often, and only when he had something significant to say. So that every time he spoke it was significant, and it made an impact."[3] Ramsey had some quixotic favourites among television personalities. He thought Jimmy Savile was particularly good value, and thoroughly enjoyed appearing on television in New York with David Frost. They were once in full flood when it was time for a break for the advertisements, and Frost said, "We must take a break here. Stay with us. We'll be back in two minutes." Ramsey had no idea how commercial television was run, and convulsed the studio audience by saying, "Why have a break? Why have a break? It's going rather well!"

"It is important from a public relations point of view that Lambeth should be seen to be a competent place", in the opinion of a former bishop of Lincoln.[4] But Michael Ramsey was congenitally incapable of organizing himself, let alone his staff, on rational administrative lines. The idea of a weekly staff meeting at Lambeth Palace attended by members of his household would have been anathema to him, and communication between the various departments was conducted on an *ad hoc* basis. Inevitably, in the heat of the moment some crucial decision would fail to be shared. The way in which Ramsey dealt with correspondence was totally haphazard. At breakfast a porter would appear with neatly arranged piles of letters in a basket. Mrs Ramsey would be given hers, the domestic chaplain his, and then the Archbishop would descend on his own post like a schoolboy attacking a pile of doughnuts, ripping some letters open, stuffing others into his cassock if the envelope looked threatening, reading some out loud, spreading marmalade across the contents of others. Then suddenly he would scoop them all up (all save those that had dropped on to the floor) and disappear to his study. Some letters (like those adorned with the Trent postmark) would go into the wastepaper basket; others he would reply to in his own hand. Some would receive dictated replies later in the day; those he found too difficult to deal with were surreptitiously "lost".

This sense of doom or threat that seemed to hover over him, induced by some unwished for interview or by boring correspondence, was a very marked aspect of Michael Ramsey's complex personality. Overseas he once seriously believed that a man was chasing him through a church, and he had clearly been very frightened. At Lambeth Palace he became obsessed by Mr Robert Maxwell and his business affairs. This was at the time of the Leasco takeover of Pergamon Press. A photographer was due from an agency, and after the photographic session Michael became extremely agitated, called his press officer back and asked, "Were those Maxwell's men?"

His physical health, on the other hand, seldom let him down. He loved swimming, went for long walks on holiday, and even on the rare occasions when he was ill refused to succumb. He left for a month-long tour of the West Indies suffering from a severe virus attack, but sailed through services in the open air comforted by nothing more than cough sweets. In 1969 he had to send a letter to the Prince of Wales, whose birthday he shared, to explain that he would not be able to attend his twenty-first birthday party at Buckingham Palace because of a bad cold, but generally his physical stamina was remarkable.

As Ramsey was getting out of a car outside the bishop of Trinidad's house the driver carelessly started up the car again, the car moved off as the Archbishop was still getting out, and his leg was badly grazed. Obviously he was in pain, and Mrs Ramsey was all for cancelling a dinner engagement that evening. But after his leg had been bathed and he had been fortified with a drink, Michael suddenly leapt up the stairs two steps at a time to prove that he was well enough to go out.

He was in fact alarmingly accident prone. While staying with the bishop of Puerto Rico he announced before breakfast that he was going to inspect the view, and walked smack into a pane of glass dividing the sitting room from the verandah. That evening, just before a supper party, he repeated his desire to inspect the view, got up and walked smack into the same pane of glass. On departing the next morning for the airport, he said goodbye to all the staff and relations – "Well, goodbye, goodbye", hand outstretched, down they went, to genuflect and kiss his ring, "goodbye, goodbye" – and stepping backwards over a ledge not more than three inches high he toppled on to a concrete path, folding up like a porcupine.

Not all his "accidents" ended in physical injury. He once stopped off at what he thought was a book shop in Bond Street, with time to kill on his way to see the Queen, only to discover after several embarrassing minutes that he had burst into a dress shop for outsize ladies.

There was inevitably a routine annual round of entertaining at Lambeth, dinners for the Lord Mayor, lunches for the Estates Commissioners, Nonconformist Church leaders to be received along with cardinals and patriarchs, and always a dinner party for the family of newly appointed bishops on the eve of their consecration. Michael took these duties seriously but not too seriously.

"Tomorrow I'm going to consecrate two suffragan bishops", he one day remarked. "I've never seen them before
and I shall probably never see them again!" One of these
occasions, in 1973, took a decidedly surrealistic turn.
Hewlett Thompson was due to become suffragan bishop
of Willesden (in 1985 he became bishop of Exeter), and
John Easthaugh was to be made bishop of Hereford. "The
night before the consecration we had the usual dinner
party", Michael Ramsey recalled. "Very nice, very nice.
And after dinner Hewlett Thompson pulled out of his
pocket a piece of music and played and sang *Come into
the Garden Maud*. Well, we were a good deal surprised,
we were very surprised indeed. Very, very surprised. But
apparently what had happened was this. A few days before
the party Hewlett Thompson had telephoned John Easthaugh to ask what would be expected of them, and John
Easthaugh had said, 'Oh, you'll be expected to take your
music and to sing after dinner.'" Not for nothing does
John Easthaugh, who had played this wicked but very
funny joke on Thompson, list his interests in *Who's Who*
as music and the theatre.

Some members of Michael's family had attended his
enthronement at York, but they saw very little of him at
Lambeth. He married his nephew Michael Barcroft at
Aldborough, inviting him and his finacée to choose the
cope he was to wear, and his sister Bridget Barcroft
remembers "We once went to a very grand lunch at
Lambeth and I sat next to some mayor of a London
borough. Also I went to tea there once or twice informally,
but not in a sort of friendly way. I wasn't close to Michael
at all."[5] It was to Joan Ramsey that Michael was close. In
the back of the official Daimler they would sit holding
hands. She more or less made sure that he was properly
dressed, although on one occasion in Newcastle he very
nearly appeared on television with a cleaner's tag attached

to his suit. Except on occasions when Joan was recuperating from illness or Michael was in retreat they spent very little time apart. It was in effect a morganatic marriage, for the wife of an archbishop of Canterbury shares in none of her husband's precedence or honours.* One day in Guyana Joan found herself accidentally walking ahead of the Archbishop, and stepping aside said, "Sorry darling, I didn't mean to walk in front of you." The debt he owed to her management of Lambeth and Canterbury, to the degree of amusement, fun, wit and gaiety with which she enlivened occasions, to the way she shared his particular brand of humour, and to her readiness to mimic and make fun of pretentious people in such a way as to make him roar with laughter, cannot be exaggerated. One very rare occasion on which he reproved her was when she began, with her feet splayed out, to imitate across the drawing room the flat-footed, clod-hopping walk of an evangelical clergyman at Church House whom neither of them cared for; he did so simply by a long and deep intake of breath, accompanied by a shaking of his head. Informed that the same evangelical clergyman was engaged in writing a book on sex, the Archbishop confined his comments to a precisely identical long and soulful intake of breath, an act that spoke volumes of disquiet rather than outright disapproval.

Joan Ramsey's self-effacement extended to a refusal to give interviews to the press, for she believed it was her job to support the Archbishop in private and simply to be by his side in public. But she would draw his attention incessantly to items of interest and to people wanting to meet him, and it was she who provided the "human" and informal touch to encounters which, for those perhaps

---

* Perhaps to compensate her, the domestic chaplains addressed Mrs Ramsey as "Ma'am".

meeting the Archbishop for the first and only time in their lives, could have been rather nerve-wracking. It was she too who took endless pains to thank their hosts and hostesses, writing assiduous letters after every engagement. She was well aware that members of the household worked hard, often under extremely difficult conditions abroad, when schedules went awry and the weather was appallingly hot, with very few words of thanks from the Archbishop, sometimes with none, and she always made a point of thanking them herself when they returned to England. Many of the problems encountered overseas were the direct result of hopelessly inefficient planning when tours were being arranged. For example, once a week, or every ten days at the most, it was considered essential that the Archbishop should have a day off. That meant twenty-four clear hours without a single engagement, formal or informal, when he need not dress up, make small talk or get into a car, but could sit around reading, swimming, having a snack off a tray if that was what he fancied. But again and again some bishop overseas would see on the programme "Free Day" and immediately arrange for the Archbishop and Mrs Ramsey to go to lunch with the Speaker of the local Assembly or some such luminary. That meant they did have to get dressed up, get into a car, and make small talk. It also meant that the household had somehow to try to break off the engagement, at the risk of causing offence, or break the news to the Archbishop that some well-meaning local dignitaries had messed up his one day off. The Archbishop always caved in and fulfilled these extra and unwelcome engagements, but it was his own fault they had come about; the Palace never issued sufficiently firm instructions about the Archbishop's wishes. The most elementary arrangements went by the board, with the Archbishop and his chaplain staying in

Government House, whilst his press officer stayed else-where. Indeed, administration was so inept that the press officer was never even involved in the planning of an overseas tour, for the Church's attitude was that press officers existed to plug gaps not to initiate events, and a good deal of the press officer's time was spent unscrambling potentially disastrous situations. For instance, in Bermuda he discovered that the bishop had arranged for the Archbishop to appear on a television station run by whites, although there was also a black television station, which the bishop had decided to ignore. To the fury of the bishop and the delight of the Archbishop, invitations to appear on both stations were speedily fixed up.

Michael Ramsey's seeming lack of concern for those who served him, even though he knew they loved him, was one of the hallmarks of life at Lambeth Palace. "He has to struggle very hard to be good", a chaplain once remarked to a colleague. That struggle took place to some extent, presumably, in the chapel, where each day began with Matins and Holy Communion. "You know, I could be swinging from the bannister one morning," the same chaplain remarked, "and the Archbishop would never notice." There was an insensitivity towards others in his make-up that was born perhaps of a deep fear of emotional commitment. His feelings about the pain and unhappiness of other people were something he found almost impossible to express. When a police motorcyclist crashed while escorting his car in Jamaica he just sat paralysed, when the first instinct of any priest should have been to see whether his services were needed; the man might easily have been dying. Later he paid a visit to the policeman's bedside, gave him his blessing and prayed for him, but he had had to be reminded even to do that. In dispensing with the services of his household, Michael Ramsey gave no thought for their future employment or welfare. "I don't really think that he had any clear idea about what a senior chaplain might be or do", Dean Noel Kennaby has written. "He told me eventually that he found me embarrassing – but he didn't explain why. So it was really rather a relief to be offered the Deanery of St Albans."[6] It was the easing of Noel Kennaby from Lambeth Palace in 1964 that had finally ensured the supremacy there of John Andrew.

One has to hope that Robert Beloe, one of the Church of England's great public servants, was never aware of the contempt in which he was held by Michael Ramsey. His appearance in the VIP lounge at Heathrow Airport on Ramsey's return from some visit overseas was quite simply dreaded, for Beloe was cast as the harbinger of bad news, come what may. He was bound to be waiting to offer advice about a speech in the House of Lords, a debate in the General Assembly, a call about to be arranged on a member of the government or the royal family – all the areas of public life that Ramsey dreaded and from which, overseas, he had made such a welcome if temporary escape. "Yes, it's true," he would admit in retirement, "it's perfectly true, I didn't give my mind to the royal family. The Duke of Edinburgh thought I was very donnish. Well I am. And I thought he was very boorish, and he is."

Michael would speak often, and with feeling, of "how awful" the Duke of Edinburgh was, and claimed that in order to show how much Prince Philip despised him the Prince had read a book throughout Prince Charles's confirmation service. Michael had been called in by the Queen, along with Earl Mountbatten, to discuss plans for Prince Charles's education, but she found communication with him difficult. She was, after all, a woman and no intellectual, and Michael's interest in women, horses and corgis was minimal. "He occasionally stayed with us in Highgate," his sister Bridget recalls, "and he got very upset because we had a dog and he was so afraid the dog would eat some of his clothes he always locked his door every time he went out."[7] Prince Charles, however, called on Michael Ramsey when he was eighteen, and made a characteristically astute observation afterwards. "I thought he was a very deep person but I couldn't get very far down."[8]

CHAPTER NINE

RETIREMENT

The first hope of every Christian is the hope of heaven:
Address at Great St Mary's, Cambridge in 1970

One day, as Michael Ramsey entered Church House in Dean's Yard, Westminster, where most of the Boards and Councils of the General Synod are housed and where the Synod meets,* he was told that a member of the House of Laity from Liverpool was ninety, and he was asked if he would like to wish him a happy birthday. "He shouldn't be in the Synod at ninety," said Michael, and refused. He himself had decided to retire when he was seventy, and on 15th November 1974, the day after his seventieth birthday, he and Joan went to live at the Old Vicarage at Cuddesdon. The prime minister, Harold Wilson, offered him a life peerage, which he accepted, but although between 1975 and 1981 he attended the House of Lords on twenty-eight occasions (sixteen times during the 1978–79 session) he never spoke in parliament in retirement. The Queen presented him with the Royal Victorian Chain, an exclusive order of chivalry in her personal gift, founded by Edward VII in 1902, and after some tactful prodding by the

* The General Assembly always met at Church House. Since the introduction of synodical government, meetings of the General Synod also take place in York.

Duchess of Kent she also gave him a farewell luncheon. The Duke of Edinburgh did not attend.

"It was a very nice lunch, very nice", he used to recall. "The Duke wasn't there, just the Queen and the corgis." The very last thing he had done as Primate of All England was to steer through the House of Lords the Worship and Doctrine Measure, which gave to the General Synod a right not enjoyed by the Church of England since the reign of Henry VIII, namely to revise its liturgy, thus reducing quite drastically the State's powers of intervention in the affairs of the Church. It was an Act to which the Queen had just given the royal assent, and apparently Michael blotted his copybook by referring to the fact.

"Well," he used to say, "I shouldn't have mentioned it. I shouldn't have mentioned it. Her face went all governessy", a brilliant pun on the fact that the Queen in Supreme Governor of the Church of England.

Michael was never at a loss to explain the intricacies surrounding the appointment of his successor. Since the death in 1972 of Ian Ramsey (to whom Michael Ramsey referred at his memorial service at St Margaret's, Westminster as a dear friend and a great man), a void had opened up in the ranks of eminent diocesan bishops. This may have occasioned relief to the Queen and the Duke of Edinburgh, who could now anticipate with something like impatience the appointment as archbishop of Canterbury of a no-nonsense, down-to-earth chap like Donald Coggan, archbishop of York, a man with whom One might be expected to have an intelligible conversation. Michael claimed to have seen Dr Coggan's popularity with the royal family growing steadily over the years, and he used to recount that "In 1974, against all the advice, the Queen dug her little toes in. She dug her little toes in and she said, 'We'll have *this* one'!"*

* Dr Coggan's tenure at Canterbury, five and a half years, was one of the

Now that Michael was Lord Ramsey and no longer an archbishop the question arose as to how he should be addressed. Very shortly after his retirement he fulfilled an engagement to conduct a retreat for clergy from the Coventry diocese, and when the bishop of Coventry, Cuthbert Bardsley, opened his front door "there he stood, looking radiantly happy. He shook all over, like a jelly, his eyebrows went up and down, his small pudgy hands acted like the fins of a fish, and finally he said, 'I'm free, I'm free'. My wife ventured to say to him, 'Your Grace, what shall I call you? I believe you don't want to be called Archbishop.' Whereupon he startled her by saying, 'Just call me Michael'."[1] It was as Michael Ramsey (not Ramsey, as he could have done as a baron) that he now signed letters, with an episcopal cross before his signature, and he much preferred to be addressed as Bishop Ramsey or Dr Ramsey than as Lord Ramsey. In every respect he reverted, quite properly, to the rank and style of a bishop, and it even became quite common for people to refer to him, certainly among themselves, as Bishop Michael – a very Orthodox thing to do.

Michael Ramsey had purchased the Old Vicarage at Cuddesdon about six years before he retired, chasing the owner down the High Street after church one morning in

---

shortest in modern times. William Temple was archbishop only two and a half years; Charles Longley, who became archbishop in 1862, six years. William Juxon, who as bishop of London kept Charles I company at his execution, only survived three years as archbishop of Canterbury, as did the sixteenth-century archbishop, Reginald Pole. Infirmity and disease carried off medieval and Anglo-Saxon archbishops at an alarming rate. St Augustine himself survived only seven years. Those whose claims to be appointed archbishop of Canterbury were considered in 1974, in addition to Dr Coggan, were Bishop John Howe, executive officer of the Anglican Communion and a former bishop of St Andrews; Kenneth Woollcombe, bishop of Oxford only since 1971; and Robert Runcie, who had been bishop of St Albans only four years.

his impetuous eagerness to buy it. This he proceeded to do without giving heed to the most basic considerations, and when Joan came to give the three-hundred-year-old house a proper survey she found a saw mill at work within earshot, and dry rot in the one beam supporting the dining room ceiling. But Michael had been determined to recreate his links with the theological college where he had trained, and soon, to his own embarrassment as much as anyone else's, he found the students sitting at his feet rather than those of the Principal. One of his guests at the Old Vicarage was Victor Stock, who in 1974 was twenty-nine and priest in charge of the University Church of Christ the King in Bloomsbury; he is now rector of St Mary-Le-Bow, Cheapside. It had been Michael's custom to visit the University Church once a year when he was archbishop, and he did so for the last time on Ash Wednesday 1974, when he presided at a Sung Eucharist and Father Stock ashed him, with the awesome words, "Remember oh man that dust thou art and unto dust shall thou return." A remarkably warm friendship developed between the old bishop and the young priest during the next few years, and Father Stock's recollections[2] must rate among the most vivid and warm-hearted concerning what everyone regarded as an exemplary retirement. But one of Father Stock's earliest encounters with Michael at the Old Vicarage in Cuddesdon was rather alarming.

"In 1975 a group of chaplains went to lunch, and afterwards I was sitting upstairs in the study and Michael began to talk about the Pope's attitude towards sex. He had reasserted traditional teaching in his encyclical *Humanae Vitae*. 'How very foolish of the Pope to lump together very, very important things, like abortion and homosexuality and divorce, with very, very trivial things like masturbation,' Michael said. 'Masturbation, masturbation, so silly of the Pope to make such a fuss about masturbation. It's the sort of thing we all do, and we hope one day something more interesting will come along to take its place.' Well, it was a warm day and the windows were wide open, and I thought, what on earth will people think if they hear all this!"

While he was living at Cuddesdon Michael thought nothing of undertaking an eighty-mile journey to visit the university city he loved, Cambridge, there on occasions to stay with Walter Hamilton, the Master of Magdalene.* He and Joan travelled by bus, and Michael used to concoct his own account of his arrival at the bus station, where Hamilton would be waiting with "a large car" which Michael automatically imagined was a Rolls Royce, although he would have had difficulty distinguishing a Rolls Royce from a Mini. "When you come off the bus," he used to say, "the people are very nice in Cambridge. They smile at you. They're very nice, very nice indeed. Now they're not so nice at Oxford. If you get off a bus in Oxford they don't smile at you. But in Cambridge they're very amiable, very amiable indeed. So you get off the bus and you look for Walter Hamilton. Now the bus station is full of rather ordinary people, rather ordinary people in from the Fens with their shopping bags, with chickens and things. And there in the corner of the car park you can see Walter Hamilton, rather grand, and rather confused by being among so many ordinary people!"

He seems always to have delighted himself by imagining everyone far grander than he, when of course as archbishop of Canterbury he had ranked as a duke. It was also to conduct Holy Week services at Little St Mary's that Michael returned to Cambridge, and to stay with the vicar, James Owen, with whom, as with Victor Stock, he formed an intimate relationship during his retirement. "Michael

* Master from 1967 to 1978.

was to me a real don," Canon Owen has said, "an integrated person who used every inch of his personality to convey truth. In that sense he was a don in the way that Sydney Smith was a don."[3] Michael was always intrigued by the fact that in the hall of Canon Owen's elegant eighteenth-century vicarage, where the Ramseys were assured of just that degree of attentive hospitality (comfortable furniture, good wine) that they enjoyed, there stood a massive punt pole. But he never ventured out on the river in Canon Owen's punt. "That's the sort of thing the Cog might do. Yes, Cog and Ma Cog, going along in the punt together, very nice, very nice." When in 1980 Donald Coggan retired, the house into which he and Lady Coggan moved became a godsend to Michael. "They're living," he used to say, "in a public house in Sissinghurst. She's so glad it's been converted."

He never failed to find humour in Donald Coggan's evangelical brand of Christianity. He claimed, in his very donnish way, to have been to breakfast at Lambeth Palace while Lord Coggan was archbishop, but very well may not have been. Nevertheless he did not hesitate to pretend that "everybody knows that he likes prunes. And every time he puts a prune in his mouth he says, 'Here's another missionary to the dark interior.' It gets rather tedious at breakfast!"

There was one anecdote Michael told about Donald Coggan that rather backfired, unless – which is perfectly possible – he was deliberately making fun of himself, for no one repeated phrases more than he. "Have you noticed how the Archbishop of Canterbury is repeating himself over and over again?", he used to ask. "Well, I notice it, I notice it a good deal, a good deal. I heard him the other day saying over and over again, 'The family that prays together stays together, the family that prays together stays together.' It's very irritating, very irritating indeed."

During the course of his life Michael Ramsey became an honorary fellow of three Oxford colleges, Merton, Keble and St Cross, and of Selwyn College, Cambridge, and he received honorary doctorates from Durham, Leeds, Edinburgh, Cambridge, Hull, Manchester, London, Oxford, Kent and Keele. The pattern of his retirement very soon fell into one of accepting invitations to lecture overseas, in America frequently, and in Canada, Japan and Australia (he was at Trinity College, Melbourne in 1977), in fostering informal relations with undergraduates, primarily in Durham, where in 1976 he gave four lectures on Pastoral Theology, and in the writing of books. His prose style and punctuation never received the close attention they deserved, and had he taken the time and trouble to polish the literary aspect of his writings he would have produced books on theology even more memorable and readable than he did. But writing gave him enormous pleasure and satisfaction. One day, like a schoolboy let out on an extra half holiday, he suddenly burst from his study at the Old Palace to say, "Well, what do you think, I've started a book! I've started a book!", and he had seldom looked or sounded happier. In 1977 he produced a biblical study called *Holy Spirit*, with the object of examining "the experience which the Christians of the first century ascribed to the Holy Spirit, and the theology with which that experience was linked", and in 1980 he published *Jesus and the Living Past*, in effect his second series of Hale Lectures, delivered at Seabury-Western Theological College Seminary two years earlier. In an attempt to encourage the "supreme importance" of stillness and silence, for he believed their neglect to be damaging to the Christian life, in 1982 Michael produced a paperback called *Be Still and Know*. Within four years it had gone into four editions and has now sold nearly 60,000 copies. It was in the series known as "the Archbishop of Canterbury's Lent Book", and is still the best selling of them all.

It was while he was in Canada that Michael wrote to William Surtees, who lived at 50 South Street in Durham, to ask if he could buy his house, and the sale was completed on 25th April 1977. Strangely enough, it tran-spired that Michael had been taught at Repton by Mr Surtees's uncle, Alec Surtees, the housemaster of Brook House; Bill Surtees had in fact been born at Repton, and his mother had been a great friend of Rosamund Fisher. Fifty South Street, with Alan Richardson's widow, Phyllis, nearby as a neighbour, stood on one of the steepest hills in Durham, with a magnificent view of the cathedral on the other side of the river Wear. Built in 1852, the house looked, according to Mr Surtees, like a disused Methodist chapel, which may well have appealed to Michael. But it was a good steady walk from the cathedral, and proved on closer examination to be as unsuitable as a retirement home as the Old Vicarage at Cuddesdon, for as Michael and Joan grew older they found the daily walk from South Street to the cathedral, and to the University and the shops, increas-ingly irksome. So in 1978 they sold 50 South Street and moved again, to the ground and first floor of 16 South Bailey, accommodation they rented from the Cathedral Chapter. The house was almost next door to the cathedral, where Michael and Joan attended Holy Communion every morning. Audrey Heaton, their housekeeper from Canter-bury, continued to look after them. In 1977 the University of Durham had honoured Michael by making him an emeritus professor, and now he forged particularly close links with St Chad's College, which in 1980 repaid his devotion to their students by making him an honorary Fellow.

One of Michael's favourite overseas assignments at this time was to stay for several months at a stretch, six years running, at Nashotah House in Wisconsin (he first went there in 1975), an extreme Anglo-Catholic seminary, where he lectured on systematic theology, the Anglican tradition and those aspects of the spiritual life – redemption and the Resurrection – which had always claimed his particular attention. And one of his most comical stories concerned a private visit he paid in retirement to Pope John Paul II. The Pope was due to make an official visit to the Archbishop of Canterbury in 1982, and Dr Runcie, it seems, invited Michael to call on the Pope to brief him about the Church of England, on the grounds that a Pole very possibly did not even know where England was. "Well," Michael used to recount, "I asked if I could see him, and I got an appointment. Very nice. And I found myself walking into the Pope's study. Well, he looked at me. He looked at me – and I could have been an Eskimo!" Nothing daunted, Michael reminded the Pope of his own official visit to Paul VI. "I told him about my great friend Pope Paul, and what progress we'd made, and how much he had to live up to. I thought that would be all right coming from an older man!" When eventually the Pontiff arrived in England there was a service at Canterbury Cathedral to which Michael Ramsey was invited. Afterwards, in a state of great excitement, he told James Owen he had been given no fewer than nine kisses during the service. "Did you notice how many Bob Runcie got?" he asked. "He only got two!"

In the way that Michael's close proximity to Cuddesdon proved slightly embarrassing for the College, it might have been thought that to have a former bishop of Durham at worship in the cathedral every day could have seemed like an intrusion to the present bishop. But Dr Jenkins says, "I was actually more haunted by Ian Ramsey's ghost, because he had been a great friend of mine. By Michael Ramsey I was in fact warmly encouraged and supported. On the occasions that I met him he somehow made it clear that he supported what I was doing, and he knew I did it from faith. That was quite clear. He was actually an amazingly humble man, and not a threat in the least. People did complain to him about me, but it was quite plain he did his best to explain what I was up to. It was lovely to have him around."[4]

The City of Durham, on the other hand, seems to have remained largely unaware that it now had living in its centre one of the most distinguished academics and Churchmen alive anywhere in England, but Michael did make some contact with the local community, becoming president of a Professional and Businessmen's Club, attending their Christmas lunches and addressing their annual general meeting. But apart from the cathedral, where Michael not only attended Communion daily but celebrated perhaps three times a month, his affections were primarily focused on St Chad's College, where he celebrated Holy Communion at 8 a.m. every Thursday, staying on afterwards for breakfast with the students. At 16 South Bailey he conducted prayer and meditation studies, Joan serving wine and cheese to the students beforehand. One such series was on the Lord's Prayer. "I know it sounds hackneyed," an American zoology student, Nils Halker, recalls, "but I could feel the intense sincerity and true sense of holiness coming from him."[5] Most of the students called him Father.

One of the undergraduates at St Chad's, Wayne Plimmer, who went on to be ordained after training for the priesthood at St Stephen's House, Oxford, says: "I suppose basically we wanted to pick his brains. We managed to drag along one or two atheists to South Bailey. Bishop Michael would introduce a topic and talk for a bit. He loved the questions. He enjoyed them most of all. He liked difficult questions, and he rejoiced that atheists and agnostics came along. He talked about the ordination of women but I could never quite work out what he felt. He was very cagey about it."[6] Remembering how Fisher had interfered by making public statements on Anglican-Methodist Reunion, Michael Ramsey in retirement was always careful never to speak out on controversial issues his successors were trying to cope with.*

Mr Plimmer summed up his impressions of these informal gatherings in Ramsey's study by saying, "You came away feeling strengthened, really. I found he was a great anchor to help me through periods of doubt. It was clear when he spoke to us that he too had had to struggle. We thought of him not so much as a theologian as in terms of his spirituality and what he had to offer in the way of helping us with our prayer lives. I felt there was a great depth there."

Those who only saw Michael Ramsey out of doors in Durham recall him wearing a Russian fur hat "like a tea cosy" to go to the post, and a quilted green waistcoat over his purple stock. He wore buckled shoes, and could sometimes be seen in the garden, which was overlooked by neighbours, drinking a glass of Guinness. David Webster, vicar of Belmont, remembers him "ambling through the Market Place . . . You could see the eyes of the Durham folk watching him with deep affection. Sometimes he would want to talk to anyone around. At other times he was in another world."[7] He took the funeral service of the owner of the post office, and when the dean gave a party for his eightieth birthday the guests included Michael's gardener.

---

* Michael Ramsey did in fact communicate his views on the ordination of women, and how he would have dealt with the situation, to the present Archbishop of Canterbury, but they remain private.

But it was of course only those who stayed at South Bailey who were able to comprehend the disciplined, almost monastic, routine that enabled Michael to accomplish so much in old age. Victor Stock had been an assistant curate in Pinner when, in 1969, Michael was celebrating the fortieth anniversary of his ordination to the priesthood, and he wrote Michael a letter "which I posted with a feeling of trepidation really, and embarrassment. I thought, what have I done, writing to the Archbishop of Canterbury? I came back from visiting a few days later and there on the mat was a handwritten reply. It seemed simply amazing that the Archbishop of Canterbury should write a letter to a curate. 'Why,' he wrote, 'should I not write and thank you for your gift of love and trust in me?'"

The friendship blossomed through Bloomsbury, and in retirement Michael invited Father Stock to stay once a year. "He was exceptionally responsive to affection, and a very, very affectionate man. He was physically very affectionate. He always kissed me at the station. I think if you were not frightened of him and loved him he was very responsive.* He valued the opportunity to ask what was going on in the Church of England. He had a sort of ritual conversation. We often talked about politics, but essentially I regarded him as a kind of mentor. I would go to him with problems.

"And we'd do things like move the pictures about. We had endless giggles about where to put the dining room table. He couldn't do anything like arrange the furniture. He didn't know what a dining room table was. Within a very rigid timetable the days were always the same. And within that very secure and very small world he felt able to let people in and exchange an affectionate, attentive

* "He loved to be loved and he needed it terribly": Bishop John Hughes in conversation with the author.

intimacy. What he needed from the other person was sparking off, and he needed you not to be frightened of him. I knew when to leave him alone.

"I used to tease him, and once he told me off. I was complaining about the calibre of bishops, and he said, 'Don't go on about it, it's too late now, it's too late to blame me now.' In some ways he was a very sophisticated man and in some ways unworldly or naïve. He blocked out whole areas of life, and one of the things he blocked out was the concept that people were no good. He would assume that his close scholarly friends like the Chadwicks* or Christopher Evans† were the run of the mill, that the Cambridge common room was the world. It was a very donnish attitude to take. Cardinal Bea, Pope Paul VI, these were the people he knew, and they were decent and prayerful. He had an unrealistic and exaggerated view of other people's intellectual and spiritual abilities. He was rather intrigued but slightly hurt by criticism made by others of people like bishops. He viewed them like a kindly old headmaster, and he was very shocked when he discovered that a bishop was a real fool, or had done something wrong.

"He once made us both laugh so much we had to lean against the wall. He felt guilty about being worked up, but enjoyed it. But this was mixed with intense seriousness and helpfulness. I once went to stay when I was quite sure there was nothing called God, and I was really quite worried about it because after all, I was a priest, and I couldn't go on for ever not believing in God, so he said we'd go for a walk at three o'clock and he'd tell me what

* Dr Owen Chadwick, Fellow of Selwyn College, Cambridge, and his brother, Professor Henry Chadwick, Master of Peterhouse, Cambridge.
† Professor Christopher Evans, Lightfoot Professor of Divinity at Durham from 1959 to 1962.

to do. He would walk very fast, ahead of you, down the tow path, while dealing over his shoulder with your problems, and on this occasion he said, 'If you do not believe in a personal God just jettison the idea, don't worry about it at all, take on some much more abstract concept of ultimate goodness, or the striving for love, or the wanting to be good, or the wanting to be kind, but go on saying your prayers, and when you pray, pray to Christ, and speak to Christ, and say, Give me a share in your courage. Give me a share in your own patience. That sort of thing. Do that when you come to the Holy Communion.'

"And it worked. You have to be exceptionally narrow-minded or fearful not to have doubts. Ramsey certainly had his. And he was able to lift away guilt, the very opposite of the Bishop of London, who produces a whole list of things you're supposed to believe in and very few people can believe in. But Ramsey would meet you exactly where you were, which I thought was an amazing thing for a man whose academic background and little donnish world and the immense privilege of his life made him so very different from a young suburban clergyman."

Once he had relinquished the trappings of office Michael Ramsey had no yearning for privilege and luxury. If an airline sent him first class tickets, all well and good, but he travelled in taxis and buses, and the lack of servants was merely a reversion to a more normal way of life. Victor Stock recalls how a typical day would begin. "He would always bring me tea in bed, in pyjamas, looking like some sort of old haystack, all the buttons done up wrong. He'd come stumbling into the bedroom carrying a tray of tea. 'The maid has brought the tea, the maid has brought the tea. We're going to the cathedral in half an hour. The bathroom's vacant, the bathroom's vacant.'

"And in the cathedral he would sink down into a kind

of heap at the back of the chapel. He often complained that the clergy never went to church. When he was a canon of Durham they all did. Breakfast was always a great feast, usually porridge and always eggs and bacon, lots of toast, lots of coffee. He would seize the post and then go to the study for the morning. Twenty minutes before lunch he would emerge for sherry and pour out two huge glasses, some of which went over the carpet. For lunch there was always soup, then a joint or chops, and a pudding or stilton. He sometimes ate apple pie. We usually had wine or cider. Then he would lie down, and then the ritual walk. There was always a huge tea, and friends would drop in. Then a bit more sitting in the study, then Evensong in his own chapel, a converted bedroom. Over the altar was a crucifix given to him by the people of Tanzania. After Evensong there was more sherry, then dinner, and after dinner back to the study. Then at about ten o'clock a tray of tea. Within that timetable he read, and dealt with a huge correspondence."

The large meals at regular intervals, the sherry and the cider, the open house at teatime was all a re-creation of the pattern of his Cambridge childhood; this was simply the way that dons and clergymen and schoolmasters lived. "One of the clues to his character", says Victor Stock, "was a strange kind of asceticism about being in the world at all. Lots of aspects of the world were held at arm's length; the theatre, the novel, music, travel.* But he was the sort of father-in-God to whom the clergy could turn. I think he was very shrewd. Underneath this kind of pared-down range of interests he was very deeply in touch with some things. He was interested in the way people ticked, and very good in the confessional. But I think he

---

* He meant travel for pleasure or on holiday.

was a deeply isolated person. He went on collecting much younger friends right up to the end."

There was always a danger, however, that the current young friend in favour might turn out only to be the flavour of the month, and as with royalty, it never did to overstep the mark. Ramsey needed privacy in which to avoid large areas of reality, and only one person at a time was permitted anywhere near him. He was almost entirely absorbed in his own personal quest for godliness, an essentially selfish occupation, and those who positively seek sanctity generally do so at the expense of others. But Father Stock has a very charitable view of his own relationship with Michael Ramsey. "I think it's so unusual and wonderful that somebody so distinguished should have made close friendships with people who were not distinguished, and should have wanted to see them. It was very easy to become pushy." But most people had their own life to return to. "For Joan, being his wife was her vocation. She did it perfectly. She provided him with exactly what he needed, to be the man he was, and I think he knew that. I think that's why he loved her so much."

Among the contemporary Church topics covered at South Bailey was, inevitably, the ordination of women. Father Stock says, "He was unenthusiastic about it because he thought it would wreck our relations with Rome, but it was something he didn't feel he could oppose. He was embarrassed about it, by not being able to be either enthusiastic or against it. He had no difficulty in relating to women priests in America, and he encouraged the vocations of several women in America. He never spoke nastily about women as so many men do, including Anglo-Catholic clergy."

By 1981 Michael's eyesight was such that notes for a sermon he left behind at the Master's Lodge at Magdalene, now in the Pepys Library, were totally illegible, and he underwent an operation in Sunderland for cataracts, which gave his eyesight a new if temporary lease of life.* By 1986 he was again complaining of poor eyesight, but at lunch one Sunday that year, when he was entertaining his former press officer, the only untoward event that occurred was when Michael got up to pour out some more hock from a bottle on the sideboard and picked up a bottle of port instead. But mishaps were a part of his life. He would lock himself out by forgetting his front door key, and one day he fell over on the front door steps. The top floor flat at 16 South Bailey was occupied by a schoolmaster, Cyril Watson, who purchased a washing machine without having it properly plumbed. "One dreadful evening," he remembers, "the telephone rang. 'Bishop Ramsey here. We're a little concerned about the water that's cascading through the ceiling.' It happened again, I'm sorry to say, about five weeks later, when my machine flooded one of the Ramseys' bedrooms."8 But the worst accident in which the Ramseys were involved while in Durham occurred in 1986 when they were on their way one Sunday morning to St Oswald's Church, where Michael was due to preach. Their car had stopped at traffic lights when a police car ran into the back of them. Joan was cut and Michael badly shaken.

There was a day when Michael had to break off in the middle of a sermon, and his doctor, Wilfred Chapman, advised him to cut down on public engagements. A real crisis in the management of domestic affairs brewed up when Audrey Heaton, whose dandie dinmonts had somewhat over-run the house, injured her leg and was finally

---

* He was perfectly capable of preaching without any notes at all. In Barbados a local reporter, having failed to catch every word of a sermon preached by Ramsey out of doors, enquired if there were any notes he might borrow. The Archbishop produced a single phrase, in Greek, scribbled on the back of an envelope.

compelled to retire. To begin with, Joan made do with temporary domestic help, but no attempt seems to have been made to hire a new resident housekeeper, with the result that she and Michael began to feel they could no longer manage to live at South Bailey. Almost every street in Durham is a hill, and Joan was finding it a struggle to get to Marks & Spencer, where the staff would help her do the shopping. So plans were laid for them to move to a house in the grounds of Greatham Hospital at Hartlepool. Roses were transferred from the garden at South Bailey and the house was decorated, but at the last minute Dr Chapman advised them not to move because he thought they would be too isolated. Then they thought of living on the ground floor of South Bailey only. All they would have needed to be comfortable was a new housekeeper.

But the Archbishop of York, John Habgood, offered to make a flat available at Bishopthorpe, and after selling most of his library, Michael returned in 1986 to the house where he and Joan had lived from 1956 to 1961. As he stood in the hall of 16 South Bailey for the last time, Michael was heard to say, "I think I like this house much better now the furniture's gone."

In the event, they were nearly as isolated at Bishopthorpe as they would have been at Greatham Hospital. Michael found there was no daily Communion, and he missed the undergraduates at Durham. A party of ten students from St Chad's did go to Bishopthorpe for lunch one day, taking their own sandwiches; among them was Richard Murray, to whom Ramsey was to write three letters later from Oxford, still asking for information about St Chad's. Another visitor was Phyllis Richardson, who remembers "One got such a welcome in the last days, the outstretched arms, and when we said goodbye I think we probably both knew it was for the last time."[9] It seems probable that Michael suffered a series of minor strokes

240

while at Bishopthorpe, and one day, Lady Ramsey recalls, "We got on to the subject of old folks' homes with the doctor, and I said I suppose we'll have to think about putting our name down for one, and the doctor said, rather smartly, 'Yes, and don't leave it too long'."[10]

In September 1987 the Ramseys said goodbye to Bishopthorpe for the second time and stayed for six weeks in Oxford with the Dean of Christ Church, Eric Heaton, who had been dean of Durham from 1974 to 1979, while rooms were prepared for them at St John's Home in St Mary's Road. They went to lunch with Michael's sister, Margaret, who lives in Oxford, who thought "By then Michael had got fearfully decrepit. He got into rather a funk coming down the steps at Christ Church. He was terrified he would fall."[11]

At St John's Home they had a bedroom and a small sitting room. Michael still got about, and made friends with a Muslim from Bangladesh from whom he bought stamps at a local post office. Shortly before Michael died, the Bangladeshi went to see him, and asked how long he had been ordained. "Nearly sixty years", Michael told him, and he was delighted by the Muslim's reply. "That's a very long friendship", he said.

Wayne Plimmer, now round the corner at St Stephen's House, resumed his friendship from Durham days. "I was quite shocked when I saw Bishop Michael for the first time in Oxford", he says. "He had lost a lot of weight. I felt St John's was going to be a sad end."[12] Some people who saw Michael Ramsey at this time, and noticed how badly he now shuffled and how shaky he was, believed he had developed Parkinson's Disease. Professor Macquarrie was present when John Taylor, the former bishop of Winchester, had Michael and Joan to lunch. "He was very shaky and tottered along," he recalls, "but his mind was clear. He talked about David Jenkins."[13]

Indeed, until the very end Michael Ramsey retained his insatiable interest in ecclesiastical events, personalities and gossip. Victor Stock went to see him three weeks before he died, when they discussed the antics in the General Synod of a clergyman who was determined to have homosexual clergy hounded. Father Stock suggested to Ramsey that had he been in charge he would have sent for the clergyman and commended him for reading the Book of Leviticus, but would have reminded him that the pastoral care of the clergy was the responsibility of the bishops, and that there were souls to be saved in his own parish, given him his blessing and told him to go home, thus saving the Synod from an awful mess. Michael roared with laughter and said, "Indeed, I would. But whether it would have made any difference I do not know. I rather fear not."

On the wall at the end of the bed was the crucifix from the chapel at South Bailey. Michael's eyes were constantly upon it. Father Stock says, "He knew he was dying, and he spent a lot of his energy helping Joan to face it. He was very, very tired. But he didn't actually go to bed until very near the end." Michael was anointed by the chaplain to St John's, and nine days before he died he received a farewell visit from the Archbishop of Canterbury, who prayed for him and gave him his blessing. The day before he died, Owen Chadwick, with whom he had often stayed when he was Master of Selwyn College, Cambridge, went to tea, and read to him. Earlier, Michael had written to the dean of Canterbury, asking if he could be buried in the cathedral cloisters, and the dean had replied asking whether he would mind being cremated. "I wrote back," Michael recalled, "and said I didn't mind being cremated in the least, but the stone over my ashes was to be sufficiently large that future generations wouldn't think I was William Temple's cat." He died on Saturday 23rd April 1988. "M was so happy and peaceful when he died," Joan wrote to the author, "as if he saw Glory & there it was – as he'd known. And no long nasty illness ahead – it was really heaven-sent." At the foot of the crucifix stood two sherry bottles. When Victor Stock went over in the morning Joan said she thought that somehow the juxtaposition of the crucifix and the sherry bottles summed Michael up. "He looked very peaceful," she told Father Stock, "but he had an expression on his face that rather suggested he was going to give God a piece of his mind about one or two things."

A POSTSCRIPT

Michael Ramsey's body was embalmed and laid out in his cassock in the chapel at St John's Home. Several students from St Stephen's House stood around the coffin and prayed. "It was a very bizarre experience", says Wayne Plimmer. "The undertakers had trimmed his eyebrows. It wasn't him at all. There was a veil over his face. We removed that."[1]

For the funeral service at Canterbury Cathedral, Lady Ramsey stayed at the Old Palace. "†Robert was a wonderful host," she wrote afterwards, "& I enjoyed finding curtains etc which had 'rested' during Cog's time but reappeared, nicely pressed, and made me feel at home. So did the sounds, unchanged, from the school houses' open windows behind & the bells above – all very comforting."[2]

The Pope and the Ecumenical Patriarch were represented. The choir sang the Russian Contakion of the Departed. Afterwards, Michael was cremated privately at Barham.

Memorial services were held in Westminster Abbey and in Durham Cathedral, and at the latter Michael was referred to on the service sheet as Scholar, Bishop, Friend.

While he had been living in Durham there had been a Post Office strike, affecting among other things the delivery of Giro cheques, and it was commented upon by Chapter staff how perturbed Michael seemed at not receiving his weekly pension. He had had no children to feed, clothe or educate, and for twenty-two years he had lived in episcopal palaces, paid for by the Church Commissioners. It would have seemed a reasonable conclusion that with so few expenses, and being in receipt of three of the highest stipends paid to anyone in the Church of England, he would, over the years, have accumulated capital which, when invested, would have added a comfortable private income to his Church and State pensions. But during the Post Office strike he had had good cause for concern. His pension was the only income he had, for either through a degree of unworldliness almost impossible to comprehend, or else because he truly did believe, as he had so often told ordinards, that wealth was always dangerous to its possessor and that "the rich man can only with difficulty be saved", he had retained in a current account every penny of the savings he could have made since 1952. By the time he entered St John's Home his pension as a former archbishop of Canterbury was £13,000 a year; fees payable to the Home for him and his wife – and these were being paid partly out of capital which had never earned a penny of interest – were £16,000 a year. As a result, he left about £45,000.

He signed a Will on 9th June 1987, shortly after moving into the North Wing Flat at Bishopthorpe, and only ten months before his death. Books and papers deposited at Lambeth Palace he bequeathed to the Palace Library. His two trustees received £500 each. The same sum went to Audrey Heaton and Dr Owen Chadwick. But he left no instructions for the distribution of any of his episcopal regalia, not even the ring given to him by the pope. This has been presented by Lady Ramsey to the Archbishop of Canterbury, who intends to ensure it descends to archbishops of Canterbury in perpetuity. His original episcopal ring, given to him on his consecration by Magdalene College, was returned by Lady Ramsey to Magdalene, together with a mitre. A cope, stole and alb went to York Minster. A purple cloak and black scarf were offered to the Suffragan Bishop of Sherborne, John Kirkham, Michael's chaplain from 1972 to 1974, and the Bishop distributed other vestments among overseas bishops.

All final judgements are passed by history, but already it is possible to meet clergy and laity who look back to Michael Ramsey's primacy with rather more than fleeting nostalgia.

"Michael Ramsey was first and foremost the clergy's archbishop. He was widely respected and valued and loved among the clergy. They valued his scholarship and his sense of humour. They trusted his pronouncements and felt secure under his leadership. He was not so widely known or deeply valued by the laity, although many of them came to appreciate his obvious holiness. Here, in their opinion, was a man of God who said his prayers and sought to proclaim the love of God." A retired diocesan bishop.

"It's only talking here, now, I realize how great a man I think he was. Will he go down as a great archbishop? Yes. He deserves to do that." A retired suffragan bishop.

"The clergy thought they had a great archbishop in touch with God." A parish priest.

"He was a great man in his own way, and by definition a great archbishop. He walked with God." An evangelical member of the House of Laity.

"He made it clear from the highest official post that the whole matter of spirituality and prayer were more important than anything else." A diocesan bishop.

"I think he was a great man, and I think he may go down in history as a great archbishop." A central church lay member of the General Synod.

"If you could have combined his good-hearted simpleness with intelligent political understanding he would have been unstoppable." An evangelical theological college Principal.

"Michael comes over consistently as a man *par excellence*: his sheer goodness and devotion to our Lord, and his humility." A diocesan bishop.

"Where his archbishopric was quite great and quite distinct was the spirituality that lay behind it. The attention to God which he happened to display was what lay behind the progressive attitude he usually brought to issues that lay before the Church." A retired diocesan bishop.

The Archbishop of Canterbury's abiding remembrance and impression of Michael Ramsey, as a man and as archbishop, is of "A serenity which triumphed over extreme vulnerability. I think," Dr Runcie adds, "Michael Ramsey was effective by giving the Church confidence and in communicating the spiritual quality which he undoubtedly had. That itself was leadership."

But let the last word remain with another fellow liberal catholic, a parish priest in the diocese of London. "Michael Ramsey would have made a great abbot of a large European community. Being washed up on the shores of Canterbury was all very odd in a way. The whole thing was a sort of dream. He was a great man *precisely* because he was so odd and weird. I think it's done a lot of people a lot of good to see anybody so crazy at the top of public life. Because really, he was raving! Dotty in every way! How ever he became archbishop of Canterbury is beyond belief."

Of two things we can be absolutely certain. As the hundredth successor to St Augustine, Arthur Michael Richard Ramsey was unique. And for better or worse, we shall not see anyone like him in public life again for a very long time indeed.

NOTES TO TEXT

CHAPTER ONE: CHILDHOOD

1 *Eighty Years and More* by A. M. Ramsey (unpublished)
2 Ibid
3 Ibid
4 Ibid
5 Ibid
6 Ibid
7 Ibid
8 Ibid
9 Mrs Margaret Paul in conversation with the author
10 *The Christian Priest Today* (SPCK, 1972; revised 1985)
11 Dr Bridget Barcroft in conversation with the author
12 Ibid
13 *Eighty Years and More*
14 In conversation with the author
15 Ibid
16 *The York Quarterly*, May 1957
17 In conversation with the author
18 In conversation with the author
19 The Reverend Donald Harris in conversation with the author
20 In conversation with the author
21 *Memories* (Gollancz, 1981)
22 In conversation with the author
23 *King's College Choir School* by R. J. Henderson (King's College School, 1981)
24 Ibid

25 In conversation with the author
26 In conversation with the author
27 Michael Ramsey in conversation with Laurie Kahn-Leavitt, 13th July 1982
28 Ibid

CHAPTER TWO: REPTON

1 *Eighty Years and More*
2 Dr Bridget Barcroft in conversation with the author
3 Mrs Margaret Paul in conversation with the author
4 *Eighty Years and More*
5 Mr Hampton Gervis in conversation with the author
6 Ibid
7 Ibid
8 *First Beginning* (Highgate Publications, 1987)
9 Letter to the author, 19th February 1989
10 Letter to the author, 19th March 1989
11 In conversation with the author
12 In conversation with the author
13 In conversation with the author
14 In conversation with the author
15 *Boy* (Jonathan Cape, 1984)
16 Undated note to the author
17 *I Left my Grandfather's House* (Allison & Busby, 1984)
18 Bishop Stockwood in conversation with the author
19 In conversation with the author
20 In conversation with the author

CHAPTER THREE: MAGDALENE

1 Magdalene *College Magazine & Record* 1986/7
2 Ibid
3 *Lewis Namier: A Biography* by Julia Namier (OUP, 1971)
4 Dr Bridget Barcroft in conversation with the author
5 Sir Norman Anderson in conversation with the author

6 Retailed by Michael Ramsey to Lady Ramsey
7 *King's College Choir School*
8 In conversation with the author
9 *Cantuar: The Archbishops in their Office* (Cassell, 1971)
10 Roger Wilson, bishop of Chichester, in conversation with the author at a Conference of European Churches at Pörtschach in Austria in 1967
11 In conversation with the author
12 In conversation with the author
13 In conversation with the author
14 Mrs Margaret Paul in conversation with the author
15 Information supplied by Mrs Margaret Paul
16 Information supplied by Mr Michael Barcroft
17 *Durham Essays and Addresses* (SPCK, 1956)
18 Speaking in Cambridge on Christianity and Violence, 23rd February 1972
19 Information supplied by Mrs Phyllis Richardson
20 *The York Quarterly* February 1959
21 *Memories*
22 In conversation with the author

CHAPTER FOUR:
THE MAKING OF A THEOLOGIAN

1 In conversation with the author
2 Stated in his obituary of Michael Ramsey for Magdalene College
3 *From Gore to Temple* (Longmans, 1960)
4 *Crucifixion-Resurrection: The Pattern of the Theology and Ethics of the New Testament* (SPCK, 1981)
5 *Introducing the Christian Faith* (SCM Press, 1961)
6 The Reverend Philip Crowe in conversation with the author
7 Ibid
8 Professor Leslie Houlden in conversation with the author
9 *God, Christ and the World* (SCM Press, 1969)
10 *The Christian Priest Today*
11 An address in Manchester, 28th June 1960
12 The Reverend Victor Stock in conversation with the author

13 In conversation with the author
14 In conversation with the author
15 Ibid
16 Mrs Simon Phipps in conversation with the author
17 In conversation with the author
18 In conversation with the author
19 Ibid
20 Lecture at All Saints Church, New York, 1988
21 In conversation with the author
22 In conversation with the author
23 Ibid
24 In conversation with the author
25 In conversation with the author
26 In conversation with the author
27 In conversation with the author
28 *From Gore to Temple*
29 In conversation with the author
30 In conversation with the author
31 In conversation with the author
32 In conversation with the author
33 In conversation with the author

CHAPTER FIVE: PARISH PRIEST AND BISHOP

1 In conversation with the author
2 And passed on to the author in a letter from Canon Peter Fluck
  dated 15th February 1989
3 *Eighty Years and More*
4 Lady Ramsey in conversation with the author
5 In conversation with the author
6 Mrs Rebecca Hurry in conversation with the author
7 In conversation with the author
8 Dr Bridget Barcroft in conversation with the author
9 In conversation with the author
10 In conversation with the author
11 Lady Ramsey in conversation with the author
12 In conversation with the author

13 In conversation with the author
14 In conversation with the author
15 See *The Christian Priest Today*
16 Ibid
17 In conversation with the author
18 Canon Frank Chase in conversation with the author
19 May 1961
20 In conversation with the author
21 In conversation with the author
22 In conversation with the author
23 Letter from the Reverend David Webster to the author dated 13th February 1989
24 "The Parish Communion": *Durham Essays and Addresses*
25 An anecdote retailed to the author by Father Harry Williams, CR
26 In conversation with the author
27 Mrs Rebecca Hurry in conversation with the author
28 In conversation with the author

CHAPTER SIX: CANTERBURY

1 The author
2 Mrs Rebecca Hurry in conversation with the author
3 In conversation with the author
4 Retailed to the author by Ludovic Kennedy
5 In conversation with the author
6 "Church and State in England": *Canterbury Pilgrim* (SPCK, 1974)
7 In conversation with the author
8 In conversation with the author
9 In conversation with the author
10 The Archbishop of Canterbury in conversation with the author
11 In conversation with the author
12 Letter from Bishop Bardsley to the author dated 25th April 1989
13 In conversation with the author
14 *Durham Essays and Addresses*

15 In conversation with the author
16 *The Church of England and the Eastern Orthodox Church: Why Their Unity is Important* (SPCK, 1946)
17 Ibid
18 Ibid
19 *Great Christian Centuries to Come*, Ed. by Christopher Martin (Mowbrays, 1974)
20 *The Dialogue of East and West in Christendom* (1963)
21 *Sobornost*, Series 4, No 12, Winter-Spring 1965
22 In conversation with the author
23 Ibid
24 In conversation with the author
25 In conversation with the author
26 In conversation with the author
27 Canon Eric James in conversation with the author
28 Quoted in *The Church of England* by Paul Ferris (Gollancz, 1962)
29 Letter from Bishop Bardsley to the author dated 4th March 1989
30 The Archbishop of Canterbury in conversation with the author
31 "The Call of Christ": *Durham Essays and Addresses*

CHAPTER SEVEN: FERMENT

1 Preface: *Canterbury Pilgrim*
2 Bishop Hughes in conversation with the author
3 In the Sheldonian Theatre, Oxford
4 *The Christian Priest Today*
5 The motion commending the Report was proposed by the author
6 In conversation with the author circa 1968
7 Ibid
8 *God, Christ and the World*
9 See Archbishop Fisher's letter to the Bishop of Southwark dated 19th February 1959, quoted in *A Life of Bishop John A. T. Robinson* by Eric James (Collins, 1987)
10 In conversation with the author

11 In conversation with the author
12 Bishop Stockwood in conversation with the author. The bishop declined to reveal what Michael Ramsey said his other major mistake had been
13 "Ramsey wanted to get Robinson back to Cambridge and persuaded Butler [Lord Butler, Master of Trinity] to take him." Canon Eric James in conversation with the author
14 *A Life of Bishop John A. T. Robinson*
15 In conversation with the author
16 "Whither Theology?": *Great Christian Centuries to Come*
17 In conversation withthe author
18 The Archbishop of Canterbury in conversation with the author
19 In conversation with the author
20 In conversation with the author
21 In conversation with the author
22 In conversation with the author
23 The Duke of Richmond & Gordon in conversation with the author
24 In conversation with the author
25 Professor Macquarrie in conversation with the author

CHAPTER EIGHT: THE ARCHBISHOP AT HOME

1 Bishop John Hughes in conversation with the author
2 Bishop Mervyn Stockwood in conversation with the author
3 The Reverend Philip Crowe in conversation with the author
4 Bishop Simon Phipps in conversation with the author
5 In conversation with the author
6 Letter from the Very Reverend Noel Kennaby to the author dated 14th April 1989
7 In conversation with the author
8 Private information

CHAPTER NINE: RETIREMENT

1 Letter from Bishop Cuthbert Bardsley to the author dated 25th April 1989

2 In conversation with the author
3 In conversation with the author
4 The Bishop of Durham in conversation with the author
5 In conversation with the author
6 In conversation with the author
7 Letter from the Reverend David Webster to the author dated 13th February 1989
8 In conversation with the author
9 In conversation with the author
10 In conversation with the author
11 Mrs Margaret Paul in conversation with the author
12 In conversation with the author
13 In conversation with the author

A POSTSCRIPT

1 In conversation with the author
2 In a letter to the author

MAJOR CHRONOLOGY

1904	(14th November) Born 71 Chesterton Street, Cambridge
1909	(aged 4) Family moves to Howfield, Buckingham Road, Cambridge
1914–16	King's College Choir School, Cambridge
1916–18	Sandroyd Preparatory School, Oxshott
1918–23	Repton
1923–27	Magdalene College, Cambridge
1925	2nd, Classics
1926	President, Cambridge Union
1927	1st, Theology
1927–28	Cuddesdon Theological College
1927	Mother killed
1928	(aged 23) Ordained deacon
1928–30	Assistant curate, the Church of St Nicholas, Liverpool
1929	Ordained priest
1930–36	Sub-Warden, Lincoln Theological College
1930	Brother dies aged 26
1936–38	Lecturer, St Botolph Church, Boston
1938–40	Vicar, St Benedict's Church, Cambridge
1940–50	Van Mildert Professor of Divinity in the University of Durham and a canon residentiary of Durham Cathedral
1942	Married Joan Hamilton
1950–52	Regius Professor of Divinity in the University of Cambridge and Fellow of Magdalene
1951–52	Canon and Prepandary of Lincoln Cathedral
1952–56	(appointed aged 47) Bishop of Durham and takes his seat in the House of Lords

1956–61	(appointed aged 51) Archbishop of York and Primate of England. Sworn a member of the Privy Council
1961–74	(appointed aged 56) Archbishop of Canterbury and Primate of All England
1961–68	A president of the World Council of Churches
1966	Received at the Vatican by Pope Paul VI
1968	Chairs the Lambeth Conference
1974	Created Baron Ramsey of Canterbury and receives the Royal Victorian Chain
1974–77	Lives at the Old Vicarage, Cuddesdon
1977	Moves to 50 South Street, Durham
1978	Moves to 16 South Bailey, Durham
1986	Moves to North Wing Flat, Bishopthorpe
1987	Moves to St John's Home, Oxford
1988	(23rd April) Dies at St John's Home, aged 83
	4th May, Funeral Service at Canterbury Cathedral, followed by cremation at Barham

BOOKS BY
MICHAEL RAMSEY

1936 *The Gospel and the Catholic Church* (Longmans)*

1945 *The Resurrection of Christ* (Geoffrey Bles)*

1949 *The Glory of God and the Transfiguration of Christ* (Longmans)*

1951 *F. D. Maurice and the Conflicts of Modern Theology* (Cambridge University Press)*

1956 *Durham Essays and Addresses* (SPCK)

1960 *From Gore to Temple* (Longmans; published in America as *An Era in Anglican Theology*)*

1961 *Introducing the Christian Faith* (SCM Press)*

1964 *Canterbury Essays and Addresses* (SPCK)

1965 *Sacred and Secular* (Longmans)*

1969 *God, Christ and the World* (SCM Press)*

1970 *The Future of the Christian Church* (with Cardinal Leon-Joseph Suenens; Morehouse-Barlow, New York)

1972 *The Christian Priest Today* (SPCK)

1974 *Canterbury Pilgrim* (SPCK)

1977 *Holy Spirit* (SPCK)

1980 *Jesus and the Living Past* (OUP)

1982 *Be Still and Know* (Collins)

1988 *Gateway to God* (Darton, Longman & Todd)

* Written under the name Arthur Michael Ramsey

TWENTIETH-CENTURY ARCHBISHOPS OF CANTERBURY

1896   Frederick Temple
1903   Randall Davidson
1928   Cosmo Lang
1942   William Temple
1945   Geoffrey Fisher
1961   Michael Ramsey
1974   Donald Coggan
1980   Robert Runcie

INDEX

261

INDEX

INDEX